For

HILTON C. BULEY LIBRARY
SOUTHERN CONNECTICUT STATE UNIVERSITY
NEW HAVEN, CONNECTICUT 06515

**AFRICAN HISTORICAL DICTIONARIES**
**Edited by Jon Woronoff**

1. Cameroon, by Victor T. Le Vine and Roger P. Nye. 1974

2. The Congo, by Virginia Thompson and Richard Adloff. 1974

# HISTORICAL DICTIONARY OF CAMEROON

by
Victor T. LeVine
and
Roger P. Nye

*African Historical Dictionaries, No. 1*

The Scarecrow Press, Inc.
Metuchen, N.J.      1974

Ref
DT
563
.L48

**Library of Congress Cataloging in Publication Data**

Le Vine, Victor T
  Historical dictionary of Cameroon.

    (African historical dictionaries, no. 1)
    Bibliography: p.
    1. Cameroon--History--Dictionaries.  2. Cameroon--
History--Chronology.  3. Cameroon--Bibliography.
I. Nye, Roger P., joint author.  II. Title.
III. Series.
DT563.L48     967'.11'003     74-901
ISBN 0-8108-0707-6

Copyright 1974 by Victor T. Le Vine
and Roger P. Nye

To
the memory of Harry Rudin,
who set the standard of
Cameroon historical scholarship

and to
Paul E. Nye,
whose generous support
through the years is
gratefully acknowledged

## CONTENTS

|  | Page |
|---|---|
| Editor's Foreword, by Jon Woronoff | vii |
| A Note on the Spelling of "Cameroon" | ix |
| Abbreviations and Acronyms | x |
| The Dictionary | 1 |
| A Chronology of Cameroon History | 131 |
| Introduction to the Study of Cameroon: A Bibliographic Essay, by V. T. Le Vine | 139 |
| Bibliography<br>  Books<br>  Articles and Pamphlets (by Author)<br>  Articles and Pamphlets (Anonymous)<br>  Public Documents | 151 |

EDITOR'S FOREWORD

With this book, Scarecrow Press introduces its series of African Historical Dictionaries, which we hope will prove as successful as the Asian and Latin American series. There is no doubt that it will fill some gaps in the documentation on Africa, not by providing new material so much as by assembling much of the existing information in a handy form, and by helping readers find further information through an extensive bibliography.

This series will cover the whole African continent, on both sides of the Sahara, treating individually countries of differing languages, races, religions and colonial heritages. It is perhaps symbolic that the first volume should be devoted to Africa's bilingual nation--Cameroon. The dictionary is all the more welcome in that it comes after the recent restructuring of the state as the United Republic of Cameroon, and can give considerable insight into the many changes in governance as well as the fate of those in power.

Certainly one could not find a better author for this book than Victor T. Le Vine, Professor of Political Science and Chairman of the African Studies Committee at Washington University, St. Louis, Missouri. He has travelled extensively in Africa and was for two years Head of the Department of Political Science at the University of Ghana, Legon. Along with numerous articles in books and scholarly journals, he has published four books, including two on the subject of this volume: The Cameroons from Mandate to Independence and The Cameroon Federal Republic. Roger P. Nye, his co-author, received his Ph.D. degree in Political Science at Washington University. After carrying on research and teaching in Turkey, he has turned to the economic and political situation in Africa, and particularly Cameroon, as part of his continuing concern with the politics of development.

Finally, a brief word about these dictionaries, which offer considerably more than may appear at first sight.

Through the listing of major persons, places, events, expressions and other useful items, it is possible both to pinpoint specific subjects and to derive an overall view of the situation. A chronological listing of events sums this up most succinctly, and the list of acronyms will help the reader through the maze of essential, but often quite incomprehensible abbreviations. The bibliography is sufficiently complete to provide further works on nearly any issue and, in this case, may be the only really extensive one available on Cameroon.

> Jon Woronoff,
> Series Editor

## A NOTE ON THE SPELLING OF "CAMEROON"

Various ways of spelling "Cameroon" will be used in this book; each is correct in its context. To avoid confusion and indicate the context appropriate to each spelling, the following key is offered:

Cameroon: Anglicized version designating (a) the country in general; (b) the whole of the Federal Republic, or either of its component states (West or East Cameroon); (c) the United Republic (after 1972).

Cameroons: Anglicized version designating (a) the two Cameroon mandates, or the two trusteeships, or the British Cameroons Mandate or Trusteeship and the Cameroun Republic; (b) either or both (Northern and/or Southern) British Cameroons Trusteeship(s); (c) generally, the country before 1960.

Cameroun: Gallicized version designating (a) the Cameroon area under French control; (b) the Cameroun Republic; (c) that spelling used by French-speaking Cameroonians in referring to either (a) or (b), as well as the former East Cameroon and the Cameroon Federal Republic and the Cameroon United Republic.

Kamerun: German version designating (a) the German protectorate, 1884-1916; (b) the spelling adopted by some nationalist groups, particularly those in the former West Cameroon, as a symbol of the unity of the two Cameroons.

Camarones: Spanish version, used in the Spanish territories and by Spanish writers.

Camaroes: Portuguese version, used by Portuguese writers.

## ABBREVIATIONS AND ACRONYMS

| | |
|---|---|
| ALCAM | Legislative Assembly of Cameroun |
| ALNK | National Army of Kamerunian Liberation |
| ANCAM | National Assembly of Cameroon |
| ARCAM | Representative Assembly of Cameroon |
| ATCAM | Territorial Assembly of Cameroon |
| ATUC | African Trade Union Confederation |
| BDC | Bloc Démocratique Camerounais |
| CAN | Courant d'Action Nationale |
| CCSC | Confédération Camerounaise des Syndicats Croyants |
| CDC | Cameroons Development Corporation |
| CDCWU | Cameroons Development Corporation Workers' Union |
| CFA | Communauté Financière Africaine |
| CFAO | Compagnie Française de l'Afrique Occidentale |
| CFTC | Confédération Française des Travailleurs Chrétiens Camerounais |
| CFU | Cameroons Federal Union |
| CGCT | Confédération Générale Camerounaise du Travail |
| CICAM | Cotonnière Industrielle du Cameroun |
| CNF | Cameroons National Federation |
| CNU | Cameroon National Union (see also UNC) |
| CPNC | Cameroons Peoples' National Convention |
| CUC | Cameroon United Congress |
| CUN | Courant d'Union Nationale |
| CWU | Cameroons Welfare Union |
| CYL | Cameroons Youth League |
| EDF | European Development Fund |
| EEC | European Economic Community |
| Esocam | Evolution Sociale Camerounaise |
| FAC | Fonds d'Aide et de Coopération |
| FCWU | French Cameroons Welfare Union |
| FIDES | Fonds d'Investissement pour le Développement Economique et Social |
| FNU | Front National Unifié |
| FPUP | Front Populaire pour l'Unité et la Paix |
| FSC | Fédération des Syndicats du Cameroun |
| FVO | Forces Vives de l'Opposition |
| ICFTU | International Confederation of Free Trade Unions |

| | |
|---|---|
| IFCTU | International Federation of Christian Trade Unions |
| Indécam | (Coordination des) Indépendants Camerounais |
| IOM | Indépendants d'Outre-Mer |
| JC | Jeunesse Camerounaise |
| JDC | Jeunesse Démocratique Camerounaise |
| Jeucafra | Jeunesse Camerounaise Française |
| KFP | Kamerun Freedom Party |
| KNC | Kamerun National Congress |
| KNDP | Kamerun National Democratic Party |
| KPP | Kamerun Peoples' Party |
| KUNC | Kamerun United National Congress |
| KUP | Kamerun United Party |
| MANC | Mouvement d'Action Nationale Camerounaise |
| MRP | Mouvement Républicaine Populaire |
| NCNC | National Council of Nigeria and the Cameroons |
| NKDP | Northern Kamerun Democratic Party |
| NPC | Northern Peoples' Congress |
| OAU | Organization of African Unity |
| OCAM | Organisation Commune Africaine et Malgache |
| OK | One Kamerun (Party) |
| PDC | Parti des Démocrates Camerounais |
| PMC | Permanent Mandates Commission |
| PSC | Parti Socialiste Camerounais |
| PTC | Parti Travailliste Camerounais |
| Racam | Rassemblement Camerounais |
| Rapeca | Rassemblement du Peuple Camerounais |
| RDA | Rassemblement Démocratique Africain |
| UC | Union Camerounaise |
| UCTU | Union Camerounaise des Travailleurs Croyants |
| UDEAC | Union Douanière et Economique de l'Afrique Centrale |
| UDFC | Union Démocratique des Femmes Camerounaises |
| UGTAN | Union Générale des Travailleurs d'Afrique Noire |
| UGTC | Union Générale des Travailleurs Camerounais |
| UNC | Union Nationale Camerounaise (see also CNU) |
| UNEK | Union Nationale des Etudiants Kamerunais |
| Unicafra | Union Camerounaise Française |
| UPC | Union des Populations du Cameroun |
| USAC | Union des Syndicats Autonômes Camerounais |
| USC | Union Sociale Camerounaise |
| USCC | Union des Syndicats Confédérés du Cameroun |
| USCC | Union des Syndicats Croyants du Cameroun |
| USLC | Union des Syndicats Libres du Cameroun |
| UTC | Union des Travailleurs Camerounais |
| WCTUC | West Cameroon Trade Union Congress |
| WFTU | World Federation of Trade Unions |
| Zopac | Zone de Pacification |

# CAMEROON

-A-

ABBIA. A bilingual cultural journal (first issue February 1963) published in Yaoundé with UNESCO support. Abbia has been the prime vehicle for the discussion of the sensitive issue of bilingualism (q.v.). See also FONLON, BERNARD; HARMONIZATION, POLICY OF.

ACCORD DE COOPERATION ECONOMIQUE MONETAIRE ET FINANCIERE. A bilateral agreement signed with France in November 1960 by which the Cameroun Republic entered the Franc Zone (q.v.). In addition, in exchange for French financial, administrative, and technical aid, the Cameroun Republic agreed to give French products preferential tariff treatment, to keep Cameroun's foreign exchange in the Bank of France, and to consult French officials in drawing up her annual import program. See also CFA FRANC; COMMUNAUTE FINANCIERE AFRICAINE.

ACTION NATIONALE see MOUVEMENT D'ACTION NATIONALE CAMEROUNAISE

ACTION PAYSANNE. One of Cameroon's many multi-functional organizations, the Action Paysanne was not only an agricultural interest group representing a well-defined sector of farmers and planters, but also a social organization that sponsored local and regional business meetings and more festive gatherings. It was organized in 1957 to advance the agricultural interests of its members (mostly Bulu and Fang farmers) but evolved into a political party. See PAYSANS INDEPENDANTS. In the 1956 general elections it won nine seats in the East Cameroun Assembly. Action Paysanne's president, Gaston Médou (q.v.), was one of the deputies. Action Paysanne later merged with the governing Union Camerounaise (q.v.) party.

ADAMA, MODIBBO, 178?-1848. Fulani nobleman who carried the jihad (holy war) of Uthman dan Fodio east

1

from northern Nigeria to Yola and the northern Cameroon area. He founded the Emirate of Adamawa, whose principal subdivisions became Yola (the capital), Maroua, Garoua, and Ngaoundéré. Adamawa received his standard from Dan Fodio in 1806, and until his death was engaged in extending the sway of his emirate over the diverse animist peoples southeast and northeast around Lake Chad. Adama was the son of an educated man named Hassana, of the Ba family, which lived at Gourin, on the Faro river; educated in Bornu, he acquired a reputation as a teacher (modibbo) and a fervent mystic. See DAN FODIO, UTHMAN.

ADAMAWA (or ADAMAOUA). An administrative region in north Cameroon inhabited by the so-called Kirdi (pagan) peoples and the Muslim Fulani. It is named after Moddibo Adama who, with his successors over the next several decades, carved out an empire over much of what is today northern East Cameroon. The headquarters of Adama's emirate at Yola still remains the traditional capital of Adamawa. See DAN FODIO, UTHMAN. The Adamawa plateau region is one of the Cameroon's five geographical zones. It is an area between 50 and 150 miles wide and is generally cooler and drier than the tropical rain forest to its south. Rainfall averages between 40 and 50 inches per year in the Adamawa region, which has a mean altitude of 3,400 feet above sea level.

ADMINISTERING AUTHORITIES. Under the League of Nations mandate system (q.v.) and the United Nations trusteeship system (q.v.), France and Great Britain were given the authority to oversee the development of their respective territories. As Administering Authorities, France and Great Britain provided administrative frameworks in their territories which represented their own notions of imperial responsibility and the "correct path" of cultural and political development. For British policy toward the Cameroons, see GREAT BRITAIN, COLONIAL POLICY AND LEGACY OF; NATIVE AUTHORITIES. For French policy toward the Cameroun, see ASSOCIATION, POLICY OF; FORCED LABOR; MISE EN VALEUR.

AFRICAN TRADE UNION CONFEDERATION (ATUC). A continent-wide trade union organization founded in 1962. The Fédération des Syndicats du Cameroun and the

Union des Syndicats Croyants du Cameroun (both q.v.) were affiliated with the ATUC.

AHIDJO, AHMADOU, 1924- . President of the United Cameroon Republic, President-General of the Cameroon National Union party. Born August, 1924, in Garoua, he attended the Ecole Primaire Supérieure in Yaoundé. From 1942 to 1946 he served as a radio operator for the Posts and Telegraph Service. In 1947, he was elected a delegate to the first Cameroun Representative Assembly (ARCAM); when that chamber became the Cameroun Territorial Assembly (ATCAM) in 1952, he was again elected to serve in it; in 1956 he was re-elected to the Cameroon National Assembly (ANCAM) in 1960. From 1953 to 1957 he served as a member of the Assembly of the French Union. In 1955 he was elected Vice-President of ATCAM, and in 1957, became President of ALCAM. In May, 1957, he was appointed Vice-Prime Minister in the cabinet of the first Cameroon government of André-Marie Mbida, acting as Minister of the Interior. Upon Mbida's resignation in February, 1958, Ahidjo became Prime Minister. In May, 1960, he was elected President of the Cameroon Republic. Following the unification of the Cameroon Republic with the former British Cameroons in 1961, he remained as President of the new Cameroon Federal Republic, and was re-elected to that position in March, 1965, and again in March, 1970. When the Cameroon Federal Republic became the United Cameroon Republic in 1972, Ahidjo remained as President, combining the functions of Head of State and Government. Ahidjo was one of the founders of the Union Camerounaise party, which later became the Cameroon National Union, and the country's principal (and only) active political party. He has travelled widely, including visits to the United States and European capitals. Ahidjo is a Fulani, Muslim, and married to a daughter of the Lamido of Garoua. He has two children.

AKWA. 1) A clan of the Douala peoples, one prominent member of which was R. J. K. Dibongué (q.v.), an initiator of the reunification movement in British Cameroons.

2) The "King" of Douala who signed a protectorate treaty with Germany in 1884. See NATCHTIGAL, GUSTAV; BELL, "KING." His grandson, Betote Akwa,

was a one-time leader of the Douala "traditional" council, Ngondo, and a member of the "old guard" nationalist leadership. See NGONDO.

3) A coastal village on the eastern side of the Wouri River which the Germans in 1909 planned to relocate further inland, thus touching off almost three decades of controversy over land rights. Douala chiefs in this period sent a steady stream of petitions to both the French administration and the League of Nations demanding the return of the expropriated lands or adequate compensation. Such demands eventually evolved into a condemnation of the colonial system and stimulated early Cameroon nationalism.

AKWA, BETOTE, 1892-1965(?). Former Minister and Douala politician. Akwa was born August 15, 1892 in Douala. Educated locally, he succeeded to the Chieftaincy of the Akwa clan of the Douala, and helped organize the quasi-traditional organization, Ngondo, which helped run candidates in the Wouri district during the 1940's and 50's. He served in the East Cameroon legislature from 1959 to 1960, when he lost his seat. Between 1959 and 1960 he served as Minister of State without Portfolio in Prime Minister Ahidjo's cabinet. Following his electoral defeat in 1960, he resumed his commercial activities in Douala.

AKWA, (KING) DIKA MPONDA. Traditional chief of the Douala, one of the principal signatories to the German protectorate treaty of July 12, 1884. He was confirmed as the successor to his father, Mpond'a Ngando, in November, 1882 by Edward Hyde Hewett, British consul for the Bights of Benin and Biafra. King Akwa died in 1884. The title of "king" was an artifact of British recognition. See BELL, KING.

ALL-PARTY CONFERENCE ON THE CONSTITUTIONAL FUTURE OF SOUTHERN CAMEROONS see BAMENDA "ALL-PARTY" CONFERENCE (1961)

ALUMINUM. Cameroon's third largest export. The aluminum is produced from bauxite imported from Guinea and processed at the Alucam plant at Edea. The large bauxite deposit at Martap in northern Cameroon has not been fully exploited due to transportation difficulties which the Trans-Cameroon Railway (Transcam) should alleviate. See BAUXITE; EDEA; TRANSCAM RAILWAY.

5          Anloo Society

ANLOO SOCIETY (also ANLU). A traditional secret society of Bikom women in the Kom area of Wum Division, which was revived by the KNDP in the late 1950's to stir up "grassfields" political support for Foncha's party in West Cameroon. This support became at times violent against the opposition KNC. Loosely structured, the Anloo developed into a centralized organization with local branches, and was in good measure responsible for a large turnout and the KNDP's electoral victory in the area in 1959.

ASSALE, CHARLES, 1911- . Former Prime Minister of the Cameroun Republic, Mayor of Ebolowa. Born on November 4, 1911, in Ebolowa, Assalé trained as a male nurse and served twelve years as an Infirmary Assistant at the Joss Sleeping Sickness Center. In 1946 he helped organize the Cameroun branch of the French Confédération Générale de Travail (General Labor Confederation), and in 1947 he was designated as a representative to the French Economic Council. Assalé was a co-founder (in 1948) of the Marxist political party, the Union des Populations du Cameroun (UPC), but left the party in 1957 because it had turned to violence and rebellion to gain its ends. In 1948 he was elected to the Cameroun Territorial Assembly (ARCAM), was re-elected to the Legislative Assembly (ALCAM) in 1956, and again to the National Assembly in 1960. Between February, 1958, and April, 1960, he served as Minister of Finance in Prime Minister Ahidjo's cabinet. Designated Prime Minister by President Ahidjo in 1960, he remained in that position until 1961 when the Federal Republic came into existence. He was then named Prime Minister of the new East Cameroon State. He served in that post until 1965, when he was replaced by Dr. S. P. Tchoungui.

ASSEMBLEE LEGISLATIVE see LEGISLATIVE ASSEMBLY

ASSEMBLEE NATIONALE see NATIONAL ASSEMBLY

ASSEMBLEE NATIONALE FEDERALE see FEDERAL NATIONAL ASSEMBLY

ASSEMBLEE REPRESENTATIVE see REPRESENTATIVE ASSEMBLY

ASSEMBLEE TERRITORIALE see TERRITORIAL ASSEMBLY

ASSIMILATION, POLICY OF. One of the two main tendencies that dominated France's colonial policy, the policy of assimilation sought to integrate France's colonial subjects politically and culturally with the homeland. In pursuit of la mission civilatrice et providentielle (the civilizing and providential mission), French statesmen held the belief that France and her colonies were indivisible, and they sometimes conferred French citizenship with all its rights and benefits on those natives who acquired the French language and customs (e.g., evolués). Assimilationist policy was embodied in Article 109 of the French constitution of 1848 which stated that the colonies were French territory and enjoyed the same rights in private and public law. When the great cultural gap between France and her black African colonies was finally realized, the policy of assimilation changed to one of "association," which put greater stress on economic development and political cooperation between the metropole and the colonies rather than the integration of political and social institutions. See ASSOCIATION, POLICY OF.

ASSOCIATION, POLICY OF. Applied throughout the French colonial empire after World War I, this policy sought practical, functional collaboration between the French rulers and the indigenous elites with France remaining the dominant force but with some measure of indigenous participation through indirect administration. "Association" assumed that the indigenous community could only develop slowly toward eventual assimilation to French culture. There was no thought of eventual colonial independence or even of self-administration. See ASSIMILATION, POLICY OF. Also involved in the policy of association was a dual system of law and an administrative separatism which operated to differentiate between the indigenous elites and masses (see INDIGENAT). The latter were to be paternalistically educated and guided, though not too rapidly, to cultural fulfillment in la civilisation française. Planned economic development of the colonies was also a principal component of this policy. See MISE EN VALEUR: PROTECTORATE POLICY.

ASSOCIATION TRADITIONELLE BANTOUE EFOULA-ME-YONG. A powerful local political group on a Bulu ethnic base organized by Charles Assalé (q.v.) in 1952. It proved a success in driving all other parties out of

Bulu land and electing Assalé to ATCAM in 1952. Other politicians took his lead and established their own "traditional" associations with varying success, such as the Kolo among the Ewondo, the Koupé among the Fulani, and the Union Bamoun among the Bamoun. See also KUMSZE; NGONDO. By 1952 Assalé's organization had been absorbed by the Union Camerounaise (q. v.).

ATANGANA, CHARLES, 1885-1943. Paramount chief of the Ewondo. Atangana was born at Mvolye. In 1896 his paternal uncle gave Atangana and his brothers into the service of the German explorer, Major Hans Dominik, whom he accompanied to Kribi. There, Atangana completed primary school, becoming proficient in German, and was later employed as a schoolteacher, infirmary assistant, and interpreter. He was one of the first baptized Christians in Yaoundé. From 1904 to 1910 Atangana accompanied Major Dominik on a series of punitive expeditions, acting as interpreter and on occasion intervening to save the lives of local chiefs threatened with execution. In early 1911, he was brought to Germany where he was received by the Kaiser and the Pope. Upon his return to Kamerun, he was chosen paramount chief of the Ewondo and Bané, the ethnic groups inhabiting the areas in and around Yaoundé. During the First World War, Atangana continued to serve the Imperial administration, eventually joining the defeated German forces in detention. When Atangana returned home after the war he was placed under house arrest. In 1921 the French administration recognized his title as Chief of the Ewondo and permitted him to return to Yaoundé. Under the new regime, Atangana helped recruit laborers for the Douala-Yaoundé railway project, effectively administered the Yaoundé area, supported the work of Dr. Jamot in suppressing sleeping sickness, and became quite wealthy in his own right. He was much honored by the French, who brought him and other traditional chiefs to Paris several times, but some of his subjects felt he abused his powers by using strong-arm methods. He is now considered one of the founders of modern Cameroon, and a statue was erected to his memory in Yaoundé.

ATLANTIKA MOUNTAINS. A mountain range extending along part of the western side of the Cameroons triangle. The physical separation of the two parts of the

British Northern Cameroon trust territory occurred just where the valley of the Benue River (q.v.) passes between the Atlantika Mountains and the Mandara Hills to the north.

AUJOULAT, (DR.) LOUIS-PAUL, 1910- . French medical doctor, politician, author. Dr. Aujoulat was born August 28, 1910 in Saida, Algeria. He first came to Cameroun in 1936, serving as a physician and lay missionary. In this latter capacity he was a co-founder, and later President, of the Catholic mission society Ad Lucem. Between 1945 and 1955 he represented Cameroun in the French National Assembly, and between 1949 and 1955 he served in the cabinet of French Prime Minister Pierre Mendes-France as Secretary of State for Overseas France. He was mainly responsible for the passage of a new, reformed Overseas Labor Code in 1952. Between 1952 and 1956 he also served in the Cameroun Territorial Assembly, and was the founder and first President of the Bloc Démocratique Camerounais, a political party to which (the later President) Ahidjo and Cameroun's first Prime Minister, Mbida, belonged. Dr. Aujoulat retired to France in 1957, turning to writing and work on medical-welfare problems. His most important book is Aujourd'hui l'Afrique (1958).

AYMERICH, (GEN.) JOSEPH GEORGES, 1858-1937. French General who led the French forces in the Kamerun Campaign, 1914-1916. Gen. Aymerich led French forces from the French Congo, one of the three prongs of the attack on Kamerun. He participated in the assault and submission of Douala, and in 1916, was named Commissioner of the French portions of the conquered protectorate. He left Cameroun in October, 1916.

-B-

BAFANG. A former département in East Cameroon, also a town inhabited primarily by Bamiléké. A Catholic secondary school exists at Saint-Paul in Bafang.

BAFOUSSAM. A former département in East Cameroon, also a town inhabited primarily by Bamiléké. The fifth national congress of the UC was held in Bafoussam in December 1965.

BAFUT. A "grasslands" tribe of the Tikar Peoples. The Bafut are the subject of a book by Gerald Durrell, The Bafut Beagles.

BAKOKO. An ethnic sub-group of the large Fang culture, who inhabit the forest and plateau areas around Edéa and Eseka. Their origin is shrouded in myth. See BASSA-BAKOKO.

BAKOSSI. An ethnic group in the Mungo Valley; the group straddles the former boundary between East and West Cameroon. See MOLONGO; TOMBEL MASSACRE.

BAKWERI (same as KPE). A coastal people related to the Douala in West Cameroon which, along with the Douala and Bulu, acted as middleman in the slave trade with the Europeans during the seventeenth and eighteenth centuries. The Bakweri were subjugated militarily by the Germans in 1894 and their plantation lands (over 330 square miles) surrounding Mount Cameroon expropriated. See BAKWERI LAND CLAIM COMMITTEE.

BAKWERI LAND CLAIM COMMITTEE. A Bakweri organization that petitioned the Trusteeship Council of the United Nations in August 1946 for the return of all the lands around Mount Cameroon which the Germans had expropriated in the 1890's. In the fifty years since the lands had been alienated to German plantation interests, native migrants had settled in the area and the Nigerian government had leased much of it to the Cameroons Development Corporation (q.v.). The Trusteeship Council argued that in fact the land was actually already in "native hands," in effect denying the Committee's petition. The Committee was founded by E. M. L. Endeley (q.v.), a medical doctor and son of an important Bakweri chief, who later became Premier of the Southern Cameroons.

BAKWERI UNION. One of three Nigeria-based Cameroonian political groups that aided in the founding of the National Council of Nigeria and the Cameroons (q.v.) in 1944. The purpose of the Union was to preserve Southern Cameroonian identity and autonomy within the Nigerian political groups being formed in the mid-1940's. See BAMENDA IMPROVEMENT ASSOCIATION; CAMEROONS YOUTH LEAGUE.

BALI. A tribe in the Bamenda highlands and the traditional enemy of the Widekum peoples. See BALI-WIDEKUM "WAR." They are an offshoot of the Chamba of East Cameroon and Nigeria and adopted certain cultural institutions (e.g., language, political structures) of the Bamoun and Tikar peoples whom they conquered. The Germans used the Bali as their principal ally in the area.

BALI-WIDEKUM "WAR." A conflict between the Bali and Widekum clans in 1951, in which seven people lost their lives. The violence demonstrated the old hostility between the two West Cameroon groups. Both Bali and Widekum straddle the geographical "boundary" between the southern rain forest and the northern grassfields, and have a record of conflict dating back to the beginning of the nineteenth century.

BALLA, BENOIT, 1924- . Former federal Foreign Minister. Balla was born September 5, 1924 in Akono, near Yaoundé, and was educated in Akono, Ebolowa, Yaoundé, and Paris, where, in 1951, he completed legal studies at the Sorbonne. He also earned a Diploma in Political Science at the School of Political and Administrative Sciences, Paris (1956), and attended the École Nationale de la France d'Outre-Mer in Paris (1957-59). He returned to Cameroun with the rank Administrateur des TOM, and served two months in 1959 as Director of the Cabinet of the Finance Ministry before being posted in Ebolowa as a Prefect (1959-60). From 1960 to 1962 he served as Director of President Ahidjo's Cabinet, then, 1962-63 as Prefect and Federal Inspector in Ebolowa, and in 1963, was named Foreign Minister. From 1964 to 1965 he was a Minister Without Portfolio, and in 1965, out of political favor, was posted as Sub-Prefect to Kribi.

BAMBOKO. A Bantu-speaking people distantly related to the Douala and found in West Cameroon along the coast.

BAMENDA. A grassy highlands region and a province in West Cameroon inhabited mainly by the Tikar peoples. Bamenda was one of four administrative divisions in the southern part of the British Cameroons. See GRASSFIELDS.

BAMENDA "ALL-PARTY" CONFERENCE (1961). A meeting of the political leaders of the Southern Cameroons lasting from June 26 to 28, 1961, held to discuss the nature of the union with the Cameroun Republic and to prepare proposals for a meeting the following month with the eastern delegation. See FOUMBAN CONFERENCE. The Bamenda proposals called for a loose federation between the British Cameroons and its eastern neighbor, with the principal governmental powers to be exercised by the legislatures of the constituent states, not by a centralized federal authority. The lack of unity, understanding and preparation among the Bamenda conferees probably insured the eventual acceptance of the Republic's conception of federal union.

BAMENDA CONFERENCE (1955). A meeting of the UPC and KNDP in November to further their dual aims of complete secession from Nigeria and eventual unification with the French Cameroun. The two parties formed a "reunification committee," which functioned only briefly, since the more conservative KNDP leadership became disenchanted with the extremism of the UPC.

BAMENDA IMPROVEMENT ASSOCIATION. A proto-nationalist organization among the Cameroon intelligentsia in Lagos during the mid-1940's which militated against continued Southern Cameroon association with Nigeria. Along with the Bakeweri Union and the CYL (both q.v.), it supported the founding of the National Council of Nigeria and the Cameroons (q.v.) in 1944, which it saw as a means of giving the Southern Cameroons separate status within Nigeria.

BAMILEKE. A collective term referring to a loose agglomeration of tribal groups living on the plateau areas southeast of the Bamboutos Mountains and west of the Noun River. They are the most populous of the "Cameroon Highlanders." Most of the ca. 800,000 Bamiléké are agriculturalists living in the Bamiléké administrative divisions (formerly départements). Here they are organized into about 100 autonomous chiefdoms ranging in size from more than 30,000 to about 50 members. Social organization revolves around the chieftancy. The chief is not only the head of the extended tribal family, but also the titular owner of all land and the dispenser of justice. A large number of age-grade associations, secret societies of socio-religio-political purpose, and inter-tribal associations, exist among the Bamiléké. Admission into the associations and secret societies is controlled by the local chiefs, themselves heads of the societies. At least seventeen languages and dialects are spoken by the Bamiléké. More than 100,000 Bamiléke have emigrated from their villages to towns such as Douala and Yaoundé where they have managed, because of their aggressive commercial skills, to dominate local retailing and transport. See DOUALA; LE PROBLEME BAMILEKE. The resulting socioethnic tensions have occasioned periodic violence and bloodshed. See BAMILEKE REBELLION; TOMBEL MASSACRE. Mathias Djoumessi, an important Bamiléké chief, was the first president of the UPC.

"BAMILEKE" (or UPC) REBELLION. A guerrilla campaign conducted between 1955-1962 by the militant wing of the outlawed UPC. The insurgents, mainly unlettered peasants from the heavily populated Bassa and Bamiléké regions in the southwest, were directed from abroad by several exiled UPC leaders (Moumié, Ouandié, and Kingue) and from within Cameroun by Um Nyobé (all q.v.). See NATIONAL ARMY OF KAMERUNIAN LIBERATION; UNION DES POPULATIONS DU CAMEROUN.

The rebellion can be said to have started on April 22, 1955 when the militantly nationalistic UPC, together with its affiliate organizations (the JDC, UDFC, USCC), issued a Joint Proclamation declaring the termination of the French trusteeship and calling for general elections. During May and June the UPC launched a series of demonstrations and riots which caused massive property damage and the loss of twenty-six lives. With its proscription in July, 1955 the UPC went underground, resorting to guerrilla warfare, which continued sporadically until 1970.

Some UPC guerrilla fighters were trained in Communist China, and arms and munitions made in Czechoslovakia and the USSR found their way through Conakry and Accra to the Cameroun Guerrillas. See CHINA, PEOPLES REPUBLIC OF. Tens of thousands of UPC supporters among the Camerounian populace permitted the rebels to control large sections of the countryside at various times. Various maquis units engaged in sabotage, arson, terrorism, murder of the so-called "valets des colonialistes," and voter intimidation during the uprising. Their strategy was to force the government to take counter-measures that would antagonize the population and lead to disapproval by the United Nations, thus forcing concessions to the UPC. The worst property damage and loss of lives occurred in the Bamiléké and Sanaga-Maritime areas. Cooperation between French and Cameroonian officials on military and police action, together with political and administrative measures by the Ahidjo government, undercut insurgent aims, resources and prospects. The rebellion tapered off with the death or surrender of its leaders, a government amnesty program which prompted many defections, and the advent of Cameroonian independence. See MAQUIS; RALLIEMENT; OUANDIE; MOUMIE; UM NYOBE; KINGUE; MAYI-MATIP.

BAMOUN (same as BAMUN). One of the main tribes of the ethnic grouping known as "Cameroon Highlanders." The Bamoun, who numbered about 80,000 in 1971, are a people of mixed origins who descended from early eighteenth-century Tikar invaders and the indigenous Bamiléké peoples of the plateau region west of the Mbam River. They claim to have lived under unbroken dynastic monarchical rule through forty-four descendants of their founder. In 1895 a remarkable Bamoun sultan, Njoya, came to the throne. See NJOYA, SULTAN. Due to Njoya's shrewdness and political abilities, the Bamoun were able to retain their cultural and religious solidarity in the face of colonial rule. Another Bamoun sultan, Seidou Njimoluh, played host to the constitutional conference at Foumban in 1961. See FOUMBAN CONFERENCE.

BANANAS. An important East Cameroonian export crop in the 1950's. Banana production in the Southern Cameroons took place principally on the plantations operated by the Cameroon Development Corporation (CDC). Production declined in the 1960's, however, due to crop diseases and terrorist activity in the principal banana-growing areas. It is now only the country's sixth ranking export.

BANDJOUN CHIEFDOM. The largest (over 30,000 people) of the more than 100 chiefdoms existing in the five former Bamiléké (q.v.) départements in the Western part of East Cameroun.

BAPTIST SECT see PROTESTANTISM

BARTH, HEINRICH, 1821-1865. German explorer. In the company of an expedition led by James Richardson and including another German, Herman Overweg, Barth left Tripoli in 1849 to explore the southern Sahara and make contact with the Muslim states in the area. Richardson died in 1851, Overweg in 1852, but Barth went on. In his wanderings, he reached Lake Chad (1851), discovered the upper Benué, visited Yola, Katsina, Sokoto, and Timbuctu. He was expelled from Yola by the Emir Lawal, who suspected him of espionage. Eventually, he recrossed the Sahara, regaining Tripoli in 1855. Barth's journey is one of the greatest feats in the history of African travel, and the huge book in which he described it one of the masterpieces of the subject.

BASEL (BASLER) MISSION SOCIETY. The most important of the several missionary bodies asked by the German government to take over the work and property of the English Baptists in Kamerun in 1886. See SAKER, ALFRED; PROTESTANTISM. The Basel missionaries worked closely with some mission groups, such as the American Presbyterians, but did not conceal their antipathy toward the presence of Catholic missionaries or toward the "Mohammedan tide" in the north. See CATHOLICISM; ISLAM. Besides inveighing against polygamy, nakedness, alcohol and trial by ordeal, the Basel Mission Society defended native interests against the unjust land policies and harsh labor practices of the German administration. See GLEIM, OTTO; FORCED LABOR. By 1914 the Basel Mission had developed a network of twelve main stations extending into the hinterland, had a school enrollment of 22,818 pupils, and had made over 15,000 converts. The First World War witnessed the sequestering of German mission holdings, but in 1924 the Basel Mission was allowed to resume its activities in the Cameroons.

BASSA-BAKOKO. The most numerous ethnic unit of the northwestern and coastal Bantu. They number about 200,000 and generally occupy the southern area of the Sanaga River Valley. Before the coming of the European traders, the Bassa were engaged in subsistence agriculture, supplemented by ocean and river fishing. They later acted as middlemen and collectors in the trade with the Europeans for slaves, ivory and vegetable oils. The Bassa staged an armed rebellion against German inland penetration but were defeated between 1892 and 1895. See ZIMMERER, EUGEN VON. Their territory was occupied by the Germans and their men used as laborers on the Douala-Yaoundé railway. See FORCED LABOR. American Presbyterian missionaries converted most of the Bassa to Christianity.

The Bassa-Bakoko were the first of the southern ethnic groups to participate in the UPC-inspired political violence, largely due to the continuous social and economic dislocations they had experienced with German conquest, forced labor, missionary activity, the French prestation system, and the industrialization around Edéa. The Bassa areas were a stronghold of UPC support during the civil violence of 1955-1958 because Reuben Um Nyobé and Theodore Mayi Matip, UPC leaders and themselves Bassa, were able to mesh their rebel organization with the Bassa traditional clans and institutions, such as the secret Ndog-Njoue Society. See "BAMILEKE" REBELLION. Bassa maquisards under Um Nyobé ranged throughout the Sanaga-Maritime division. Massive numbers of Bassa rallied to the government after Um Nyobé's death in 1958. See RALLIEMENT.

BAUXITE. One of the largest known deposits of bauxite in Africa (estimated at over one billion tons) was discovered in 1959 at Martap, on the Adamawa Plateau, near Tibati. The deposit is too far from the coast (approximately 500 miles from Edéa, where it would have to be processed) to be presently exploitable. Plans for railway connections to the site have been completed, but the initial high costs of rail transportation and the unpredictable state of the world aluminum market make exploitation of the Martap deposits problematic. See ALUMINUM; EDEA; TRANSCAMEROON RAILWAY.

BEECROFT, JOHN, 1790-1854. British consul and agent in Cameroon. A merchant of mixed Black-White parentage, Beecroft became Governor of the British settlement on Fernando Po in 1836. See FERNANDO PO. When the Spanish took over the island again in 1844, he was named Consul and General Agent for the British government in the Bays of Benin and Biafra, a post he filled until his death in 1854. Beecroft was responsible for the pact of April 29, 1852, which regulated the relations among the several national trading groups at Douala; he became a source of legitimation of Douala chiefs; and on January 14, 1856, he established the Douala Court of Equity, designed to settle conflicts among the traders, and between the traders and the Douala populations.

BELL, ("KING") NDOAMBA LOBE, 1838(?)-1898. A powerful chief of the Douala in the late nineteenth century. Chief Bele (corrupted by the English to "King" Bell) at first enjoyed a commercial monopoly with the European traders along the Cameroon coast. The resulting friction among the Douala caused other chiefs (e.g., Akwa, Priso) to leave Bell's jurisdiction and create their own "kingships." Bell was one of the Douala "kings" who signed the protectorate agreements with Germany in 1884. A section of Douala city today is named New Bell. King Bell was the grandfather of Prince Rudolph Douala Manga Bell, who was hanged by the Germans in 1914.

BENUE (or BENOUE) RIVER. The eastern extension of the Niger running through the northern savanna region of Cameroon. The valley of the Benue passes between the Atlantika Mountains and the Mandara Hills in the west and divided the former (British) Northern Cameroons Trust Territory. The navigability of much of the Benue has enabled northern Cameroon to maintain economic ties with the northern parts of Nigeria and the Nigerian port of Burutu. (The Benué was closed to traffic, however, during the Nigerian civil war of the late 1960s.) As part of the economic development of northern Cameroon, a major bridge, financed by the European Development Fund, will be built across the Benué at Garoua.

BETAYENE, JEAN-FAUSTIN, 1922- . Former Foreign Minister of Cameroon, attorney. Betayené was born on September 23, 1922 at Komo-Ebala. He was educated at Yaoundé until 1939, when he joined the Free French military forces, serving in Equatorial Africa and in the north African campaigns. In 1942 he became a clerk to the Haut-Nyong subdivisional administration, and in 1944 was named President of the Native Court in Doumé. From 1945 to 1953 he worked in the Political Affairs Section of the French High Commission in Yaoundé, and from 1953 to 1958 served as Assistant to the High Commission Delegate in Paris. During this period he attended the University of Paris (earning a licence en droit) and the École Nationale de la France d'Outre-Mer (earning the brevet of Administrateur d'Outre-Mer). During 1958 he served as the Delegate of the autonomous Republic of Cameroun in Paris, returning to Yaoundé to serve (until 1960) as counselor for foreign affairs to Prime Minister Ahidjo. After independence (1960) he was appointed General-Secretary for Administration in the Foreign Ministry, in October, 1960, was named Foreign Minister, in which capacity he remained until 1963, when he stepped down to become director of the newly-created National Investment Bank.

BETI-FANG see BETI-PAHOUIN

BETI-PAHOUIN (or BETI-FANG). The most numerous (approximately 700,000) component of the Equatorial Bantu; a widely dispersed linguistic agglomerate which includes the ethnic groups inhabiting the Yaoundé area. The Beti-Pahouin are principally composed of the Ewondo groups (the largest with about 470,000 speakers), the Bulu, and the Fang. In Yaoundé the local Beti have succumbed to the economic domination of the Bamiléké immigrants. See LE PROBLEME BAMILEKE. The Beti-Pahouin were deeply influenced by Christian missionary activity, as evidenced by their relatively high literacy rate. See CATHOLICISM; PROTESTANTISM.

BEYBEY-EYIDI, MARCEL, 1914-1966. Physician and politician. Dr. Beybey-Eyidi was born on November 21, 1914 in Douala, and was educated at the Yaoundé Primary School and the École Preparatoire de Médicine in Joss. He finished his medical studies in Paris in 1950. During the Second World War he served in the medical sections of the Free French forces, and from 1951 to 1955 practiced in the Government medical services in France and Cameroun, serving 1954-55 as medical advisor to Louis-Paul Aujoulat, Secretary of State for Overseas France (q.v.). In 1956 he opened a clinic in Doula. He became active in oppositional politics during 1956, publishing a journal, l'Opinion au Cameroun, and appearing at the UN as a petitioner in

1957 and 1959. In 1960 he was elected to represent the Wouri constituency in the Cameroun National Assembly. In 1962, along with three other opposition leaders, he was tried, convicted, and sent to prison for alleged conspiracy and sedition. Released in 1965, he returned to his clinic, and died in Douala in 1966.

BILINGUALISM. Cameroon is formally recognized as a bilingual country, but only a small fraction of the population speaks both French and English. Most instruction in West Cameroon schools continues to be in English, that in East Cameroon in French. Several factors hamper the realization of true bilingualism in Cameroon: the lack of trained bilingual personnel, local resistance to the idea and adherence to native vernaculars, and the fear on the part of many educated Cameroonians that bilingualism will result in a loss of cultural identity and their authentic African heritage. The learning of both French and English became compulsory at the secondary school level in 1963. The only secondary school, however, in which all instructors are bilingual is the Federal Bilingual Grammar School at Man o' War Bay, Victoria, in West Cameroon. The Federal University (q.v.) at Yaoundé also attempted to create a genuine bilingual institution, but it is still heavily francophone and monocultural due to its location (i.e., in East Cameroon) and its dependence on French foreign aid. Dr. Bernard Fonlon (q.v.), a West Cameroonian, was the earliest and most effective and articulate advocate of bilingualism. See "HARMONIZATION," POLICY OF.

BIMBIA. 1) A Cameroon ethnic group, part of the Northwestern Bantu configuration; the Bimbia, more commonly known as Isuwu (also, Isubu, Subu), are directly related to their neighbors, the Douala, and the Bakweri (q.v.).

2) Bimbia village, the seat of the minor chieftaincy of the Bimbia people, located at the mouth of the estuary of the Wouri River, near present-day Victoria. Bimbia was the site of John Beecroft's (q.v.) first trading station (set up in 1832), as well as one of the two Baptist missions established by Joseph Merrick (q.v.) (in 1844). Bimbia became a bone of contention between England and Germany after agents of the Woermann firm (q.v.) signed a treaty of annexation with the Bimbia chief on July 11, 1884. The document ceded the

territory around Bimbia (including various creeks and rivers) to the Germans, much to the irritation of the British, who felt that because of Bimbia's proximity to their Victoria colony, the village ought properly to belong to them.

BINDZI, BENOIT, 1924- . Former Foreign Minister of the Federal Republic. Born at Ekok, Bindzi attended schools in Mbalmayo and Yaoundé, as well as the Catholic Seminary in Akono, before joining the customs service in 1944. He held senior posts, including Deputy Controller at Douala, and was appointed Principal Secretary to the Minister of Economic Affairs in 1958. After being attached to the French Foreign Office for special training, and later to the French Embassy in Bonn, he returned home in 1960 to become Principal Secretary to the Foreign Minister. He headed the Cameroun delegation to the United Nations from 1961-64, and again in 1966. In 1963 he was Vice-President of the UN General Assembly's 18th session. In 1964 he became Minister of Information, and in July, 1966, took over the Foreign Ministry, a post he filled until 1967.

BIYIDI, ALEXANDRE see MONGO BETI

BLOC DEMOCRATIQUE CAMEROUNAIS (BDC). A political party organized in July 1951 by Louis-Paul Aujoulat (q.v.). Its strength was found principally among Catholics in the central area of Cameroun. The BDC was not sympathetic to the goals of the UPC and had no real commitment to the Kamerun Idea (q.v.). Aujoulat, who proposed the creation of a single electoral college (four years before it became an actuality) and the enlargement of ATCAM's powers, himself became Assembly president after his party's success in the March 1952 elections to ATCAM. Aujoulat drew into the BDC such diverse personalities as Ahmadou Ahidjo and André Mbida (both q.v.). The BDC, virtually extinct by 1955 due to party splits and mergers, was the lineal precursor to the Parti des Démocrates Camerounais (q.v.).

BORORO. A pastoral Foulbé family, powerful in the Cameroon north. See VOLLARBE.

BRAZZAVILLE CONFERENCE. Convoked by the Free French under General de Gaulle in January 1944 and presided over by Felix Eboué, the Governor of Chad, the conference was attended by colonial administrators concerned with tropical African territories and set the stage for the postwar political evolution of Cameroon. The recommendations of the Conference, many incorporated into the Constitution of the Fourth French Republic in 1946, were: (1) continuation of the traditional assimilationist aims of French colonial policy with some administrative decentralization, but a rejection of any conception of autonomy for French dependencies or their evolution outside the French empire; (2) the creation of some type of federal structure uniting France and its overseas territories with territorial representation in the political bodies of the new Fourth Republic; (3) the abolition of the indigénat, all forms of forced labor, and the distinctions between citoyens and sujets and between evolués and indigènes.

BUCHNER, DR. MAX. Gustav Nachtigal's (q.v.) assistant in the early colonization of the Cameroons' coastal area. After Nachtigal raised the German flag over Douala in July, 1884, he left Buchner as the temporary official German representative in the region until a permanent government could be installed. Buchner, alone representing the whole German government in the Cameroons, found himself in immediate conflict with the British merchants and missionaries, most of whom refused to accept German rule. A native uprising in December, 1884 prompted Buchner to call in German Admiral Knorr, who put down the rebellion with naval gunfire and marines. He then took over from Buchner, determined to establish German rule firmly. One of Knorr's first acts was to dissolve the British-controlled Court of Equity (q.v.). See HEWETT, EDWARD HYDE; LOCK PRISO, CHIEF; WOERMANN, ADOLF.

BUEA. The former capital of West Cameroon, on the slopes of Mount Cameroon. The Germans raised their flag over Buea in December 1885 and later made the city the capital of their protectorate. As part of Southern (British) Cameroons, Buea was under the authority of the Lieutenant Governor of the Southern Provinces of Nigeria. Buea has a population of ca. 5,000, most of which are Bakweri, since Buea is also the seat of the Paramount Chief of the Bakweri. Gov. Jesco von Puttkamer (q.v.) erected a building in the style of a mansion on the Rhine (it is still known as the Schloss) which served successive German, British, and Cameroonian territorial executives.

BULU (or BOULU). A Bantu language spoken by some 150,000 Beti-Pahouin in southern and central Cameroon. The Bulu-speakers were prominent among the coastal tribes which acted as middlemen in the European slave trade in the seventeenth and eighteenth centuries. See SLAVE TRADE. They rose in armed rebellion against German colonial penetration into the interior in the 1890's but were defeated with considerable loss of life. The Bulu were converted to Christianity by Presbyterian missionaries. The Bulu have a history of ethnic antagonism against the neighboring Bassa-Bakoko. In addition, in an outburst of economic frustration in 1956, the Bulu rioted against the immigrant Bamiléké in the southern town of Sangmélima, injuring seven Bamiléké and destroying their market stalls. See ETHNIC CONFLICT; LE PROBLEME BAMILEKE. The Bulu's principal leader during the 1950's was former East Cameroon Prime Minister Charles Assalé.

BURTON, (SIR) RICHARD F., 1821-1890. English explorer, orientalist, writer, and Consul. Burton served as British Consul at Fernando Po between 1861 and 1865. During his service in that post, Burton supervised British exploration along the Nigerian and Cameroon coasts, and lent his support to several British entrepreneurs who sought to establish factories (stations) at Douala.

-C-

CALABAR. A town about eighty miles west of Mount Cameroon on the coast near the Rio del Rey which, by the beginning of the nineteenth century had become famous as a center for the purchase and export of slaves. It is now a Nigerian port. See SLAVE TRADE.

CAMARÕES, RIO DOS (literally RIVER OF PRAWNS). The name given the Wouri River by the first Portuguese explorers who reached the Cameroon coast near the site of modern Douala, ca. 1472. The Portuguese caught and ate--mistaking them for prawns--a variety of crayfish found occasionally in the Wouri estuary. The name Rio dos Camarões stuck and subsequently

Cameroon

was generally applied to the entire coastal area between Mount Cameroon and Rio Muni (formerly Spanish Guinea). The name Cameroon is derived from this early misattribution.

**CAMEROON CHAMPION.** A weekly pro-CPNC newspaper which appeared in Victoria, West Cameroon in 1960 but ceased publication in 1962 following the death of its founder, Peter Motomby-Woleta.

**CAMEROON DEVELOPMENT CORPORATION (CDC).** Created in 1946 under a Nigerian Government Ordinance to manage and develop the former German plantations in West Cameroon, the CDC is the largest statutory corporation in the United Republic and plays a vital part in the country's economy, both with its production for export (mainly bananas but increasingly tea and rubber) and its taxes to the West Cameroon government. The CDC employs 15,000 workers and provides them with free health care and housing, as well as educational and recreational services. Its operations include administering ports, roads and a railway system, in addition to 19 plantations. Financial grants and budgetary subsidies from Great Britain and Nigeria were needed, however, to offset the CDC's erratic record of profitability in the 1950's.

With federation and the shift away from reliance on Nigeria, Great Britain and the Commonwealth market came a loss of almost 2 billion CFA francs by the CDC. West Cameroon's total exports and whole economy suffered a severe setback. It took a £3 million loan from the World Bank and a £2 million loan from the Development Fund of the Common Market to set "Camdev" back on its feet. The federal government took over CDC operations in 1962-63. Negotiations with World Bank and EDF were concluded in 1967 for loans to further develop CDC holdings and to increase the total area planted from 21,600 to about 33,000 hectares.

**CAMEROON DEVELOPMENT CORPORATION WORKERS' UNION (CDCWU).** One of the two principal trade unions in West Cameroon, the CDCWU was founded in 1947. Its first general secretary was E. L. M. Endeley (1947-1950) who built the union into an influential organization. Endeley's successor as general secretary was N. N. Mbile. The CDCWU claimed a membership of ca. 10,000 workers in 1965.

Cameroon

CAMEROON HIGHLANDERS. The largest ethnic grouping in Cameroon. It is composed principally of the Bamiléké (about 800,000); the various related tribes of the Bamenda Plateau, most of them of Tikar origin (about 400,000); and the Bamoun (about 85,000). See BAMILEKE; BAMOUN; TIKAR.

CAMEROON NATIONAL UNION see UNION NATIONALE CAMEROUNAISE

CAMEROON PEOPLES NATIONAL CONVENTION (CPNC). A political party formed in May, 1960, by the merger of the KNC and the KPP, in order to counter the growing dominance of the KNDP in West Cameroon politics and to offer an alternative to the latter's position in the February 1961 UN plebiscite. The CPNC was led by Endeley, Mbile and Motomby-Woleta (all q.v.) and was electorally strongest in the forest areas of the Kumba, Nkambe and Victoria Divisions. The CPNC's pre-plebiscite campaign raised the spectre of widespread maquisard terrorism if the voters chose unification with Cameroun. See BAMILEKE REBELLION. CPNC leaders variously advocated integration with Nigeria, a period of nominal independence for Southern Cameroons or, failing these, a partition of Southern Cameroons according to the results of the plebiscite in each Division. The voters chose unification with Cameroun. See PLEBISCITES, UNITED NATIONS; MOLONGO.
In the first general elections to the 37-seat West Cameroon Legislative Assembly in December 1961, Dr. Endeley's CPNC won ten seats to the KNDP's twenty-five. The CPNC as the opposition party pressed for the early formation of a single national party. See PARTI UNIFIE. The CPNC's last electoral contest was its unsuccessful challenge to the KNDP in 1964 for ten seats in the Federal Assembly in which it won less than 25 per cent of the total vote and no seats. In August 1965 the CPNC and KNDP formed a "national government" within which Endeley became leader of the (West Cameroon) legislature. The CPNC, like the KNDP, UC and CUC, dissolved itself when the new Cameroon National Union (q.v.) was born on September 1, 1966.

CAMEROON TIMES. Launched as the weekly Kamerun Times in 1960 in Victoria with the financial assistance of Paul Soppo Priso (q.v.), the Cameroon Times (after 1961) became one of the principal English-language newspapers of West Cameroon. The Times supported the KNDP and its policy of unification with Cameroun. It ceased publication in April 1968 for what were claimed to be "financial reasons" but resumed operations two or three times a week in 1969 under new management. The Times had a limited circulation of about 5,000.

CAMEROON UNITED CONGRESS (CUC). A small party or parliamentary clique founded in 1965 by S. T. Muna and E. T. Egbe after they, along with eight others, had been expelled by Foncha from the KNDP. The CUC formed the opposition to the governing KNDP/CPNC coalition in the West Cameroon Assembly after August 1965 and maintained close ties with the Ahidjo government in Yaoundé. The CUC stressed the need to quickly achieve a truly unified national party. See PARTI UNIFIE. As a result, Egbe was chosen to chair the Drafting Committee which during the summer of 1966 prepared the statutes for the new single national party, the Cameroon National Union (q.v.). In addition, President Ahidjo appointed Muna as Prime Minister of West Cameroon in 1968. Various other members of the former CUC also gained employ in the federal government.

CAMEROONS FEDERAL UNION (CFU). A loosely-knit Southern Cameroons political group (1947-1949) that grew out of the Cameroons Youth League (q.v.). Led by Dr. Endeley, the CFU advocated reunification of the two Cameroonian trust territories, although Endeley's real concern was greater administrative autonomy and separate regional status for the Southern Cameroons within the Nigerian framework. See CAMEROONS NATIONAL FEDERATION.

CAMEROONS NATIONAL FEDERATION (CNF). A Southern Cameroonian political grouping of various tribal improvement unions and land committees which emerged out of the May 1949 conference in Kumba. The conference was attended by nineteen Cameroonian groups, including the CFU and CDCWU, only one of which, the Baminyang Improvement Union, was made up of French Camerounians residing in the British trust territory. The CNF's leaders were Endeley, Mbile, Muna, and George (all q.v.). The CNF made the first written demand for Cameroon reunification in a petition to the 1949 UN Visiting Mission (q.v.).

The memoranda of the CNF and its constituent organizations often advocated the removal of all frontier restrictions and customs barriers between the British Cameroons and French Cameroun, and the teaching of French and English in the schools of both Cameroons. But the CNF's (and Endeley's) real objective was the creation of an autonomous Cameroons Region within Nigeria, free from administrative subordination to the Eastern Region of Nigeria. Some sections of the CNF, however, thought that unification should be the prime concern of their organization. See KAMERUN UNITED NATIONAL CONGRESS. Southern Cameroons did achieve quasi-federal status within Nigeria in 1954 with its own House of Assembly at Buea and representation in the federal legislature at Lagos. See KAMERUN NATIONAL CONGRESS; "LYTTLETON CONSTITUTION"; and NORTHERN PLEBISCITES, UNITED NATIONS.

CAMEROONS WELFARE UNION (CWU). One of the earliest political groups in the Southern Cameroons. It was formed in 1939 in Victoria and in its brief existence attempted unsuccessfully to replace Chief Manga Williams with one of its own nominees in the Nigerian Legislative Council. The Lagos branch of the CWU was the nucleus from which the Cameroons Youth League (q.v.) was formed.

CAMEROONS YOUTH LEAGUE (CYL). A small, Lagos-based Southern Cameroon nationalist group founded in 1939 and modeled on the Nigeria Youth Movement (q.v.). Several of its early members (CYL President Peter M. Kale, First Secretary E. L. M. Endeley, and J. N. Foncha--all q.v.) later became prominent in Southern Cameroonian politics. Initially, its purposes were solidaristic and welfare-oriented, the main concern being the protection of a distinctive Cameroonian identity under administrative integration with Eastern Nigeria. More overtly political aims were developed after some contact with various Nigerian and Cameroonian nationalist groups such as the National Council of Nigeria and the Cameroons, and the Cameroons Federal Union (both q.v.). The CYL played a leading part in the campaign against the 1946 "Richards Constitution" (q.v.), by urging home rule for the Cameroonians.

CATHOLICISM. The first Catholic mission in Kamerun was opened by the Pallotine Fathers in 1890. By 1913

Catholics operated 151 schools with over 12,500 pupils. Vigorous and effective proselytism, especially among the Ewondo and Eton peoples, resulted in large proportions of Catholics by 1961 in Yaoundé (almost half the population), in Douala (over one-third) and in East Cameroon as a whole (almost one-fifth). Catholics continue to run several fine secondary schools in Cameroon including Sacré-Coeur in Makak and Saint-Paul in Bafang. Contrast: ISLAM; PROTESTANTISM.

In politics, the Catholic hierarchy generally opposed the UPC because of its militancy and alleged Communist underpinnings, supporting instead Aujoulat's centrist BDC and later, Mbida's PDC. In January 1962, however, the newly enthroned Archbishop of Yaoundé, Jean Zoa, was reported to have purged the Yaoundé Catholic hierarchy of pro-Mbida followers, dissociating the Church from the Démocrates and officially declaring its neutrality in partisan matters. That neutrality has been difficult to maintain, however, in the face of political developments. The Church has come into open conflict with the government several times. See NDONGMO AFFAIR; L'EFFORT CAMEROUNAIS.

CFA FRANC. The standard currency of the French-speaking African states. CFA stands for Communauté Financière Africaine. The CFA franc was introduced as the federation's currency in 1962, replacing the Nigerian pound in the West. See FRANC ZONE.

"CHICK FORMULA." A financial arrangement worked out in 1955 by the Nigerian Financial Secretary, Sir Louis Chick, to subsidize the budget of the Southern Cameroons government. When Southern Cameroons became a separate administrative entity within Nigeria in 1954, a study showed that it could not develop without Nigerian financial aid. The "Chick formula" was devised to guarantee a Nigerian government subsidy to Southern Cameroons in the event of a budget deficit by the latter. Budget deficits did occur in the following years, and the system of revenue allocations was deemed unsatisfactory. Intended to stabilize Souther Cameroonian finances, the formula had failed to account for the fluctuations in CDC revenues and thus was abandoned in favor of new arrangements. See CAMEROON DEVELOPMENT CORPORATION; PHILLIPSON REPORT.

CHINA, PEOPLES REPUBLIC OF. The Communist Chinese government was sympathetic to and financially supported the radical nationalist UPC party during the late 1950s and early 1960s. Moumié, Kingué and Ouandié were guests of the Peking regime in November 1959 and again in July 1960. UPC guerrilla fighters, perhaps as many as 300 in 1961, were openly trained on the Chinese mainland. They received ideological indoctrination along with instruction in sabotage operations and guerrilla combat tactics. The UPC's "struggle for national liberation" was the subject of laudatory articles in Chinese, Soviet and East European publications. After the collapse of UPC resistance and the advent of the Cameroon federation, the Ahidjo government remained cool toward the Peking regime. On April 2, 1971, however, the Cameroon government broke its diplomatic ties with the Nationalist Chinese government on Taiwan and recognized Peking. This reversal was partially in response to changing international conditions and partially due to the fact that Peking had ceased supporting the UPC.

CHRISTALLER, THEODOR, 1840(?)-1896. German educator. Christaller came to Kamerun in 1887, and in 1888 opened the first German school. He prepared the first German-Douala dictionary, edited several vernacular textbooks, and wrote a Douala grammar.

CLAPPERTON, HUGH (1788-1826), LANDER, RICHARD (1804-1834), DENHAM, DIXON (1786-1828), and OUDNEY, WALTER (1801-1824). British explorers. Oudney, Clapperton, and Denham were the first Europeans to see Lake Chad (1822). Denham explored the Shari river, and Clapperton and Oudney explored the Hausa states of northern Nigeria. In 1825 Clapperton and Lander proceeded from Fernando Po to the mouth of the Niger, which they followed north and northwest to Bussa and Yaouri, and then northwest to Zaria, Kano, and Sokoto. Denham, Clapperton and Oudney's journals were published in 1829.

COCOA. The most important crop in East Cameroon and the country's leading export commodity; cocoa represented about 25 per cent of the total value of exports in the 1960s. Cocoa farmers in the south and center of the country constitute 13 per cent of the Cameroon population. The production of cocoa, unlike the organized plantation production of coffee and cotton, is still largely a family enterprise. Cocoa prices on the world market have fluctuated considerably, causing economic dislocation and political difficulties in Cameroon.

COFFEE. An important export crop of both East and West Cameroon and Cameroon's second leading export commodity. Two varieties of coffee are produced: Robusta, most of which is grown in the coastal areas; and Arabica, which grows mainly in the Bamiléké and Bamoun country in the West. Coffee and cocoa together account for over 50 per cent of the East's exports.

COLLEGE OF ARTS, SCIENCE AND TECHNOLOGY. An important pre-university level institution in West Cameroon, located in Bambili (Bambui). It was involved in the 1960s controversy concerning federal-state division of authority over education. Federal control was eventually established, but the prolonged controversy impeded the rapid development of the College.

COMMISSIONERS AND HIGH COMMISSIONERS OF FRANCE IN CAMEROUN, 1916-1959. (The dates of their arrival in Cameroon are given):

| | | | | |
|---|---|---|---|---|
| Aymerich, Georges | 1916 | Cournarie, Pierre | 1940 |
| Fourneau, Lucien-Louis | 1916 | Carras, Hubert | 1943 |
| Carde, Jules | 1919 | Delavignette, Robert | 1946 |
| Marchand, Théodore-Paul | 1923 | Hofherr, René | 1947 |
| Bonnecarrere, Auguste-François | 1932 | Soucadaux, André | 1949 |
| | | Pré, Roland | 1954 |
| Répiquet, Jules | 1934 | Messmer, Pierre | 1956 |
| Boisson, Pierre | 1936 | Ramadier, Jean | 1958 |
| Brunot, Richard | 1938 | Torre, Xavier | 1958 |
| Leclerc, Philippe | 1940 | | |

COMMITTEE OF LADIES AND GENTLEMEN TO PROMOTE FRIENDSHIP BETWEEN FRENCH AND BRITISH CAMEROONS. A West Cameroon society established in Victoria late in 1956 by supporters of reunification to promote contacts among high-level politicians and civil servants across the Cameroon borders. A complementary society, les Amis du Cameroun britannique, was set up in Douala. The Western hosts included such notables as Endeley, Dibongué, and other KNC leaders. Eastern and Western delegations exchanged visits, but these contacts lacked scope and continuity.

**COMMUNAUTE FINANCIERE AFRICAINE (CFA).** The African Financial Community comprises all the states, except Guinea and Mali, which were part of French West and Equatorial Africa, plus Cameroon, Togo and Madagascar. The monetary reserves of the CFA countries are held in French francs in the French treasury. Exchange is effected on the Paris market, where CFA francs are freely convertible to French francs. Foreign assets earned by the member countries are pooled in an Exchange Stabilization Fund where part of the reserves earned by richer members can be used to offset the deficits incurred by poorer members. Cameroon is also a member of the Franc zone (q.v.).

**CONFEDERATION FRANÇAISE DES TRAVAILLEURS CHRETIENS (CFTC).** A French Catholic group of trade unions. Louis Paul Aujoulat (q.v.) founded a territorial branch of the CFTC (Confédération des Travailleurs Chrétiens) in 1952 in Yaoundé, specifically to counter the UPC-dominated Confédération Génerale Camerounaise du Travail, a branch of the CGT, France's largest trade union. See also UNION DES SYNDICATS CONFEDERES DU CAMEROUN.

**CONFEDERATION GENERALE CAMEROUNAISE DU TRAVAIL (CGCT).** Like the USAC and UGTC, one of the more radical of East Cameroun's trade unions. The CGCT was at one time the local branch of the Communist-dominated French Confédération Générale du Travail. The CGCT also had close relations with UGTAN (the "militant" black pan-African trade union) and with the Communist WFTU. In 1963 the CGCT merged with other East Camerounian unions to form the Fédération des Syndicats du Cameroun (q.v.).

**CONFERENCE ON THE CONSTITUTIONAL FUTURE OF THE SOUTHERN CAMEROONS** see FOUMBAN CONFERENCE

**CONFERENCE ON THE PLEBISCITE QUESTION** see MAMFE CONFERENCE; UNITED NATIONS, "CAMEROONS SESSION" OF GENERAL ASSEMBLY

**CONGRESS OF BERLIN.** The international conference held in Berlin between November 15, 1884 and February 26, 1885, and attended by fourteen countries, of which Germany, France, Great Britain, the United States,

Belgium and Spain, were the most important. Though the principal outcome of the Congress was to regulate navigation on the Congo and Niger Rivers, and though territorial matters were little discussed, its practical effect was to ratify various colonial spheres of interest in Africa and to dampen future conflict over such issues. The Germans felt that the Congress had also solidified their hold over the Kamerun and Togo protectorates, established in 1884.

CONSTITUTION OF THE CAMEROUN REPUBLIC (1960). The 1960 constitution was drafted by the Consultative Committee in a brief three months in order to meet the deadline for independence on January 1, 1960. The document was ratified by popular referendum on February 21, 1960, by 797,498 affirmative to 531,000 negative votes. The constitution created a unitary state with a unicameral national assembly elected by direct universal suffrage. See NATIONAL ASSEMBLY OF CAMEROUN. In its sections dealing with the presidency, the constitution was remarkably similar to that of the Fifth French Republic. Because of the Cameroun Republic's short existence, many of the constitution's administrative provisions were not implemented nor its delegated powers exercised to their full extent. Indeed, much of the Cameroun Republic's existence was taken up with preparing for its demise, or evolution into a federal system. See FOUMBAN CONFERENCE.

CONSTITUTION OF THE FEDERAL REPUBLIC OF CAMEROON (1961). On October 1, 1961, when the British Southern Cameroons became a part of the new Cameroon Federal Republic, the Constitution of 1961 came into effect. The document created a federal system with two states, the East and West Cameroon, each with its own Government, headed by a Prime Minister, and legislature. The West Cameroon legislature included a House of Chiefs. The Federal Government was headed by a President and Vice-President, a cabinet, and a federal legislature of 50, in which ten seats were reserved to West Cameroon. Broad powers were given the federal government, and provision was made for the gradual incorporation of most important state domains into the national (federal) system. The 1961 Constitution was amended twice; in 1969 (which changed the succession procedure, permitted the Federal Assembly to prolong its life, and changed the procedures whereby the state Prime Ministers were chosen and the State Legislatures could be dissolved) and in 1970 (which made the function of Vice-President incompatible with any other position, a move designed to permit J. N. Foncha to be divested of his post as West Cameroon Prime Minister).

CONSTITUTION OF THE UNITED REPUBLIC OF CAMEROON (1972). Following the referendum of May 20, 1972, the new Constitution of 1972 came into effect. The country's third basic document since 1960, it radically altered the structure of power and government. Under the new law, the states were merged into a new national government, and their governments and powers superseded. The locus of power is clearly in the Presidency (the office of Vice-President having been eliminated), and the sole legislative organ is the National Assembly, which meets for two thirty-day sessions per year. The new Constitution was followed by a reorganization of the country's administrative system, as well as new dispensations for integrating its diverse educational and legal systems. In effect, the 1972 Constitution restores the unitary regime created in 1961, but with strengthened Presidential powers.

CONSULS, BRITISH, FOR THE BIGHT OF BIAFRA (FERNANDO PO).
1853 James Beecroft
1855 T.J. Hutchinson
1861 Capt. Richard J. Burton
1864 C. Livingston
1873 G. Hartley
1878 D. Hopkins
1880 Edward H. Hewett

COORDINATION DES INDEPENDANTS CAMEROUNAIS (INDECAM). Like Esocam and Renaicam, Indecam was a short-lived government-backed anti-UPC political group. It was organized on November 8, 1952 in Edéa after a vigorous pamphleteering campaign, but was weakened by leadership rivalries and vanished by 1959.

COTONNIERE INDUSTRIELLE DU CAMEROUN (CICAM). If expansion plans are completed, the Cameroon Cotton Industry will be the largest textile complex in francophone Africa. Partially financed by the European Development Fund, the plans call for raising the capacities of the weaving factory in Garoua and the bleaching, dyeing and printing factory in Douala in order to produce 6,000 tons of cloth per annum. See COTTON.

COTTON. First introduced into Cameroun in 1950 by the Compagnie française pour le Développement des Fibres Textiles (CFDT), which established experimental stations and provided seeds, equipment and training to local peasant farmers. By 1965 cotton was Cameroon's third largest export crop, but far behind coffee and cocoa. New ginning factories, cotton seed oil pressing plants and processing plants have expanded cotton production and aided in the economic development of the north. See COTONNIERE INDUSTRIELLE DU CAMEROUN.

COURANT D'UNION NATIONALE (CUN). On June 6, 1956, seventeen days before the loi-cadre (q.v.) was to go into effect, Soppo Priso (q.v.) launched CUN, the purpose of which was to unite all the political parties in Cameroun on a common "minimum program." Its main themes were rejection of the loi-cadre, reunification of the Cameroons, and proclamation of a general amnesty (for the banned UPC). Although initially warmly received in the south and joined by many prominent people, extremists and moderates clashed at the congress at Ebolowa in November 1956, over whether or not to boycott the forthcoming elections to ATCAM. This split led to the CUN's disappearance only five months after its inception. However, CUN was significant in drawing together the most important political personalities in the Territory on a basic nationalist program of independence, unification and reconciliation.

COURT OF EQUITY. Established by agreement between white traders and the Douala chiefs in the late 1850s, the Court of Equity sat in Douala and was composed of German and British merchants as well as local chieftains. The Court was created in order to settle peacefully disputes between the traders and among the continually warring native chiefdoms. It could levy fines and penalties or, if necessary, call in British gunboats to enforce law and order and restore the calm necessary for the white man's trade. The English consul Hewett (q.v.) revived the somewhat moribund Court in 1883. With the establishment of the German protectorate in July 1884, Nachtigal and Buchner (both q.v.) tried unsuccessfully to gain control of the Court from its incumbent British merchants. Finally in December 1884 the German admiral Knorr, having put down a native rebellion (see LOCK PRISO, CHIEF), forcibly abolished the Court of Equity, thus removing the last vestige of English authority in the Cameroons. The following year under the Kamerun's first governor, Julius von Soden (q.v.), the Germans established a dual court system (one for whites and one for Africans) to replace the Court of Equity.

-D-

DAN FODIO, UTHMAN (OTHMAN, OSMAN, USUMAN), 1754-1817. Founder of the Sokoto Fulani empire. Dan Fodio was born at Marafa, in the Gobir area of what is now northern Nigeria, then one of Hausa states of the region. He studied in Agades, Morocco, and returned home to serve as tutor to one of the royal princes of the Hausa king Wawa Zangworo. In 1802, a new Hausa king who feared Fulani influence had Dan Fodio dismissed from the court, and he returned to his village to teach Islamic law and to preach the purification of the faith, which he considered had been debased by the Hausa rulers. Despite efforts to silence him, he succeeded in rousing the Fulani population, and in 1806 declared a jihad (holy war) against unbelievers and in particular, against the Hausa kingdoms. His cause was everywhere victorious, and by the time of his death he had founded an empire that stretched some 1,250 miles east-west from Masina on the upper Niger to Adamawa on the Benué. Dan Fodio fixed Sokoto as his capital, and it remained the principal town of the empire (though not its official capital) until its final dissolution during the early decades of the twentieth century. Following Dan Fodio's death, the empire was divided among his three sons. See ADAMAWA.

DAOUDOU, SADOU, 1926- . Minister of Defence. Daoudou was born in 1926 at Ngaoundéré; he was educated at Garoua and at the Collège de Bongor (Chad). From 1948 to May 1957 he was an administrative assistant at Maroua, then becoming Deputy Subdivisional Chief of Kaelé. In 1958 he moved to the Prime Minister's office as Chef du Cabinet (Principal Secretary) and in 1960, won a seat in the National Assembly as deputy from Adamawa. In May, 1960, he was appointed Secretary of State for Information in Prime Minister As-

salé's cabinet, and in June, 1961, became Minister of
Armed Forces, a position he retained in the Federal
cabinet and in the cabinet of President Ahidjo's government after Cameroon became a unitary state in 1972.
M. Daoudou is considered one of Cameroon's political
"old timers, " and is a close confidant of President
Ahidjo.

DE GAULLE, CHARLES, 1890-1969. Statesman, general,
and President of France. On October 8, 1940, after
Free French representatives had "rallied" Equatorial
Africa and Cameroun to his cause, de Gaulle landed in
Douala to symbolize Free French return to French
soil. Thereafter, de Gaulle visited Cameroun three
times: in 1944 before opening the celebrated Brazzaville Conference (which radically altered the premises
of French post-war colonial policy); again in 1958,
when he campaigned for the ratification of his proposed
Constitution (which included provisions for a new French
Community, and an option for independence); and for
the last time in 1966.

DEMOCRATES CAMEROUNAIS see PARTI DES DEMO-
CRATES CAMEROUNAIS

DENHAM, DIXON see CLAPPERTON, HUGH

DEUTSCHE KOLONIALGESELLSCHAFT. An important German irredentist organization which in 1926 began to
propagandize for the return of the colonies Germany
lost after World War I. It had 250 branches, 30, 000
members and the participation of important government
figures in Berlin. After Hitler's accession to power,
the campaign to regain the Cameroons (and other former colonies) included the widespread publication of
colonial propaganda, radio broadcasts and diplomatic
pressures on the French and British governments.

DIBONGE, R. JABEA K. (also DIBONGUE), 1896-1963(?).
Politician. Born in October, 1896, in Douala, Dibongé was a member of the Akwa clan, one of the
most prominent in Douala. He was educated in German schools, winning the Governor Puttkammer Prize
in 1911, as top student in the German Protectorate.
By the time the Germans left the country (1916), Dibongé had risen to be the highest ranking African in
the Kamerun government, clerk to the Douala District

Commissioner. He left Douala in 1918 and moved to the British Cameroons, eventually joining the Nigerian civil service and becoming, in 1937, Assistant Chief Clerk at Buea, and in 1944, Chief Clerk in Enugu (Eastern Nigeria). He returned to Douala in 1947, and in 1949 went to Buea and joined Dr. Endeley in working on behalf of the then Cameroons National Federation, which advocated reunification of the French and British Cameroons. In Buea he helped form the French Cameroons Welfare Union, devoted to advancing the interests of Doualas in the British Cameroons, and which also favored reunification. In 1960 he shifted his position, favoring merger with Nigeria and urging his fellow Southern Cameroonians to so vote in the UN plebiscite of 1961. Mr. Dibongé was active on the Southern Cameroons Marketing Board and was, for a time, Chairman of the Southern Cameroons Development Agency.

DOBELL (GENERAL) CHARLES M. A British officer in World War I who launched a seaborne expedition against the Germans in Kamerun. Douala fell to his troops on September 26, 1914. With the collapse of German resistance in 1916, Britain and France divided Kamerun into zones of influence. Dobell took charge of the new British Cameroons possessions. See AYMERICH, JOSEPH G.

DOMINIK, (MAJOR) HANS. German officer and colonial official. Dominik arrived in Yaoundé from Germany in 1894, and under orders from Governor Jesco Puttkamer, established a military camp from which pacification expeditions could be launched to the north. In 1899 Dominik helped to put down a revolt among the Bulu; turning north and west, he led expeditions against the Bamiléké, and finally against the Fulani lamidos in the north. Maroua fell to him in 1902, as did Mora that same year. He turned the latter town into fortifications that held out against Allied troops until the end of the Kamerun campaigns of the First World War.

DO POO, FERNAŌ, (FERNANDO PO). 15th century Portuguese explorer. Not much is known about Fernando Po, though historians agree that he discovered the island that bears his name in 1472, and during the same year, visited Mount Cameroon and explored the coast along Ambas Bay, the site of present-day Victoria. It is possible that he also visited the mouth of the Wouri River, though there is little direct evidence to that point.

DOUALA. 1) A port city near the mouth of the Wouri River. Douala was the site of the first European trading activity, the first urban center to receive the full impact of the Westernization process, and has been the largest town in the Cameroon since 1884, the beginning of German colonial rule. Douala had an estimated population of 250,000 in 1971. It is the Cameroon's principal port and most important commercial center. As in many rapidly expanding urban agglomerates across Africa, Douala has undergone serious social and economic dislocations. Industrialization and urbanization have led to the breakdown of traditional social structures, a burgeoning population (quadrupled since 1947), large numbers of unemployed, and ethnic tensions between the original inhabitants (Doualas) and the increasingly numerous immigrants.

2) An ethnic group numbering about 50,000 today and located in and around the town of Douala. The Douala people were the first Cameroonians to be subjected to Western influence through European military, merchant and missionary activity. In the seventeenth century the Douala chiefs served as middlemen in dealings with the various European powers and controlled the slave traffic from the interior. With the increasing incursion of white traders, the Douala moved into other endeavors, notably the sale of land to European speculators. Since 1947 the percentage of Douala in the town has decreased from 46% to 20% as other ethnic groups, particularly the Baméléké, greatly increased in size. More important, Douala economic influence has correspondingly decreased as the immigrants have come to dominate retailing, transportation and most of the unskilled labor fields. The immigrants also made considerable inroads into previously Douala-dominated trades such as government service and education.

DOUALA MANGA BELL, (PRINCE) ALEXANDRE, 1897-1966. Politician and paramount chief of the Douala. The son of Chief Rudolph Douala Manga Bell, hanged by the Germans in 1914 on charges of treason. Born December 3, 1897 in Douala, Alexandre attended primary school in Douala, then undertook secondary and university studies in France and Germany, graduating magna cum laude from the University of Heidelberg. Although he had been a critic of French administration during the mandate period, the French regarded him so highly that they named him a member of the French delegation to the United Nations conference in San Francisco in 1945. Douala Manga Bell returned home and used his prestige to win an election to the first French Constituent Assembly. He went on to win re-election to the second Constituent Assembly, and then, to the French National Assembly in November, 1946. He was returned to the French National Assembly in 1951, and again in 1956. In 1952 he became a Councillor to the Cameroon Territorial Assembly, and when Cameroon became independent in 1960, was elected a Deputy to the country's first National Assembly.

DOUALA MANGA BELL, (PRINCE) RUDOLPH, 1873-1914.
Rudolph Douala Manga Bell was the oldest son of the Douala king Manga Ndumbe. Following his studies at the Gymnasium at Ulm, Germany, he returned home in 1896, becoming a civil servant, then, upon the death of his father in 1908, becoming paramount chief (chef supérieur) of the Douala people. Chief Rudolph came into conflict with the German administration over the expropriation by the latter of lands on the Joss plateau, allegedly in contravention of the Protectorate Treaty of July 12, 1884. Rudolph was divested of his title by the Germans in 1913, and in 1914 was accused by the administration of seeking to foment rebellion among Cameroon chiefs and of having entered into clandestine relations with enemy powers. He was charged with high treason, arrested, and hanged on August 8, 1914.

"DUCK BILL." The area between the Logone and Chari Rivers in northeast Cameroon, ceded by France to Germany on November 4, 1911, as part of the compensation for the surrender of German rights in Morocco. The area ceded involved some 275,000 square kilometers.

-E-

EBERMAIER, KARL. The sixth and last German governor of the Kamerun, from 1912 until the Allied occupation of the colony in 1916. In his first two years Ebermaier was faced with increasingly serious resistance of the Douala people, resulting from a highly unpopular attempt on the government's part to move the Douala out of their city and expropriate some of their lands. The execution of their chief, Rudolph Douala Manga Bell, made the Douala particularly bitter and rebellious. With the fall of Kamerun to the Allies, Governor Ebermaier was interned, along with the remaining German forces, by the Spanish in Rio Muni.

EDEA. The largest city in the Sanaga-Maritime province and the site of a large hydro-electric and aluminum-smelting complex built by the French-financed company Alucam in the late 1940s and early 1950s. The extremely cheap hydro-electric power produced by the generators at Edéa (on the Sanaga River) made it possible to attract foreign bauxite (principally from Guinea), which is processed into finished aluminum products by the Alucam plant. See BAUXITE.

L'EFFORT CAMEROUNAIS. A Catholic weekly newspaper founded in 1955 and published by the Paulist Fathers in Yaoundé. It followed a relatively liberal line editorially and was often critical of the government. Over the years a number of issues were confiscated when the paper presented stories that the government wanted suppressed. The newspaper ceased publication during 1970 due to "financial difficulties."

EGBE TABI, EMMANUEL, 1929- . Minister and West Cameroonian politician. Egbe Tabi was born May 24, 1929, in Bachua-Akagbe, and attended schools in Bali, Tali, and in 1949, earned his Cambridge School Certificate. From 1950 to 1951 he served as a clerk in the administrative offices in Mamfe. In 1951 he left for further studies at Fourah Bay College, Freetown (Sierra Leone), then to the University of Durham where he earned a Diploma in Business Administration. After his return to Cameroon, he served as Deputy Personnel Officer for the Cameroon Development Corporation (1956-58). As of 1958 he attended the School of Law at London University, and was called to the Bar in 1960. In 1961 he became legal counsel to the CDC, but later that year, following his election as Speaker of the West Cameroon Assembly, he was named Deputy (Federal) Minister of Justice; a post he filled until

1970, when he was named Federal Minister of Posts and Telecommunications.

EKANGAKY, NZO (EKHAH NGHAKY), 1934- . Secretary-General of the Organization of African Unity, former Federal Minister. Ekangaky was born on March 22, 1934, in Nguti. He was educated locally and in Nigeria, where he was awarded a B.A. in 1959 at the University of Ibadan. In 1960 and 1961 he studied diplomacy at the University of Bonn, Germany. From 1959 to 1960 he occupied several administrative positions in Cameroon before being named (1962) Deputy Foreign Minister. From 1964 to 1965 he was Federal Minister of Health and Population, and in 1965, became Federal Minister of Labor and Social Welfare, a position he held until 1972, when he was chosen to become Secretary-General of the OAU. Active in party affairs, he was Secretary-General of the Kamerun National Democratic Party (1962-66), and since then has been a member of the Executive Committee of the Cameroon National Union. Between 1961 and 1970 he also served in both the West Cameroon legislature and the Federal Assembly. Widely traveled, bilingual, he also published two political pamphlets.

ENDELEY, (DR.) EMMANUEL LIFAFE MBELE, 1916- . Medical doctor, former Prime Minister of the British Southern Cameroons trusteeship. Born April 10, 1916, a son of Bakweri chiefs, he attended schools in Buea, Bonjongo, Umuahia (Eastern Nigeria) completing his education at the Nigerian School of Medicine at Yaba and in 1942 entering Nigerian public service as an Assistant Medical Officer. Endeley became principal medical officer of the Cottage Hospital in Buea in 1945, and in 1947 undertook to organize the workers of the Cameroon Development Corporation. He subsequently became General Secretary of the CDC Workers' Union (1948), leading the workers in several strikes, and making representations to a visiting United Nations mission. In 1949 he and Nerius N. Mbile founded one of the first Southern Cameroons political parties, the Cameroon National Federation; he also assumed the Presidency of the Bakweri Improvement Union, an organization with political and cultural purposes. In 1950 Endeley left the CDCWU to devote his full time to politics, and in 1951 he was elected to the Eastern Nigerian Assembly as one of the Southern Cameroon's representatives. He espoused the cause of separate regional status for the Southern Cameroons, and in 1954 was named Leader of Government business in the Southern Cameroons' own House of Assembly. Endeley became Prime Minister of the Southern Cameroons in 1958, but relinquished the post to John Ngu Foncha when the latter's Kamerun National Democratic Party narrowly won the general elections of 1959. Dr. Endeley then became Leader of the Opposition. From 1959 to 1961 he campaigned actively to keep the Southern Cameroons in the Nigerian federation, but saw his view overwhelmingly rejected when, in a UN-administered plebiscite, the people voted to join the Cameroon Republic. Thereafter he remained in what became the West Cameroon Assembly, finally retiring to his medical practice in 1966.

ENGLISH LANGUAGE. The British colonists, merchants and missionaries who introduced English to the coastal Cameroonians were more concerned with spreading commerce and the rule of Britannia than in assimilating the natives into British culture. As a result, the British approached the language barrier in Cameroon in a practical, informal manner and were often satisfied with the varieties of pidgin English which sprouted out of the myriad commercial and mission contacts. Compare: FRENCH LANGUAGE. The use of pidgin English has become enmeshed in the whole controversy over a lingua franca in Cameroon. See BILINGUALISM. English courses offered by the U.S.A.I.D. program and the Peace Corps have improved both the teaching and learning of English, although there is still resistance to it among north Cameroonians and some east Cameroonian officials.

ETEKI MBOUMOUA, WILLIAM-AURELIAN, 1933- . Former federal Minister of Education. Born October 20, 1933 in Douala, he studied first in Douala, and then took both parts of the Baccalauréat in France. In 1953 he earned his licence en droit, and in 1955 entered the École Nationale de la France Outre-Mer, from which he graduated in 1959 as an Administrateur d'Outre-Mer. Upon his return to Cameroon, he was first appointed Deputy Prefect in Yabassi, then Prefect of the Sanaga-Maritime Department. In June 1961 he was named Minister of Education, Youth, and Sports, a post he held until 1968. He then joined the United

Nations Educational, Scientific, and Cultural Organization in Paris, becoming President of UNESCO's General Conference.

ETHNIC CONFLICT. The Cameroon Republic presents an unusually complex and fragmented ethnic picture. There are more than 136 identifiable linguistic groupings in the former East Cameroon and about 100 vernaculars in the former West Cameroon. Ethnic or inter-tribal conflict has had a long history in Cameroon (e.g., the Bassa-Bakoko versus the Bulu and Beti peoples). Latent ethnic hostilities periodically break out into open fighting and bloodshed (e.g., Bakossi versus Bamiléké). See TOMBEL MASSACRE. The influx of rural migrants to the larger Cameroonian cities has incited new ethnic animosities with economic overtones. See IBO; LE PROBLEME BAMILEKE. Cameroonian political parties and trade unions were often formed along tribal or ethnic lines (e.g., the Bamiléké in the Union des Populations du Cameroun). Mediating ethnic rivalries and calming ethnic hostilities are among the most difficult and yet necessary tasks of the Cameroonian government.

EUROPEAN DEVELOPMENT FUND (EDF). An agency of the European Economic Community (q.v.) which provides economic aid in the form of grants and loans to its member countries. Total EDF commitments to Cameroon by January 1970 were almost $106 million. The EDF is financing the construction of a major bridge which will cross the Benué River (q.v.) at Garoua (q.v.). See FONDS D'AIDE ET DE COOPERATION; TRANSCAM RAILWAY.

EUROPEAN ECONOMIC COMMUNITY (EEC). The Cameroon Republic is an Associate member of the Common Market through its adherence to the Yaoundé conventions of 1963 and 1969. Cameroon has benefited by the lowering of the common external tariff for a number of its primary products: coffee, cocoa, and palm oil. Cameroon's overall trade pattern is weighted heavily toward French and Common Market channels, both in value and volume. In 1969, 70% of its imports came from EEC members, while 73% of its exports went to EEC countries. See also EUROPEAN DEVELOPMENT FUND.

EVOLUE (similar to ASSIMILE). The Gallicized African elite who had become assimilated to French law, language and customs and who were accordingly granted greater rights than the indigenous masses. See INDIGENAT.

EVOLUTION SOCIALE CAMEROUNAISE (ESOCAM). An early anti-UPC political grouping, like Indecam and Renaicam, which was organized in 1948 by the French administration in Cameroun with strong Ngondo backing. Esocam's leaders, mainly Bassa notables and some Douala, attended the second KUNC conference at Kumba in December 1951, where they opposed the resolutions on independence and unification of the two Cameroons, as did Kumsze and Ngondo (both q.v.) which were also represented. Thereafter, Esocam decided to try to oppose every UPC cell in the Sanaga Maritime Region with an Esocam cell. Esocam faded away by 1955.

EWONDO. The largest unit of the Beti-Pahouin ethnic grouping. See BETI-PAHOUIN.

"EXTERNAL" UPC. The foreign-based wing of the outlawed Union des Populations du Cameroun after it was ejected from the British Cameroons. Such UPC leaders as Moumié, Kingué, and Ouandié (q.v.) attempted to guide the guerrilla and terrorist activities of the "internal" UPC in Cameroun from bases abroad in Cairo, Conakry and Accra during 1958-59. While in Cairo the exiled UPC leadership was permitted by Colonel Nasser to open an "information bureau," to publish pamphlets, and to broadcast over Radio Cairo. Presidents Sékou Touré of Guinea and Nkrumah of Ghana gave Moumié extensive financial and political support. See "BAMILEKE" REBELLION; NATIONAL ARMY OF KAMERUNIAN LIBERATION.

-F-

FANG. The language spoken by one of the main subgroups of the Beti-Pahouin; also designates the several Fang-speaking ethnic groups in Cameroon, Gabon, Equatorial Guinea, and Congo/Brazzaville. See BETI-PAHOUIN.

FEDERAL INSPECTORATES. The Cameroon Federation was divided into six administrative Inspectorates, five in East Cameroon and one for the whole of West Cameroon. Federal inspectors had headquarters in Buea in the West and in Bafoussam, Bertoua, Douala, Garoua, and Yaoundé in the East. Their job was to supervise and coordinate the work of all federal officials and departments within their jurisdiction and to report directly to the President through the Minister Delegate to the President in charge of Federal Territorial Administration and Public Service. By their almost plenary powers of supervision, investigation and control of all activities of federal officials, including the authority to call upon the police or armed forces for aid, the federal inspectors insured federal authority at the state and local levels and represented the principal guarantee of centralized government control. A new administrative arrangement was introduced in 1972, whereby West Cameroon was divided into two provinces and the East into five provinces, each headed by a governor rather than a federal inspector.

FEDERAL NATIONAL ASSEMBLY. The federal legislative body of the Cameroon Republic, 1961-1972. It was a unicameral legislature elected for five years by direct, secret, and universal suffrage in each state on the basis of one deputy for each 80,000 inhabitants. The first Federal Assembly, however, was composed of deputies selected by the two states' legislatures; there were forty deputies from the East and ten deputies from the West (all 50 were members of the ruling Cameroon National Union Party, q.v.). Elections to the Federal Assembly were held in 1964 and 1970 (the latter delayed a year so as to coincide with the presidential election), and the 4:1 East-West ratio was maintained in both instances.

FEDERAL UNIVERSITY OF CAMEROUN. Opened in 1962, the Federal University at Yaoundé moved in 1967 and 1970 out of temporary quarters and into two new sets of buildings, constructed mainly with financing from the French Fonds d'Aide et de Coopération (q.v.). Since 1963 the University has had three faculties: law (which includes economics and politics and attracts over 60 per cent of the students), letters (which includes history and sociology), and sciences.

Fédération 44

The University has a Center for African Research, a medical school under construction, and two "normal schools" which produce secondary teachers, primary school inspectors, and instructors for teacher-training institutions. Although created as a bilingual institution of higher education, it has remained heavily francophone. See BILINGUALISM.

FEDERATION DES SYNDICATS DU CAMEROUN (FSC). Created on January 23, 1963, the FSC brought together four of the largest trade unions in Cameroun (USLC, UGTC, CGCT, USAC) and several of the smaller independent ones, with a combined membership of about 60,000 workers in 1965. This figure represented perhaps 87 per cent of all East Cameroun trade-union members. With this merger the FSC became--despite the "autonomy" required by its statutes--the labor arm of the dominant Cameroon National Union party (q.v.).

FERNANDO PO. An island in the Bight of Biafra named after a Portuguese explorer who visited the area in 1472. See DO POO, FERNAO. Later Portuguese settlers on the island traded in slaves, gold and ivory with the coastal peoples and developed sugar plantations. Spain acquired Fernando Po from Portugal in 1777. Great Britain, with Spanish permission, established a small settlement on the island in 1827 in order to better police the coast in its efforts to eliminate the slave trade. The British settlement included a Baptist mission which was eventually pressured by Catholic Spain into leaving. See SAKER, ALFRED. German military and civilian personnel were interned on the island during World War I.

FLEGEL, EDUARD F., 1832-1886. German explorer. Between 1879 and 1883 Flegel actively explored the Benue River and the Adamawa area for Germany. His attempt (with Staudinger) to penetrate the Benue via the Niger was frustrated by Bismark's 1886 treaty with extended British sovereignty to Yola.

FON. Traditional designation for "chief" among the Bafut, Bali, Bamiléké, Bamoun, and Nsaw peoples.

FONCHA, JOHN NGU, 1916- . Former Prime Minister of West Cameroon and Vice-President of the Cameroon Federal Republic. Foncha was born on June 26, 1916 in Bafreng, in the former British Southern Cameroons. He was educated in Bamenda, and attended secondary school near Onitsha, Nigeria. From 1940 to 1955 he taught in various Catholic schools in Bamenda, and during this period, began his political activities by organizing and leading first a group called the Cameroon National Federation (1949-1950); then in 1951, with N. N. Mbile, the Cameroon National Congress. From 1951 to 1954 he served in the Eastern Nigerian Assembly, and in 1955, founded the Kamerun National Democratic Party (KNDP), of which he was the General Secretary during its entire lifetime (1955-1966). The KNDP won the general elections of 1959, and Foncha became the Southern Cameroon's Prime Minister, a position he held until 1961, when the two Cameroons became the Cameroon Federal Republic. A supporter of unification, his campaign helped the pro-unification position win the U.N. plebiscite of 1961. From October 1961 to 1965 he served as Vice-President of the Cameroon Federal Republic, simultaneously holding the position of Prime Minister of West Cameroon. In 1965, running with President Ahidjo in the national elections, he was returned for another five-year term as federal Vice-President, but gave up the Prime Ministership of West Cameroon. In 1970, he "retired" from political life when Mr. S. T. Muna, who had been West Cameroon Prime Minister, was chosen to run with President Ahidjo in the general elections of that year.

FONDS D'AIDE ET DE COOPERATION (FAC). The successor to FIDES, FAC is a French aid fund which has supplied both technical assistance and non-repayable grants to Cameroon for capital development projects. With the abatement of the "Bamiléké" rebellion (q.v.), FAC took an inventory in late 1962 of the damage done in the Bamiléké areas in order to determine the costs of rebuilding. It also provided about $6 million for the construction of new facilities at the Federal University of Cameroun (q.v.) and over 2,000 m. CFA Francs for the expansion of the rice growing enterprise run by SEMRY at Yagoua (q.v.).

FONDS D'INVESTISSEMENT POUR LE DEVELOPPEMENT ECONOMIQUE ET SOCIAL DES TERRITOIRES D'OUTREMER (FIDES). This French governmental "investment fund for the economic and social development of overseas territories" contributed almost 77 billion

French francs ($154 million) to Cameroun's development between 1950-1958. The aid money supported such items as the Cameroun budget, local administrative expenses, the construction of infrastructure, scientific and technical research, and social services such as health, housing and education. FIDES was later renamed Fonds d'Aide et de Coopération (q.v.).

FONLON, BERNARD NSOKIKA, 1924- . Politician, educator. Born on November 19, 1924, at Nsaw, West Cameroon, he attended various Catholic schools in the Southern Cameroons until 1939. During 1940-41 he was an assistant teacher at St. Anthony's school, and during the 1942-45 period attended secondary school at Christ the King College, Onitsha (Nigeria). From 1946-1947 he was a tutor at St. Joseph's College, Sasse (Buea). During 1948-53 he studied philosophy and theology at Bigard Memorial Seminary, Enugu (Nigeria), which was followed by a year of teaching at Christ the King College. As of 1954 he continued his studies in literature at the National University of Ireland, Dublin, where he was awarded the M.A., then undertook further study at the Sorbonne, and Oxford. In 1961 he took his Ph.D. in literature at Dublin. During 1961 he served as Private Secretary to West Cameroon Prime Minister Foncha, and later that year was appointed Chargé de Mission (Special Advisor) to President Ahidjo. In 1964 he was named Deputy Minister of Foreign Affairs; in 1968 he became federal Minister of Transportation and Posts and Tele-Communications; and in 1970, assumed the functions of Minister of Public Health and Population. He left the government in 1972, following creation of the unitary state. Dr. Fonlon is the founder and Editor-in-Chief of the cultural review, Abbia.

FORCED LABOR (also called CORVEE). The practice followed by both German and French colonialists for over half a century whereby local workers were conscripted, without adequate pay or medical supervision, to build roads, railways and other public projects. Two German rail lines, the Nordbahn (northern line) and the Mittellandbahn (central line), stretching north and east respectively from Douala for over 300 kilometers, were built with forced labor. Under the French mandate forced labor was linked to a system of taxation known as prestation (q.v.) and enforced by resort to the indigénat (q.v.). The French used corvée labor to extend the Mittellandbahn through an unhealthy forest region, resulting in a high mortality rate among the workers. The shackling and flogging of these laborers was not uncommon. This use of conscripted labor aroused a great deal of indignation abroad. As a result of the urging of the Permanent Mandates Commission (q.v.) of the League of Nations, the French administration finally diminished its use of corvée labor in 1933 and abolished it altogether in 1952. See MISE EN VALEUR.

FORCES VIVES DE L'OPPOSITION (FVO). A movement of opposition deputies launched by Soppo Priso and Marcel Beybey-Eyidi (both q.v.) in order to counter the growing strength of the northern-based Union Camerounaise (q.v.) by forming a united front of southern-based minority parties. The FVO held several conclaves in late 1959 and early 1960 which were attended by representatives of the many parties, groups and movements in opposition to Ahidjo: a number of tribal associations, the militant labor federation CGCT, some ralliés UPC and UPC affiliates, as well as MANC and and PDC members. They encouraged participation in the February 1960 constitutional referendum but advocated rejection of "Ahidjo's Constitution." With little success in the referendum, the FVO criticized both the UPC-inspired disorders and the government's harsh counter-measures, as well as the complicated new electoral procedures which the Ahidjo government had instituted for the April elections to ANCAM, procedures which, they felt, would deprive minority parties of a voice. With the continued fragmentation of the southern political arena, the defection of deputies to the UC and the defeat of Soppo Priso in the April 1960 elections to ANCAM, the FVO became another moribund movement on the path to Ahidjo's parti unifié (q.v.). See also GROUPE DE HUIT; MOVEMENT D'ACTION NATIONALE CAMEROUNAISE; PARTI DES DEMOCRATES CAMEROUNAIS.

FOUDA, ANDRE, 1930- . Mayor of Yaoundé, politician. Fouda was born in Djoungolo, near Yaoundé. He was educated in primary and secondary schools in Yaoundé, and in 1948 was employed as Postal Clerk. From 1952 to 1956 he served in the Territorial Assembly. In 1958 he was appointed Minister of National Economy, which post he held until 1960, when he was defeated for a seat in the new National Assembly. He returned to the East Cameroon Assembly in 1964, remaining a Deputy until 1970. In 1961 he also became a member of the East Cameroon Economic and Social Council. His position of longest tenure has been the Mayorship of Yaoundé, which he assumed in 1956. Fouda usually ran as a political independent, but he has had close associations with the once-important Démocrates party.

FOULBE see FULANI

FOUMBAN CONFERENCE. A post-plebiscite meeting between representatives of Southern Cameroon and the Republic of Cameroun at Foumban, July 17-21, 1961, to resolve the differences between the Foncha and Ahidjo conceptions of the nature of the forthcoming federation. Foncha's ideal was a loose federation, a highly decentralized collaborative alliance which would safeguard the powers of the states as against the federal authorities. Ahidjo's conception of a federation entailed a highly centralized, strong federal government whose powers would exceed those of the constituent states. At this conference and one at Yaoundé the following month, the differences were resolved and a draft federal constitution was produced which adhered more to Ahidjo's centralized scheme than to Foncha's looser union.

FRANC ZONE. A monetary organization based on the French franc and covering monetary transactions in countries such as Cameroon, which use the CFA franc. See CFA FRANC.

FRANCO-CAMEROUNIAN "SECRET" AGREEMENTS. Signed on December 25, 1959 by France and the soon-to-be independent Cameroun Republic, the agreements provided for a continuation of French military, monetary and economic aid to Cameroun and for diplomatic, cultural and economic cooperation between the two nations. Clauses permitting the stationing of French troops on bases within Cameroun later came under fire by some Camerounian politicians. See MINIMUM COMMON NATIONAL PROGRAM. The French military mission in Cameroun numbered 2,000 officers and men in September 1960, nine months after independence.

FRENCH CAMEROONS WELFARE UNION (FCWU). Founded originally as the French Cameroons Welfare Association in 1949, probably by R. J. K. Dibongé (q.v.), the organization was intended to strengthen the solidarity of those Douala living in Southern Cameroons and to mobilize the French Camerounian workers on the Southern Cameroons plantations. It was also concerned with securing the right of French Camerounians residing in British Cameroons to vote in elections held there. Contact with the UPC for a brief period brought Dibongé's espousal of unification. See KAMERUN IDEA, THE; KAMERUN UNITED NATIONAL CONGRESS. At one time the organization had a membership exceeding four thousand.

FRENCH LANGUAGE. The spread of French culture being one of the principal goals underlying the policy of assimilation, French colonial authorities insisted that Africans learn the French language. The teaching of French was accordingly placed at the core of the educational system outlined in the July 25, 1921 decree. Compare: ENGLISH LANGUAGE. A commitment to French was central to France's philosophy of its "civilizing mission." See ASSIMILATION, POLICY OF. Most Cameroonian officials, especially in East Cameroon, speak French today and most federal government business is carried on in French. See, however, BILINGUALISM.

FRENCH UNION. Created by the French Constitution of October 1946 (Title VIII, Articles 60-82), the French Union was a political institution designed to allow the French dependencies some measure of participation in governmental policies affecting them. A distinction was made between Associated States (e.g., Indo-China, Tunisia), which were an integral part of metropolitan France, and Associated Territories (i.e., Cameroun and Togo), which were not formally annexed to France. The French Union had legislative and executive organs: the Assembly and the High Council, respectively. The Assembly, in which Camerounian representatives participated, in actuality had little more than an advisory role in regard to legislation affecting the overseas territories. The real administrative and legislative powers regarding Cameroun were vested in the French Republic's Ministry for Overseas France. Cameroun was also placed under the jurisdiction of a High Commissioner (q.v.). The system of the French Union thus perpetuated to some extent the former colonial relationship between metropolitan France and her dependencies, and was in the eyes of some Africans clearly contradictory to the aims and spirit of the UN Trusteeship Agreement (q.v.). As if to emphasize the integration of France and her dependencies, all members of the French Union were given full rights in the French parliament itself. See ASSOCIATION, POLICY OF.

FRONT NATIONAL UNIFIE (FNU). A loose coalition of the four leaders of the East Cameroonian opposition parties formed in May 1962 to reject President Ahidjo's proposal for a parti unifié (q.v.), a unified or united party. The four leaders--Charles Okala of the PSC, Theodore Mayi-Matip of the parliamentary UPC, André-Marie Mbida of the PDC, and Dr. Marcel Beybey-Eyidi of the new PTC--issued a Manifesto on June 23, 1962 declaring that a unified party system would sabotage their own parties for the benefit of the ruling Union Camerounaise party (q.v.) and would ultimately culminate in a "fascist-type dictatorship." The Manifesto went on to label Ahidjo's call for a parti unifié as mere rhetoric to disguise single party rule or a parti unique (q.v.). Within three weeks these opposition leaders were arrested and tried for having violated a two-month old law making it a crime to "incite hatred and conflict and disseminate news prejudicial to public authorities." They were convicted and sentenced to both fines and imprisonment. One immediate political result was that ten opposition deputies in ANCAM within the next five months decided to join the UC. The short-lived Front National Unifié was one of the last attempts by opposition parties in East Cameroon to resist Ahidjo's drive toward national party consolidation and a one-party state. See also FRONT POPULAIRE POUR L'UNITE ET LA PAIX.

FRONT POPULAIRE POUR L'UNITE ET LA PAIX (FPUP). A parliamentary grouping of Bamiléké deputies (initially 18) in the 1960 National Assembly (q.v.) or ANCAM. The FPUP included a number of ex-UPC maquisards who had accepted collaboration with the government. The group complained of political and economic discrimination against the Bamiléké people, appealed to their brethren to heal their divisions, and pledged FPUP efforts toward peace and unconditional amnesty. In the face of official government pressures, the FPUP disintegrated in April 1961. Most of its members joined the Union Camerounaise (q.v.) within three months. The group's nominal leader was Pierre Kamdem Ninyim (q.v.) who continued to direct guerrilla activities in the Bamiléké districts while holding the national post of Minister of Health. The FPUP included such others as Victor Kanga and Happi Louis Kemayou (both q.v.). The erosion of the FPUP was an example of the trend toward a one-party state in East Cameroon, culminating in the formation of the Union Nationale Camerounaise (q.v.) in 1966. See also FRONT NATIONAL UNIFIE.

FULANI (also called FULAH, FOULAH, FOULBE). The dominant ethnic group in northern Cameroon, composed primarily of Muslim pastoralists and livestock farmers and numbering at least 450,000 in 1967. Believed to have originated in the Fouta Djallon and the Senegal valley in western Africa, the Fulani invaded and conquered the four centuries-old empire of Bornu at the beginning of the nineteenth century and established their own empire over much of what is today Nigeria, Cameroon and the neighboring states. See DAN FODIO, UTHMAN.

Fulani emirates, lamidates (chiefdoms ruled by a lamido or Fulani chief) and sultanates were eventually subordinated to British, German and French colonial rule, although many individual emirs and lamibé (plural of lamido) were able to maintain their local authority even to the present. In 1958 Fulani chiefs allied themselves with Ahidjo (himself a Fulani Muslim) and his party, the Union Camerounaise, and have long had political control over such principal towns of the Cameroon north as Maroua, Yagoua, Garoua, and Ngaoundéré. The language of the Fulani is called fulfuldé.

FULLER, JACKSON. British missionary. Fuller was born in Jamaica, the son of a freed slave. He arrived in Fernando Po with Alfred Saker in 1844, and went to Douala in 1858 to help the latter operate his mission. Saker ordained him a minister in 1859. Fuller is credited with opening the missions at Deido and Bonaberi.

-G-

GANTY, VINCENT. A non-Cameroonian African (probably born in Guinea) residing in Paris who became the self-appointed spokesman for the Douala chiefs in their attempts in the early 1930s to regain the lands which the Germans had expropriated during the period of their colonial rule. In 1931 Ganty sent numerous petitions and memoranda to the Permanent Mandates Commission (q.v.) of the League of Nations, backing the Douala chiefs' land claims, criticizing the French administration of the mandate in the areas of education, justice, labor and taxation, and even demanding the creation of a Cameroun Republic with himself as president. Ganty's efforts were not completely altruistic: he was reported to have raised 100,000 francs in annual subscriptions for his "organization."

GAROUA. A principal town (and capital of a Fulani chiefdom) in the Cameroon north. Its population was estimated at 30,000 in 1967. The Benué River (q.v.) passes through Garoua, making it one of the most important ports of the country. Until 1901 Garoua was one of the last holdouts against German control of the whole Kamerun. Ahmadou Ahidjo (q.v.) was born in Garoua in 1924 and thirty-four years later founded his Union Camerounaise (q.v.) there. The Union Nationale Camerounaise (q.v.) held its 1969 party congress in Garoua.

GENDARMES. East Cameroon police. Due to the scarcity of local police in West Cameroon at the time of federation, gendarmes from the East were moved in to provide "security" and to "maintain law and order." The gendarmes' activities, sometimes brutal, over-zealous and extra-legal, raised a public outcry in West Cameroon. The gendarmes came to be feared almost as much as the remaining maquisard die-hards who carried out terrorist activities sporadically and from whom the gendarmes were authorized to protect the populace. In addition, the gendarmes prompted a debate over federal-state control of internal security forces.

GEORGE, SAMPSON A., 1922-1959. West Cameroon nationalist politician. George was born in Mamfe(?), and was educated in Mamfe, Lagos, and Port Harcourt. He served as postal clerk and telegraphist 1942-45, then became active in Nigerian trade union affairs, serving as Secretary to the Lagos Town Council Workers' Union (1945-46). During this period he helped found, and became Secretary-General of one of the earliest West Cameroon proto-nationalist organizations, the Cameroons Youth League. From 1951 to 1954 he was a member of the Mamfe Town Native Authority. In 1953 he was named advisor to the Cameroons delegation to the London Constitutional Conference, at which separate regional status for the then Southern Cameroons was discussed. During this period he also served as a member of the Eastern Nigerian House of Assembly and the Nigerian national House of Representatives. In 1954, when the Southern Cameroons became a quasi-federal territory, George was elected to its House of Assembly, in which he served until his death. George was a fervent advocate of reunification of the two Cameroons, and published an important pamphlet (Kamerun Unification) on the subject.

GERMANY, COLONIAL POLICY AND LEGACY OF. In its thirty-year protectorate over the Kamerun, the German administration laid the foundation for modern Cameroon's social overhead capital (i.e., basic transportation, communication, irrigation, and power facilities): wharves and docks at Douala, Kribi, Campo, Tiko and Victoria; rail lines north from Douala to Nkongsamba and east almost to Yaoundé; many bridges, roads and paths; and well-constructed public buildings, many of which are still in use. The plantations and development projects begun by the Germans gave the subsequent French and British administrations an established basis for further economic development. In addition, German rule and law helped shape the political attitudes of two generations of Cameroonians.

Less measurable legacies include the effects of widespread missionary and educational activity, and the disruptions caused by the introduction of the money economy, the military conquest, the use of forced labor, and the expropriation of native lands. The Germans are remembered by the Cameroonians themselves as always strict, at times harsh, but usually just. Indeed, the "Kamerun Idea" (q.v.), evoking a half-mythical "golden age" when the Cameroon was one and undivided, became an important symbol for Cameroonian nationalists during the 1940s and 1950s. See BASEL MISSION SOCIETY; SODEN, JULIUS VON; and the cross-reference cited therein.

GLEIM, OTTO. The fifth governor of the Kamerun (1910-1912), following Theodore Seitz (q.v.). During his short rule the question of the German government's plan to expropriate Douala property came up. Gleim sympathized with the Douala and supported their strenuous objections to the scheme.

GOVERNORS, GERMAN, OF THE KAMERUN PROTECTORATE.

| | |
|---|---|
| von Soden, Julius | 26 May 1885 - 14 February 1891 |
| von Zimmerer, Eugen | 15 April 1891 - 13 August 1895 |
| von Puttkamer, Jesco | 13 August 1895 - 9 May 1907 |
| Seitz, Dr. Theodor | 9 May 1907 - 27 August 1910 |
| Gleim, Dr. Otto | 28 August 1910 - 29 January 1912 |
| Ebermaier, Karl | 29 January 1912-1915 |

"GRASSFIELDERS." A name often used to designate the Tikar and Bamiléké peoples, inhabitants of the Bamenda highlands. See TIKAR.

GROUPE DE HUIT. A parliamentary coalition of eight opposition deputies in ALCAM, composed primarily of MANC representatives, which tried to counter the growing strength of Prime Minister Ahidjo's northern-based party, the Union Camerounaise (q.v.) with efforts to achieve a united front of southern-based parties. The members of the Groupe were Bétoté Akwa, Charles Assalé, Gaston Behlé, Hans Dissaké, Ekwabi Ewane, Aloys Ntonga, François Obam, and Paul Soppo Priso. The Groupe's numbers and its cohesion dropped when Assalé and Ewané accepted ministerial posts in Ahidjo's preindependence government and even supported Ahidjo's demand for full powers (pleins pouvoirs) in October 1959. Behlé also broke ranks to become Minister of Labor and Social Welfare. Behlé and Assalé campaigned for an affirmative (i.e., pro-UC) vote in the February 1960 constitutional referendum. In the April 1960 elections to ANCAM, four members of the Groupe were not re-elected: Soppo Priso, Akwa, Behlé and Ntonga. See also FORCES VIVES DE L'OPPOSITION.

-H-

HADJI; EL HADJ (literally, the pilgrim). A title--and mark of respect--taken by any Muslim who has completed the obligatory pilgrimage to Mecca. (Also spelled Alhadji, El Hajj, Alhajji, etc.)

HANNO (also: HANNON). A Phoenician explorer who sailed from Carthage in the fifth century B.C. with a great expedition of sixty vessels and explored the west coast of Africa. According to some interpretations of his celebrated Periplus (Journal), Hanno sailed as far south as the Bight of Biafra where he wrote of seeing the eruptions of a large volcano which he named "The Chariot of the Gods." Later commentators sought to identify the volcano as Mount Cameroon.

HAPPI, (DR.) JEAN-CLAUDE, 1927- . (Federal) Commissioner for Public Health, physician. He was born on July 16, 1927 in Bana, was first educated locally, then went on to France where he completed his schooling at Cannes. He was awarded a scholarship to study medicine at Paris University, and presented a doctoral thesis in 1957. In 1958 Dr. Happi became medical superintendent of Yaoundé Hospital, and then served in the Ministry of Health before being appointed Director (later, Commissioner) of Public Health in 1963. Dr. Happi served a term in the Executive Council of the World Health Organization, and was President of the Organization for Coordination in the Fight against Endemic Diseases in Central Africa (OCEAC).

"HARMONIZATION," POLICY OF. An educational policy designed to integrate and synchronize the differing structures of the two states' school systems after federation. In 1965 primary education was "harmonized" by the inauguration of a six-year cycle in West Cameroon, replacing its previous eight-year cycle. By 1967, the harmonization of secondary syllabuses for languages, mathematics, history, and geography had been achieved in both East and West Cameroon. Harmonization has also involved attempts to equalize the lengths of courses, and to synchronize the school year and school holidays in both states. See BILINGUALISM. In a larger sense, harmonization also connotes the efforts of the two states after federation to standardize and integrate their disparate economic, administrative and legal systems. Harmonization has not proceeded without some fears and doubts on the part of the West Cameroonians that they may be culturally assimilated by their dominant eastern partner.

HEWETT, EDWARD HYDE. The British "itinerant consul" for the Gulf of Guinea to whom King Bell (q.v.) wrote a letter in 1881 requesting British protection and annexation. Hewett visited the Cameroons coast and reported to London his misgivings about increased French trading in the area and the need for British treaties with the coastal chiefs to prevent the cession of this territory to other foreign powers (i.e., France). Due to governmental delays and procrastination, Hewett returned to the Cameroon River to conclude treaties of annexation on July 19, 1884, only to be greeted with the news that a week earlier the Germans, under instructions from Bismarck, had established a protectorate over the Cameroons coast. Hewett remonstrated with King Bell, but to no avail, and then convoked a meeting of the Court of Equity (q.v.), at which time he instructed various British traders present to "keep in touch with" those chiefs who had not signed the German treaty. See LOCK PRISO, CHIEF. Hewett did manage to acquire Victoria (q.v.) as a British possession the week before, but having "lost" the Cameroons, he was dubbed "Too Late Hewett."

HIGH COMMISSIONER. The French official who exercised extensive political authority in each of France's overseas dependencies after 1946. The High Commissioner's reports to the French government on "his" territory's status were carefully read, and his recommendations about the pace of a territory's "progress" were usually followed. High Commissioner Jean Soucadaux presided over the Cameroun's early developments under its Territorial Assembly (q.v.). Roland Pré (q.v.) was High Commissioner at the beginning of the Bamiléké or UPC Rebellion (q.v.) in 1955. As the Cameroun headed toward independence, and as Camerounian politics, parties, and personalities became more diverse, the turnover rate of High Commissioners became high, with Messrs. Pierre Messmer (1956-57), Jean Ramadier (1957-58) and Xavier Torré (1958-59) filling the post for brief periods.

HOLT, JOHN, 1842-1904. English businessman. In 1862, the British Consul at Fernando Po, James Lynslager, himself a merchant, brought young John Holt from Liverpool to be his secretary. Lynslager died in 1864, and Holt took over his commercial activities. In 1867 he founded his own company, John Holt, Ltd., Liverpool, which established an agency at Bimbia and elsewhere along the West African coast. It eventually became one of the largest British trading firms in Africa.

HOUSE OF CHIEFS. A traditional governmental structure and part of the bicameral legislature of West Cameroon. Seats in the House of Chiefs were not elective; they went to the incumbents of the most important chiefdoms of West Cameroon. As such, the number of seats was not fixed (usually it varied from 22 to 26), but its members were given the same stipends and allowances as the elected members of the West Cameroon House of Assembly. The continued existence of the House of Chiefs was guaranteed in the 1961 Federal Constitution, but its powers were only quasi-legislative and meager. Its powers were limited to deliberation, advice, and delay of certain measures for some months. The House of Chiefs was abolished in 1972 for "efficiency's sake."

-I-

IBO. A southern and eastern Nigerian ethnic group with some 25,000 members in West Cameroon. Aggressive, enterprising and commercially adept, the Ibo tended to dominate the petty commerce of West Cameroon, especially in Kumba. See KUMBA. The anti-Ibo propaganda of the KNDP in (British) Southern Cameroons just prior to the 1961 plebiscite was undoubtedly a factor in the voters' decision to opt for unification with the Cameroun Republic, rather than with Nigeria. See PLEBISCITES, UNITED NATIONS. During the Nigerian civil war (1967-70) perhaps as many as 25,000 Ibo refugees fled from the neighboring secessionist state of Biafra into West Cameroon. The Cameroon Federal Government sheltered them in refugee camps but officially supported the Nigerian central government.

INDEPENDANTS D'OUTRE-MER (IOM). A parliamentary grouping of Black Africans in the French National As-

Indigénat 58

sembly, formed in September 1948. Dr. Louis-Paul
Aujoulat (q.v.), Léopold Senghor of Senegal, and others helped found IOM in order to gain political leverage and bargaining power in the precariously balanced French political system. By 1953 the IOM group included 14 representatives of the Black African constituencies and was loosely allied with the centrist- French Mouvement Républicain Populaire (MRP), from which Douala Manga Bell (q.v.) had defected. However, competition for leadership of the group plus disagreements during passage of the loi-cadre (q.v.) were obstacles to united action by its members.

INDIGENAT. A comprehensive set of violations and penalties which formed one basis for French colonial policy in the Cameroun during the mandate period. On the assumption that the vast mass of native subjects (sujets indigènes) should be accorded stricter treatment and fewer rights than those natives who had become Gallicized or "assimilated" into European law and customs (assimilés or évolués), French colonial administrators enforced a separate legal regime on the sujets indigènes. The indigénat restricted their civil liberties (e.g., rights of association and movement), and permitted forced conscript labor to build roads and other public works. Established by decree in 1924, the indigénat conferred on French and French-trained administrators in the mandate territory broad disciplinary powers and virtually unchecked authority to punish natives without a trial for a variety of ill-defined violations, such as vagabondage, acts of disorder, and hindering traffic. The indigénat was condemned by the French administrators attending the Brazzaville Conference in 1944 and was abolished in 1946. See also BRAZZAVILLE CONFERENCE; FORCED LABOR; ASSOCIATION, POLICY OF; MISE EN VALEUR.

INTERNATIONAL CONFEDERATION OF FREE TRADE UNIONS (ICFTU). A non-Communist international trade-union organization with which the Fédération des Syndicats du Cameroun (q.v.) was affiliated.

INTERNATIONAL COURT OF JUSTICE (WORLD COURT).
The United Nations plebiscite in Northern Cameroons on February 11-12, 1961 showed a clear desire on the part of those in the territory to unite with Nigeria.

The Ahidjo government of the Republic of Cameroun, charging that the plebiscite had been conducted unfairly and with undue pressure on the voters, contested the vote at the United Nations but was rebuffed by the General Assembly on April 21, 1961. The Camerounian government then took its case to the World Court. The appeal was more a symbolic protest than a substantive attempt at reversal, because Court cases often take years and because the two Cameroons (the Republic and the former British Southern Cameroons) were to unite in a federation just six months later. Indeed, in December 1963, the Court refused to decide on the merits of the case, contending that the General Assembly of the United Nations had already settled the issue. See PLEBISCITE, UNITED NATIONS; NORTHERN CAMEROONS CASE.

INTERNATIONAL FEDERATION OF CHRISTIAN TRADE UNIONS (IFCTU). A confessional--mainly Catholic-- group of trade unions with which the Union des Syndicats Croyants du Cameroun (q.v.) was affiliated.

ISLAM. Muslim influences have operated for centuries in the Cameroon north, but it was not until the beginning of the nineteenth century and the jihad of Uthman Dan Fodio that much of the Chad plain and the Adamawa Plateau was Islamized. See DAN FODIO, UTHMAN. There are approximately 600,000 Muslims in East Cameroon, most of them Fulani and residing north of the inland forest plateau. Proselytizing on the part of Muslim teachers still goes on, much of it directed at the large numbers of animist peoples who constitute about 45 per cent of the population in the East and about 55 per cent in West Cameroon. The Muslim Fulani of the Cameroon north established a pattern of authority and administration that resisted and even retarded the Westernization of that area. Compare: CATHOLICISM; PROTESTANTISM.

-J-

JAMOT, (DR. COL.) EUGENE, 1879-1937. French medical officer largely responsible for eliminating sleeping sickness in West Africa. Dr. Jamot was born on November 14, 1879 in Creuse, France. He earned his medical degree in 1908, and joined the military health

service in 1910. He was posted first to Chad and then
to Brazzaville. In 1922 he was sent to the French
Cameroun, charged with finding the means to overcome
sleeping sickness, which had spread over most of the
central part of the territory. Through his vigorous
efforts in research, mobile treatment centers, popular
education, and preventive medicine, Dr. Jamot succeeded, between 1922 and 1939, in lowering the inci-
dence of the disease from 25% of the population in the
affected areas to less than 1%. He was also named
chief of the anti-sleeping sickness services in French
West Africa. He retired in 1936 to France. In Cameroun, he was memorialized by having a hospital named
after him, and a commemorative stele was erected in
his honor near Ayos.

JANTZEN UND THORMAHLEN. A Hamburg trading firm involved in the early German commercial and colonial activities in the Cameroons. Johannes Voss, an agent of
the firm, was present at the signing of the German
protectorate treaties with the Cameroonian coastal
chiefs in 1884. See also HEWETT, EDWARD HYDE;
NACHTIGAL, GUSTAV; WOERMANN, ADOLF. In the
three decades prior to World War I, Jantzen & Thormählen and the Woermann company, rivals to some extent, had over 17,000 Africans working on their 58
plantations. In order to improve their commercial
capabilities, Jantzen & Thormählen invested in better
dock and rail facilities and encouraged exploration into
the interior. See ZINTGRAFF, EUGEN; KRIBI.

JEUNESSE CAMEROUNAISE FRANÇAISE (JEUCAFRA). A
French-sponsored, quasi-political, cultural-youth organization founded in 1938 by a wealthy young assimilé
from Douala, Paul Soppo Priso (q.v.). Jeucafra was
the successor to L'Union Camerounaise (q.v.) and included French members. French colonial policy and
the indigénat (q.v.) prevented mass participation in
politics, so Jeucafra remained principally a discussion
group for the Camerounian elite. Its program consisted of opposition to Nazi Germany, the furtherance
of patriotism, and the suggestion that the Cameroun
mandate be incorporated into France so that, as a
colony, it could enjoy full French citizenship. Jeucafra survived World War II as the only association
through which African Camerounians might address
themselves to political matters. It was the seminal

group from which the leadership of postwar political parties was drawn. Two of its more prominent members were André Fouda and Dr. Louis Aujoulat (both q.v.). Jeucafra became Unicafra in 1945. See UNION CAMEROUNAISE FRANÇAISE.

JEUNESSE DEMOCRATIQUE CAMEROUNAISE (JDC). One of many UPC subsidiary organizations which served as a propaganda organ and petition-writing agency in the UPC pyramidal structure. Formed in 1952, and led by T. Mayi-Matip (q.v.), the JDC (youth group) was dissolved on July 13, 1955 by a decree of the Council of Ministers after the May riots in Yaoundé. Following its proscription in Cameroun, the JDC set up its headquarters across the border in Kumba (British Southern Cameroons) and again became active in its publication of propaganda literature and its campaign to recruit members and sympathizers for the UPC's nationalist cause. See also UNION DEMOCRATIQUE DES FEMMES CAMEROUNAISES.

JOINT PROCLAMATION see "BAMILEKE" REBELLION

JUA, AUGUSTIN NGOM, 1924- . Former Prime Minister of West Cameroon. Born in Wum, Jua was educated locally, becoming a teacher and serving in the Bamenda area before turning to politics in 1952, when he became a member of the Wum Native Authority Council. In 1954 he entered the Southern Cameroons House of Assembly, and in 1955 helped J. N. Foncha found the Kamerun National Democratic Party. In 1965 he was appointed West Cameroon Secretary of State for Finance, and later that year, was designated West Cameroon Prime Minister by President Ahidjo, a position he held until December, 1967, when he was replaced by S. T. Muna.

-K-

KAMDEM-NINYIM, PIERRE, 1936-1961. Former East Cameroon Minister. Born on May 10, 1936, he was educated in Baham, and later, 1952-54, at the Lycée Pascal, Paris. In 1954 he became traditional chief of the Baham (Bamiléké) group, also at that time becoming active in the guerrilla activities of the illegal Union des Populations du Cameroun (UPC) party. In 1956 he was

Kamerun 62

arrested, divested of his chieftaincy, and imprisoned until 1959, when he was amnestied. He stood for election in 1960 under the banner of the revived (and legal) branch of the UPC, and was elected to the National Assembly. In 1960 he was appointed East Cameroon Minister of Health, a position in which he served until June, 1961. In 1962 he was implicated in the murder of a deputy, tried and shot.

KAMERUN. German transliteration of Cameroon. See CAMAROES, RIO DOS. The official name of the German protectorate was the Schutzgebiet Kamerun. Kamerun had three capitals: Douala (1885-1901), Buea (1901-1909), and Yaoundé (1909 on).

KAMERUN FREEDOM PARTY (KFP). A small party in the Northern British Cameroons that campaigned for unification with Cameroun before the 1961 UN plebiscite. See PLEBISCITES, UNITED NATIONS.

KAMERUN IDEA, THE. The belief among many Cameroonian nationalists that the 32 years of German rule had welded the peoples of the British Cameroons and French Cameroun into a cohesive unit with distinctive cultural, economic, ethnic and social affinities and common values. Thus, it was held that the two territories should be "reunited" so as to reconstitute the "Kamerun Nation." In reality there was no "Kamerun nation," no awakening of national awareness under German rule. Although The Kamerun Idea exaggerated the extent of cultural and political commonalities between the two Cameroon Trust Territories, it served a symbolic function and was utilized by Cameroun nationalists to mobilize political sentiment in the 1950s. "Reunification" was a central objective of the UPS in East Cameroun and of KNDP in British Cameroons. See GERMANY, COLONIAL POLICY AND LEGACY OF.

KAMERUN NATIONAL CONGRESS (or CONVENTION) (KNC). Created in May 1953 by a merger of the CNF, KUNC, and most of the Cameroons block in the Nigerian Eastern House, the KNC was one of Southern Cameroons' three major parties in the mid-1950s. See also KAMERUN NATIONAL DEMOCRATIC PARTY; KAMERUN PEOPLES' PARTY. The party was launched by Endeley, Muna, Foncha (all q.v.) and others in the NCNC who demanded Cameroonian autonomy within the Nigerian federal framework. In December 1953 the KNC moved closer to a position favoring integration with Nigeria and away from the position favoring secession from Nigeria and eventual reunification with Cameroun. The KNC suffered a major split in 1955 when Foncha and others resigned to form the KNDP. In the March 1957 general elections the KNC won only six of the thirteen seats in the Southern Cameroons House of Assembly, while its ally, the KPP, won two seats. Finally, in January 1959 the KNC/KPP lost its majority to the KNDP, as it took only twelve of the 26 seats in the enlarged Assembly. The KNC and the KPP merged in 1960 to form the Cameroon Peoples' National Convention (q.v.).

KAMERUN NATIONAL DEMOCRATIC PARTY (KNDP). The governing party of West Cameroon from 1959 to 1966, founded by J. N. Foncha (q.v.) in March 1955 when he split with Endeley's KNC over the question of secession from Nigeria and reunification with Cameroun. The KNDP flirted briefly with the outlawed Camerounian UPC (1955-1957) but became disenchanted with it because of its radical activism and excessive anti-imperialist stance. See BAMENDA CONFERENCE (1955). Other KNDP leaders were Jua and Muna (both q.v.).

In the January 1959 elections in Southern Cameroon, the KNDP garnered fourteen seats in the House of Assembly to the KNC/KPP's twelve. Foncha became premier and left for the United Nations to plead his case before the special session of the General Assembly. See UNITED NATIONS, "CAMEROONS SESSION" OF GENERAL ASSEMBLY. In the 1961 UN plebiscite in Southern Cameroons, the KNDP succeeded in mobilizing the grasslands peoples of the Bamenda, Mamfe and Wum Divisions and the more Westernized people in the Victoria and Kumba Divisions into voting for unification with Cameroun. See PLEBISCITES, UNITED NATIONS. One of the KNDP's principal tactics before the plebiscite was to play on fears of Ibo domination. See ANLOO SOCIETY; IBO.

At the Bamenda "All-Party" conference in June 1961, and at the Foumban conference a month later (both q.v.), Prime Minister Foncha pressed for a loose federation with the Cameroun Republic. The KNDP consolidated its governing position in West Cameroon with its electoral victory in December 1961 and its role in federal politics by winning all ten seats to the federal National Assembly in early 1964. Yet the

KNDP, beginning with its national convention in 1963, began to develop rifts over the succession to party leadership positions and over the provisions for eventual merger with the East's single party, the Union Camerounaise (q.v.). By the time of the creation of the single national party, the Cameroon National Union (q.v.) in September 1966, the KNDP and its founder, Foncha, had been eclipsed by the politics and exigencies of national unification.

KAMERUN PEOPLES' PARTY (KPP). Formed in 1953 and led by Mbile, Kale and Motomby-Woleta, the KPP was a splinter group from the Kamerun National Congress (q.v.) following the governmental crisis in the Nigerian Eastern Regional House of Assembly. See NATIONAL COUNCIL OF NIGERIA and the Cameroons. The KPP urged the retention of links with the NCNC and continued association with the Eastern Region of Nigeria. The KPP won only two of the thirteen seats in the March 1957 election to the House of Assembly. It merged three years later with the KNC to form the Cameroon People's National Convention (q.v.).

KAMERUN SOCIETY. A small group of intellectuals, all employed by the Cameroons Development Corporation (q.v.) and attracted to the KNDP's reunification policy. In 1956 the group began rendering assistance to the KNDP by drafting speeches and policy statements. One of the Society's publications in 1957, entitled Economic and Financial Problems of the Cameroons was highly critical of Nigeria's economic policy toward the British Cameroons since World War II. The authors of this pamphlet, E. T. Egbe and S. J. Epale, later became ministers in the federal government.

KAMERUN TIMES see CAMEROON TIMES

KAMERUN UNITED NATIONAL CONGRESS (KUNC). Founded in August 1951 at Kumba by R. J. K. Dibonge and Nerius N. Mbile (both q.v.) as a splinter of the CNF, the KUNC was an outspoken unificationist organization in the Southern Cameroons. It adopted the German spelling (Kamerun) to indicate its pan-Cameroonian political stance. The KUNC made several contacts with UPC leaders at Kumba and Tiko in 1951-1952 to advance the cause of reunification but became disenchanted with the UPC's communist connections and its desire for hegemony within the nationalist movement. The KUNC re-merged with the CNF in 1953. See KAMERUN NATIONAL CONGRESS.

KAMERUN UNITED PARTY (KUP). A minor party in the Southern Cameroons led by Paul M. Kale (q.v.), which urged its followers to vote for independence in the 1961 UN plebiscite. Since "independence" was not one of the two alternatives confronting the voters, Kale suggested that people show their distaste for the given alternatives by taking the "middle way" and tearing their ballots in half. Few voters followed his advice. See PLEBISCITES, UNITED NATIONS.

KAMVEU. An hereditary council of notables that advised Bamiléké chiefs (Fons) on matters of importance.

KANGA, VICTOR, 1931- . Former Federal minister, attorney, politician. Kanga was born on February 19, 1931, in Banka (Bamiléké), and attended local schools until 1946, when he went to France and the Lycée Gambetta in Toulouse. From 1949 to 1952 he studied law in Toulouse, then went on to the University of Paris for advanced studies, earning his Doctorate in Law in 1956. During his stay in Paris he also attended the Ecole Nationale des Douanes (customs), which awarded him a diploma. He returned to Cameroun in 1957, and was appointed a customs inspector in Douala. He then went on (1958) to become Principal Secretary to the Minister of Education, then Director of Customs in Douala (1958), and in 1960 was elected to the National Assembly from the Wouri constituency. In 1960 he was appointed Minister of Justice, then (1961) Minister of National Economy in the new Federal cabinet. In December, 1966, a court sentenced him to four years' imprisonment for alleged publication of anti-government rumors, i.e., pamphlets claiming misuse of funds by high officials.

KINGUE, ABEL, 192?-1964. Revolutionary politician. Not much is known of Kingue's early life. By 1948 he had apparently become involved in the newly-founded Union des Populations du Cameroun (UPC), and tried unsuccessfully to win parliamentary seats under the UPC label at the general elections of 1949, 1951, and 1952. In 1955 Kingue, with the rest of the UPC leadership, fled to the British Cameroons following the UPC's unsuccessful revolt in Cameroun in May of that year. By 1954 he had already risen to the Vice-Presidency of the UPC. After 1955, Kingue, along with Moumié, became one of the principal exile UPC leaders, attempting to direct the continuing UPC rebellion in Cameroon. From 1955 to 1959 he found haven in Cairo, and finally, in 1959, settled in Conakry with other exiled UPC members. He died in Conakry on June 16, 1964.

KIRDI. An agglomeration of eastern Nigritic, plateau Nigerian, Sudano-Nigritic, and Chadic peoples living as hill dwellers and as nomads, mainly in the areas between the Mandara Hills and the Logone River north of the central plateau region. About 800,000 Kirdi are found in the Cameroon north. They constitute the majority in the northern regions but have never constituted a voting bloc. The term "Kirdi" (Fulani for "pagan") is a convenient designation and does not denote linguistic, social or ethnic homogeneity. The Kirdi do have certain similarities, however: (1) neither Muslim nor Christian, they usually practice forms of animism and ancestor worship; (2) they are opposed to the Fulani peoples, their traditional overlords, who tried to Islamize and subjugate them in the early nineteenth century, driving many of them into the mountains (see MATCHOUBE); (3) their economy and life style remain relatively simple, many of them still clinging to seminudity, practicing rudimentary agricultural methods, and engaging in barter trade. It is among the Kirdi that economic development, literacy and life expectancy are the lowest in the country.

KOLA NUTS. A walnut-sized nut traditionally traded by West African peoples. The nut, chewed, provides mild stimulation; commercially it is today used in the production of cola drinks. The Kola nut trade in Cameroon represented one of the principal linkages for the commercially adept Bamiléké.

KOM. An ethnic unit among the Tikar peoples.

KRIBI. An important port during the German protectorate period, but now in some decline. South of Edéa on the East Cameroon coast, it is now a tropical resort area and has a large fish cannery. In 1887, a German expedition which included botanists and zoologists, set out from Kribi to explore the Nyong River and to expand German rule into the interior. By 1895 settlements had been made at Yaoundé and Ebolowa. Kribi was nearly destroyed in 1899 during a Bulu uprising.

KUMBA. The largest town in West Cameroon with an estimated population (in 1967) of 40,000. Groups of Cameroonian nationalists held several conferences at Kumba, out of which grew the Cameroons National Federation (CNF) in 1949 and the Kamerun United National Congress (KUNC) in 1951. After its proscription in 1955, the UPC set up its first headquarters in Kumba, then part of British-administered Southern Cameroons. The British expelled the UPC in 1957 for directing terrorist activities. The inhabitants of Kumba have been economically threatened by the in-migration of Ibos and others from Eastern Nigeria, who took over much of the petty trading. The indigenous Cameroonians in Kumba showed their resentment of these developments by supporting both the Kamerun National Democratic Party (KNDP), with its anti-Ibo propaganda, and the extremist One Kamerun Party (OK), as well as voting overwhelmingly in the February 1961 plebiscite for unification of the two Cameroons.

KUMSZE. A traditional secret Bamiléké society which practiced "magical" rites. In May, 1948 Mathias Djoumessi, an important Bamiléké chief in French Cameroun and first president of the UPC, "revived" the Kumsze and merged it with the newly-formed UPC for the purpose of promoting pan-Bamiléké aspirations. The new Kumsze's anti-traditional bias alienated many chiefs and its significance dwindled. See also NGONDO.

KUOH, CHRISTIAN-TOBIE, 1913- . Born on April 23, 1913, Kuoh was educated in Cameroon. He became a sub-prefect in Douala in 1958, going on to assume the functions of principal secretary to the Prime Minister (1959), then Secretary-General (Administration) to the President (1960-1964). From 1964 to 1968 he was Director-General for State Control at the Presidency, and from 1968 to June, 1970, Minister-Delegate for the State Inspectorate. He is the author of a novel, A Personal Trial (1956).

KWAYEB, ENOCH KATE, 1924-    . Politician, lawyer, judge. Born in Bazou on November 26, 1924, Kwayeb attended local primary schools and, in 1945, entered the teaching profession as a "moniteur." As of 1948 he studied in France, first at a secondary school in Aix-en-Provence, then at the University of Toulouse, and finally at the University of Paris where he received Doctorates in Laws and Jurisprudence. In 1957-58 he attended the elite École Nationale de la France d'Outre-Mer. In January, 1959, Kwayeb returned to Cameroon to assume a judgeship in Yaoundé. During 1959 he served as Director of the Cabinet of the President of the Legislative Assembly, and between July 1959 and April 1960 was Director of the Cabinet of the Minister of Justice. He then served as Director of Cabinet to the Foreign Minister (1960), Prefect in the Bamiléké Departments (1960), and Federal Inspector for the Western Administrative Region (1960-63). In 1963 he was named Minister Delegate to the Presidency in Charge of the Federal Civil Service, and in 1968, became federal Minister in Charge of Territorial Administration. He lost his portfolio in 1971, in the wake of a cabinet reshuffle.

-L-

LAMIDO (plural: LAMIBE). Fulani chiefs of the Cameroon north. The lamibé have been Muslims since the jihad of Uthman Dan Fodio (q.v.). Traditionally powerful, even autocratic, in their lamidats (or kingdoms), they are viewed by many southerners as feudalistic, reactionary and opposed to modernization. Many of the deputies in the Cameroun Assembly were themselves lamibé and others were sons of lamibé who may indeed have sought a continuation of Foulbé privilege and dominance. Yet others from the north--most notably Ahidjo and Moussa Yaya (both q.v.)--were modernists and progressives. Ahidjo's government tried to limit the power of the more traditional lamibé by co-opting some, deposing others, and cutting off their sources of strength, such as tribute and their private police forces. See OUSSOURA TAXES. The principal lamidats are those of Ngaoundéré (founded 1836), Garoua (1938), Maroua (1919), and Rey Bouba (1804). Each lamidat has an elaborate hierarchy, including a galdima (prime minister), sarkin sanou (military chief), imam (principal religious leader), alkali (judge), wajin (minister), etc.

LAMINE, YERIMA MOHAMMAN, 1927- . Born on October 20, 1927, a son of the Lamido of Kolofata (Margui-Wandala), he was educated in Mora and Garoua. Lamine began his career working as a clerk in the French administrative offices at Fort Foreau and at the Maroua court. In 1956 he was elected to the Territorial Assembly, and in 1959 was a co-founder of Ahidjo's Union Camerounaise. He was returned to the 1960 National Assembly, served in the East Cameroun government as a Secretary of State, and in 1964 was named Deputy Prime Minister of East Cameroun. He was dropped from the new government formed in 1972, but remained an important official in the Cameroon National Union Party.

LANDER, RICHARD see CLAPPERTON, HUGH

"LA VOIX DU CAMEROUN." The UPC propaganda broadcast over Radio Cairo in 1957. The broadcasts stressed the brutality of the Ahidjo government in suppressing opposition and criticized the French government for giving Ahidjo the arms, ammunition and funds for its anti-insurgent campaign. See also LA VOIX DU KAMERUN.

LA VOIX DU KAMERUN. A bimonthly journal published in Cairo by the "external" UPC. President Nasser gave Ouandié, Moumié and Kingué refuge in the UAR and permitted the rebels to open a so-called information bureau which issued, along with other propaganda pamphlets, La Voix du Kamerun. The journal railed against the alleged harshness of the Ahidjo regime and applauded the sporadic successes of the maquis (q.v.) in Cameroun. It also castigated the French for supporting Ahidjo and tried to persuade African states not to recognize the new Cameroun Republic. See also "LA VOIX DU CAMEROUN."

LA VOIX DU PEUPLE. A rallié UPC newspaper.

LEAGUE OF NATIONS. French Cameroun and the British Cameroons were mandated territories under the League of Nations, administered by France and the United Kingdom but supervised by the League's Permanent

Mandates Commission. See MANDATE SYSTEM; PERMANENT MANDATES COMMISSION.

LECLERC, PHILIPPE. French General. During the night of August 26-27, 1940, Col. Leclerc, with a group of twenty-four Free French partisans took possession of Cameroun for Gen. de Gaulle. Leclerc subsequently became Free French Commissioner in Cameroon and, between 1941 and 1943, led a series of military expeditions against the German and Italian rear in Libya.

LEGISLATIVE ASSEMBLY OF CAMEROUN (ALCAM). On May 9, 1957 Cameroun's Territorial Assembly took the name Legislative Assembly and began a period of two and one-half years of self-government within the trusteeship framework and under the provisions of the Statute of the Cameroun (q.v.). The French High Commissioner (q.v.), however, remained responsible for the Cameroun's defense and foreign relations. Cameroun was now outside the French Union (q.v.) but continued to be represented in France's National Assembly.

André-Marie Mbida (q.v.), appointed by the High Commissioner and invested formally by ALCAM, was the first prime minister. His policies of military repression of the UPC and advocacy of a prolonged period before independence (as much as ten years), reduced his support in ALCAM, and Mbida was forced to resign in February 1958. He was followed by Ahmadou Ahidjo (q.v.), during whose premiership ALCAM adopted a resolution (October 24, 1958) proclaiming the desire of the Cameroun for independence, reunification of the French and British zones, and the termination of the trusteeship on January 1, 1960.

The rise of de Gaulle to the Presidency in France and the report of the 1958 UN Visiting Mission (q.v.) helped propel Cameroun toward independence, as Ahidjo at home adroitly mixed repression of the UPC with continued appeals for amnesty and reconciliation. See RALLIEMENT; TABLE RONDE. On November 22, 1958 ALCAM accepted a new French statute covering the transitional period before independence. Effective on January 1, 1959, the new Statute provided for the Cameroun's complete internal autonomy with its own elected representatives responsible for domestic legislation, administration and justice. France retained authority only for foreign policy, defense and currency.

Camerounians were no longer to be represented in France's parliament. ALCAM's last session was a turbulent eighteen-day affair in October 1959. Virulent debate surrounded Ahidjo's proposal to give his government the power to legislate by decree for six months (the pleins pouvoirs law), but it was passed fifty to twelve with one abstention. ALCAM's last act on October 30, 1959 was to choose a twenty-one member consultative committee to help draft a new constitution for the Cameroun Republic, to become independent on January 1, 1960. The Constitution, modeled after that of the Fifth French Republic, was approved by the Camerounian people (797,498 to 531,000) in a referendum on February 21, 1960. On April 10, general elections were held for the new ANCAM or National Assembly of Cameroun (q.v.).

LE PROBLEME BAMILEKE. The most vexing ethnic problem confronting Cameroon, it has two fundamental aspects: 1) within the Bamiléké community the traditional authority structures (i.e., the power of the chiefs, customs, the rules governing land use) are being questioned by the Westernized younger generation; 2) massive Bamiléké migration to the cities (due mainly to village overpopulation and fragmented land holdings) has brought pressures on the local townspeople who have lost to a large extent their economic and numerical dominance to the energetic and resourceful newcomers. See DOUALA; YAOUNDE. These problems of the use of Bamiléké land, the power of the chiefs, the alienation of Bamiléké youth and the frictions caused by Bamiléké emigration constitute a severe social crisis in Cameroon, and one which has erupted in periodic violence and bloodshed. See KANGA, VICTOR; TOMBEL MASSACRE; UNION DES POPULATIONS DU CAMEROUN.

LIKOMBA PLANTATION. A large and prosperous banana estate of former German ownership on the Tiko plain in the former (British) Southern Cameroons. The plantation was leased from the Nigerian government by the British company, Elders and Fyffes Ltd., in 1948 and was to be administered by the Cameroons Development Corporation after a period of eighteen years. In 1955 African workers on the plantation numbered 3,435. See LIKOMBA PLANTATION WORKERS' UNION.

LIKOMBA PLANTATION WORKERS' UNION. An important
trade union organization in Southern Cameroon which
was formed by a splinter group of the CDCWU in
1949. It affiliated with the All-Nigerian Trade Union
Federation in 1954 but after unification cut its ties
with the ANTUF. In 1962 the Likomba union joined
the West Cameroon Trade Union Congress (WCTUC).

LOCK PRISO, CHIEF. A pro-British Douala chief who
ruled Hickory Town on the Cameroon River and who
refused to sign the German protectorate treaty in
1884. Instead, Lock Priso signed a treaty of his own
with the British consul, Edward Hyde Hewett (q.v.).
Lock Priso had the sympathy, if not the support, of
English traders and missionaries when, in December
1884, he rebelled against his pro-German overlord,
King Bell (q.v.), who had signed the German protectorate treaty. The uprising was quickly quelled by
German marines and Hickory Town leveled. See
BUCHNER, DR. MAX.

LOGONE RIVER. One of the major rivers of north Cameroon, the Logone is a tributary of the Chari, which
flows into Lake Chad. In the Yagoua (q.v.) area it
forms the frontier between Cameroon and Chad. The
Logone River valley is an important area for rice cultivation. See SOCIETE D'EXPANSION ET DE MOD-
ERNISATION DE LA RIZICULTURE DE YAGOUA.

LOI-CADRE (literally: outline law). The enabling law
passed by the French National Assembly on June 23,
1956, which established the institutional framework
for autonomy in France's territoires associées. The
loi-cadre marked the beginning of a new era for Cameroun, signaling the introduction of the first really
large-scale reforms made in the territory since 1946.
See BRAZZAVILLE CONFERENCE. It gave Cameroun its first important push to independence by helping minimize delays in the parliamentary process, by
recognizing the possibility that the trust territory could
follow a political development suited to its particular
circumstances, and by providing for elections to the
Cameroun Territorial Assembly (q.v.) on the basis of
universal adult suffrage. See ASSOCIATION, POLICY
OF.

LOTIN SAME. The head of the Native Baptist Church in
Douala who, during World War I, fused his church with
the German Baptist Mission and formed the United Native Church. After the war French missionaries sought
to reestablish a measure of European control in the
United Native Church, and in 1922 secured Samé's expulsion on the grounds that he baptized polygamists,
meddled in politics and refused to obey European missionaries. His expulsion split the church and occasioned battles between dissident congregations over the
possession of certain church buildings. More important, the religious fervor of Samé's supporters, combined with Garveyite black nationalism and anti-colonialism, boiled over into a religious "revolt" which kept
the town of Douala seething for months during 1922-23.
The whole affair came to a close when the elders of
the church were forced to capitulate to the French administration, the church was given over to European
control in May 1923, and Lotin Samé was permitted to
return to his pulpit on condition that his sermons remained clear of racialist doctrine.

LUTHERAN SECT see PROTESTANTISM

-M-

MAMFE. An administrative region in West Cameroon bordering Nigeria, and a city therein which had an estimated population of 12,000 in 1967. As one of four
administrative divisions set up by the British in the
Southern Cameroons, Mamfe was subject to the policy
of "indirect rule," expressed through the creation of
Native Authorities (q.v.). In the 1961 UN Plebiscite
(q.v.), the inhabitants of Mamfe voted for unification
with the Cameroun Republic. See MAMFE CONFERENCE. During the Nigerian civil war (1967-70) Cameroon troops were sent to the Mamfe division to seal
the border.

MAMFE CONFERENCE. A two-day meeting of all Southern
Cameroonian political parties in August 1959 held at
the instigation of the UN General Assembly. The conference attempted (but failed) to resolve the differences
between Foncha and Endeley (both q.v.) regarding qualifications for voting in the forthcoming UN plebiscite
(q.v.) and the alternatives to be placed before the

voters. See PHILLIPSON, SIR SYDNEY; UNITED NATIONS, "CAMEROONS SESSION" OF GENERAL ASSEMBLY.

MANDARA. A northern Cameroon people inhabiting the southern borders of Lake Chad. The Mandara were Islamized in 1715, and attained their apogee as an important state during the reign of Boukar Guiama (1773-1828). Following Boukar's death, the Mandara undertook a series of wars against the Fulani and achieved a standoff, but were finally subjugated by Rabah in 1895. See RABAH.

MANDATE SYSTEM. Set up at the Versailles Peace Conference in 1919, the mandate system was embodied in Article 22 of the Covenant of the League of Nations. The system provided international supervision over the conquered colonies of Germany (and Turkey) and was administered by the League's Permanent Mandates Commission (q.v.). The object of the system was to prevent certain abuses in the mandated territories, such as forced labor and traffic in slaves. The system was not intended to prepare dependent peoples for eventual independence. The Covenant stated that the mandatory authorities (e.g., France and the United Kingdom in the two Cameroons) were to secure "the well-being and development of [dependent] peoples."

MANDATES, BRITISH AND FRENCH CAMEROON. According to Article 119 of the Versailles Treaty (June 28, 1919), Germany formally renounced title in all her foreign possessions to the victorious Allies. The Declaration of London, signed July 10, 1919, created the Mandates System (q.v.) and gave the Cameroon mandates to Britain and France, ratifying the Anglo-British accords of March 4, 1916, which partitioned the Kamerun protectorate between the two powers. France received four-fifths of the old Kamerun, less the "Duck bill" area (q.v.), which was returned to the French Congo. Britain received two noncontiguous areas which subsequently became the British Southern and Northern Cameroons territories. The mandate agreements were finally ratified by the Council of the League of Nations on July 20, 1922, and they remained in force until 1946, when the League finally dissolved itself and turned its various obligations, including the Mandates, over to its successor, the United Nations.

The two Mandates subsequently became part of the United Nations Trusteeship System (q.v.).

MAQUIS (literally: wild, bushy land). Rebel guerrilla bands whose members (maquisards) engaged in widespread acts of terrorism and sabotage in Cameroun from 1955 on. Two kinds of Cameroonian maquis groups may be distinguished:
    1) The maquis led by revolutionary UPC leaders (e.g., Ouandié, Um Nyobé) were well-trained and equipped abroad (e.g., China, Egypt, Algeria, Congo/ Brazzaville, Ghana). They sought to eliminate the French presence and to gain independence, reunification and the legal reinstatement of the UPC and, after 1960, to overturn the Ahidjo regime.
    2) The maquis operating under ad hoc leadership without specific political motivation consisted of marauding bands of terrorists.
    Overall guerrilla activity had diminished by 1962 with the death or ralliement of the rebels and government repression, although reports of sporadic guerrilla activity in the southeast and southwest continued until 1970. See "BAMILEKE REBELLION"; RALLIEMENT; UPC; UM NYOBE. The last important UPC maquis leader in Cameroon, Ernest Ouandié, was captured by the government in 1970 and executed in 1971. See OUANDIE, ERNEST.

MARIGOH MBOUA, MARCEL, 1921- . Former President of the Federal Assembly, politician, teacher. Born in 1921 at Nguelebok, he was educated locally, and between 1940 and 1952 was a teacher and school principal of the École Principale de Djoungolo (Yaoundé). He was elected to the Territorial Assembly in 1952, and re-elected to the later legislatures in 1956 and 1960. He first served under the banner of the Démocrates Camerounais, then the Union Camerounaise, and subsequently became one of the founding members of the Cameroon National Union, serving in various leadership capacities in each party. From 1957 to 1958 he was Minister of Labor and Social Legislation in Ahidjo's cabinet; in 1960 he became Vice-President of the Cameroon National Assembly, and in 1965, President of the Federal Assembly, a position to which he was re-elected in 1970.

MASSA. A leading ethnic group inhabiting the rice-growing areas of the Logone River (q.v.) valley area near Yagoua (q.v.). The Massa are principally farmers, fishermen and stock-breeders. They grow sorghum (one of the leading cereals of the savannah in West Africa) and herd cattle, not for food or trade, but for savings, social status, and communal exchanges. In addition, horses are considered a sign of wealth among the Massa. The Massa have plots of land called "Nagaba," each controlled by a mythical "master of the land." Efforts by SEMRY to encourage the Massa to plant rice have met with moderate success.

MATCHOUBE. Kirdi slaves or those captured by the Fulani during the jihad of Uthman Dan Fodio in the early nineteenth century. See DAN FODIO, UTHMAN; FULANI. The matchoubé lived with their Fulani overlords but were neither Islamized nor accepted into Fulani society. Some of the descendants of the matchoubé remain enslaved today, despite laws forbidding involuntary servitude, while others have achieved limited civil and social status, including service on local councils. See ISLAM; KIRDI.

MAYI-MATIP, THEODORE, 1927- . Politician. Born on June 2, 1927, in Eséka, he was one of the co-founders of the Union des Populations du Cameroun Party (UPC). In 1955, following an unsuccessful UPC-led revolt, Mayi fled into exile, then returned to enter guerrilla activity with UPC leader Rueben Um Nyobé (q.v.). When Um was killed in 1958, Mayi surrendered to the government and was subsequently rehabilitated, becoming part of the "legal" opposition to the Ahidjo government. In 1959 he was elected to the Legislative Assembly in a by-election, and in 1960, was re-elected to the National Assembly as part of the "legalized" wing of the UPC. In 1962, along with three other opposition leaders, Mayi was tried and convicted for alleged conspiracy and sedition against the government. He spent the next two and a half years in prison. In 1968 Mayi helped to dissolve the UPC, joining the dominant Cameroon National Union party.

MBIDA, ANDRE-MARIE, 1917- . Former Prime Minister of Cameroun. Born ca. 1917 at Edinging, near Yaoundé, he was educated in Yaoundé, matriculating from the Roman Catholic Seminary. After being employed as a legal secretary to a French attorney, Mbida set up his own business in Ebolowa in 1951. Elected to the Territorial Assembly in 1952, he also became, in 1956, a counselor to the Assembly of the French Union and a deputy to the French National Assembly. In the general elections of 1956, he defeated the incumbent, Dr. Aujoulat, and that same year, as head of the largest group of deputies in the Territorial Assembly, was asked to form the first Cameroon government. He served as Prime Minister until February, 1958, when, following a ministerial crisis, he gave up the Prime Ministry to his Deputy and Minister of the Interior, Ahmadou Ahidjo. Mbida helped to found the Démocrates Camerounais, which formed the first government, and pursued an anti-communist and anti-UPC policy. After his departure from the government, he went into voluntary exile (1959), joining the exiled leaders of the opposition UPC party in Conakry. Benefiting from an amnesty, he returned to Cameroun to contest the April, 1960 elections, and was re-elected to his old seat in the National Assembly. Though his Démocrates entered into the ruling coalition (with Ahidjo's Union Camerounaise party), Mbida steadfastly refused a ministerial portfolio. In 1962 he was arrested for an alleged conspiracy against the government, and spent over two years in prison. Released in 1965, he made his peace with President Ahidjo, and retired from politics to go back into business.

MBILE, NERIUS NAMASO, 1923- . Minister, politician, newspaperman. Mbile was born in Lipenja, in the then Southern Cameroons, on April 4, 1923. He was educated locally and in Eastern Nigeria. Active in the early days of Southern Cameroons nationalism with Dr. Endeley, he helped found the CDC Workers Union, and was General Secretary (and later President) of the Union from 1949 to 1951, as well as serving as general secretary for Endeley's political party, the Cameroon National Union. Subsequently, he was Deputy Leader of the Kamerun Peoples' Party (1953-59), Deputy Leader of the Cameroon Peoples' National Convention (1960-67), and political advisor to the Ndian section of the Cameroon National Union. He was a member of the Eastern Nigerian House of Assembly (1952-53), the Nigerian House of Representatives (1952-53), and the Southern Cameroons Legislature from 1957 on. He served as West Cameroon Minister of Works (1958,

1965-67), Minister of Lands and Surveys (1968), and Secretary of State for Primary Education (1969-72). Mbile is considered one of West Cameroon's political founding fathers; he long supported merger with Nigeria, but after 1961 became a supporter of President Ahidjo and the dominant Cameroon National Union.

MBWE-MBWE, ca. 18th century. Tenth ruler in the Bamoun dynasty founded by Nshare (q.v.). Mbwé-Mbwé was noted for his stature and love of war. During the early part of his reign he crossed the Noun River and forced the submission of 48 chiefs, whose territories he then caused to be settled with slaves he had captured during his campaigns. Also during his reign, his kingdom was invaded by the Fulani, and Mbwé-Mbwé fled from Foumban, which he had refused to fortify. The invaders took Foumban, then left it, and the king returned, this time determined to erect the necessary fortifications. When the Fulani returned and tried to storm the town, they were repulsed and the kingdom saved.

MERRICK, JOSEPH, 1808(?)-1849. Jamaican Baptist missionary. Merrick, the son of a former slave, came to Fernando Po in 1843, and later that year founded the Cameroons Mission in Bell-Town, Douala. In 1844 he founded another mission at Bimbia. Merrick earned a reputation as an explorer, teacher, minister, craftsman. He climbed Mount Cameroon and was the first non-African to visit the Bakoko people; he opened a school at Bimbia, translated the Bible into Isubu (the Bimbia dialect), and wrote a textbook for elementary classes in that language. He also set up a printing press--on which Saker's Douala Bible was printed--and developed a machine for making bricks out of local materials. Merrick's students were among the first Christian converts in Cameroon. In 1849 he sailed for England to go on leave, but died during the voyage.

MIGRATION. Aside from nomadic pastoralists, the internal movement of ethnic groups and migrant workers within the Cameroons, usually from the hinterland and plateau regions toward the larger towns and coastal areas, has given rise to two phenomena: urbanization, with its attendant problems of increasing pressure on the ability of the towns to absorb the newcomers and provide services and opportunities for employment; and socioethnic tensions between the indigenous town dwellers and the migrants, usually with economic overtones. See KUMBA; "LE PROBLEME BAMILEKE."

MINIMUM COMMON NATIONAL PROGRAM. With the Northern-based Union Camerounaise (q.v.) holding a tenuous majority of one in the 100-seat National Assembly of Cameroun (q.v.) after the April 1960 elections, southern politicians led by Mbida (q.v.) attempted to achieve a unified opposition to the UC. In May, thirty-eight deputies elected from southern districts attended a roundtable conference at Mbida's home in Yaoundé to solidify this opposition. The conference ended with a four-point "Minimum Common National Program" which called for: (1) an unconditional amnesty for UPC leaders and followers; (2) the departure of French administrators and repudiation of the Franco-Camerounian secret agreements (q.v.) of December 1959; (3) the withdrawal of French troops; and (4) the reunification of the two Cameroons.

The first three of these objectives failed to be realized because: (1) eighteen Bamiléké deputies withdrew from the conference to form their own parliamentary grouping, the Front Populaire pour l'Unité et la Paix (q.v.), thus preventing any southern bloc strategy; (2) President Ahidjo moved quickly to enlarge his parliamentary following in ANCAM by gaining adherents from MANC; and (3) Mbida was accused of opportunism and of trying to divide rather than unite the newly independent nation. The last objective, reunification, was achieved, but it had already been a basic policy of the regime and its leaders since 1958.

MISE EN VALEUR. (Connotes: "development," a dynamic transformation and realization of potential.) The French colonial policy of planned economic development, first elaborated by Colonial Minister Albert Sarraut in 1923. The policy expressed the need for cooperation between metropolitan France and the colonies, with the latter being reservoirs of raw materials for home manufacturers. The mise en valeur was a vital component of the French policy of "association" in the period before World War II in that it sought to secure the economic interdependence of France and Cameroun. From an economic standpoint the program of mise en valeur was notably successful in Cameroun: the territory's total trade increased five-fold between 1922 and 1938 and its social overhead (i.e., transportation and communications infrastructure, education, and so on) was considerably enlarged. From a political standpoint the program left a legacy of ill-will among many Africans because of (1) the heavy tax burden required to finance various projects; (2) the use of corvée labor reinforced by the indigénat system; and (3) the displacement of local populations in the course of road-building, the enlargement of the port of Douala and the expansion of European and native plantations. See INDIGENAT.

MISSIONS, CATHOLIC. Catholic missionary activity in Cameroon dates from 1890, with the arrival of the Pallotine Fathers Vieter and Walter, who established the Marienberg mission near Edéa. By the outbreak of the First World War, Catholic mission activity brought Cameroon an apostolic prefecture, a number of missions, schools, and seminaries, as well as nearly 55,000 converts. Following the war, in 1922, the first Catholic Bishop, Msgr. Francois Xavier Vogt (q.v.), was named. The first indigenous priests were ordained in 1935. The first Cameroonian Bishop, Msgr. Etoga, was consecrated in 1955, and in 1961 Msgr. Jean Zoa (q.v.) became Archbishop of Yaoundé and the highest ranking prelate in Cameroon. The Catholic missions in East Cameroon have been principally French; in West Cameroon the Mill Hill Fathers operated the main mission for the Church. See also CATHOLICISM.

MISSIONS, PROTESTANT. The earliest Christian missions in Cameroon were Protestant, connected with the London Baptist Mission, organized (beginning 1843) by Alfred Saker, Joseph Merrick, and Jackson Fuller (q.v.). With the establishment of the German protectorate, the English missionaries gave way to the German Basel Mission, whose activities continued until they were chased from the field by the war in 1914. The Basel Mission returned to the British Cameroons, where it continued until 1957, when its branch became independent. Another German mission, the Berlin Baptist Mission, whose first pastor was Lotin Samé (q.v.), also left the field in 1916. The German Baptists were followed by the missions of the Paris Evangelical Mission; their establishments merged with the Baptists in

1957 to form the independent Cameroon Council of Baptist and Evangelical Churches. Another early mission was the American Presbyterian Mission, whose Cameroon activities began in 1842 and continued until 1957, when the independent Cameroon Presbyterian Church was established. Other important Protestant missions included the following: Adventists (since 1928), fraternal Lutheran (since 1919), Norwegian Lutheran (since 1952), United Sudanese, European Baptist, and American Sudanese Lutheran.

MOLONGO. Traditionally the supreme council of the Bakweri clan chiefs, similar to the Ngondo organization among the Douala. Moribund before 1958, Molongo was revived by Dr. Endeley and Nerius N. Mbile for the purpose of exciting xenophobic, irredentist and nationalistic fervor among the Bakweri, Bakossi and Balondo poeples and influencing the outcome of the 1961 plebiscite.

MONGO BETI (pseud., ALEXANDRE BIYIDI), 1932- . Writer. He was born at Mbalmayo, and attended primary school and the lycée in Yaoundé, taking his baccalauréat in 1951. In France, he studied literature at the Sorbonne, and in 1954, published his first works (three short novels: Sans Haine, Sans amour, and Ville Cruelle) under the pseudonym of Eza Boto. In 1956 he took the pseudonym of Mongo Beti, under which he became famous. He published in succession the novels Le Pauvre Christ de Bomba (1956), Mission to Kala (1957), King Lazarus (1958), in addition to numerous articles and literary reviews. In 1958 he was awarded the French Prix Saint-Beuve for his literary output, and is considered Cameroon's most important writer. He is now a university lecturer. [Only those works translated into English have been given their English titles; the rest were written in French.]

MOUMIE, (DR.) FELIX-ROLAND, 1926-1960. Politician and physician. Born at Foumban, Moumié was educated in Cameroon, and in 1950 took a medical degree at the Medical School of the Ecole Normale William Ponty, near Dakar, Senegal. Upon his return to Cameroun, he became involved in the newly-formed (1948) Union des Populations du Cameroun (UPC) party. In 1952 he became a co-President of the UPC, already known

as a Marxist organization. When, in the wake of an
abortive rebellion led by the UPC in 1955, the party
was outlawed, Dr. Moumié went into exile with most
of the other UPC leaders. He first took refuge in the
British Cameroons, then in Cairo, and finally, in Conakry
and Accra. During his exile, he was President
of the UPC, and submitted numerous petitions on its
behalf to the United Nations. On November 3, 1960,
during a visit to Geneva, Switzerland, he died of poisoning
under mysterious circumstances.

MOUNT CAMEROON. Originally called Mount Ambozes by
the early Portuguese explorers, this 13,350-foot semiactive
volcano is the highest point on West Africa's
coast. Buea, the capital of West Cameroon, is situated
3,000 feet up on the slopes of Mount Cameroon,
which overlooks the Bay of Victoria. In 1858 Alfred
Saker, at the head of an English Baptist mission community,
established the first permanent European settlement,
Victoria, at the foot of the mountain. Mount
Cameroon has erupted several times in the recent
past: 1909, 1922, 1959.

MOUSSA YAYA, SARKIFADA (EL HADJ), 1926- . Former
Vice-President of the Federal Assembly. Educated in
Garoua, Moussa Yaya became a veterinary assistant in
1942. He entered politics in 1958 upon his election as
a municipal councillor in Garoua, a position he held
until 1964. Elected to the Legislative Assembly in
1959, he has served in every national legislature since.
One of the founding members of the Union Camerounaise,
he became a member of the Cameroon National
Union's executive committee in 1966, and from 1970 on
was first Vice-President of the Federal Assembly. A
quiet, self-effacing man, Moussa Yaya has been considered
one of Cameroon's most astute and powerful
politicians.

MOUVEMENT D'ACTION NATIONALE CAMEROUNAISE
(MANC). A tactical alliance created by Charles Assalé
and Soppo Priso (both q.v.) from the merger of
Ngondo and the Association Traditionelle Bantoue
Efoula-Meyong (both q.v.), in March 1956. The outlawed
UPC commanded much sympathy among MANC
leaders and followers, and the MANC pressed for a
general amnesty and reconciliation throughout the late
1950s. MANC criticized the 1957 Statute of the Cam-

eroun (q.v.) because it fell short of a move to complete independence. MANC, with its eight deputies from the coastal areas of Cameroun formed the government opposition in the Legislative Assembly (q.v.) or ALCAM under Prime Minister Mbida in 1957. Within ALCAM, MANC's eight deputies were known as the "Groupe de Huit." From 1958-1960 MANC was part of the governing coalition under Prime Minister Ahidjo. Several months after the 1960 elections for the Cameroun Republic's National Assembly (q.v.) or ANCAM, MANC formally dissolved itself and fused with the Union Camerounaise (q.v.). Assalé was rewarded with the Prime Ministership of the Cameroun Republic.

MOUVEMENT DE L'UNION CAMEROUNAISE see UNION CAMEROUNAISE

MUKETE, VICTOR. From 1954 to 1957 Mukete was a Minister in the Eastern Nigerian Government. Thereafter he became President of the Cameroons Development Corporation and, after 1961, First Vice-President of the Federal Chamber of Commerce.

MUNA, SOLOMON TANDENG, 1912- . Former Prime Minister of West Cameroon and Federal Vice-President. Born ca. 1912 in the Bamenda district of then Kamerun protectorate, he attended local primary and secondary schools, then studied at the National Teacher Training College in Kumba, and later at the Institute of Education of the University of London (1949). From 1932 to 1951 he was a teacher, and later, principal, in several Southern Cameroons Protestant schools and in the Mungo area of the French Cameroun. In 1951, he left teaching to campaign for the Kamerun National Congress party, winning a seat in the Eastern Nigerian Assembly, where the Southern Cameroons was represented. He became Public Works Minister, but resigned in 1953, devoting himself to recognition of Southern Cameroons as a separate region in Nigeria. After separation from Nigeria he became (1954-1957) Minister of Resources and Public Works as well as Deputy Leader of Government to Dr. Endeley. He broke with Endeley in 1957 over the issue of reunification with the French Cameroun, joining J. N. Foncha's Kamerun National Democratic Party. When the KNDP won the general elections of 1959, Muna became first Minister of Public Works, then Minister of Trade and Industry and then Minister of Finance in Foncha's cabinet. In 1961, following reunification, he became Federal Minister of Transportation, a post he occupied until his nomination to the Prime Ministry of West Cameroon in 1968. In March 1970, he ran on the national ticket with President Ahidjo, and became Federal Vice-President; in May of that same year he added the portfolio of West Cameroon Prime Minister to his functions. When Cameroon became a unitary state in 1972, Muna lost both these positions.

MVENG, ENGELBERT, S.J., 1930- . Historian, artist, writer. The Rev. Mveng was born May 9, 1930, in Enam-Ngal, Ntem. Between 1936 and 1948 he attended mission and diocesan schools near Ebolowa and Yaoundé, and in 1949, began teaching in Akono. Also in 1949, he began theological studies at the Seminary in Akono, then went on to Otele, and during 1951-53 completed his novitiate as a Jesuit in Congo/Kinshasa. Between 1954 and 1964 he undertook advanced studies at various universities in Belgium and France, receiving licences in Theology, Letters and Philosophy, as a Doctorate in Philology at the University of Paris. Since 1965 he has taught at the Federal University in Yaoundé, and has occupied the position of Director of Cultural Affairs in the Ministry of Education, Youth and Culture. He has won prizes from the Academie Française (1964), and the International Exhibition of Religious Art in Trieste (1966), and is the author of several books, of which the most important is his History of Cameroun (1963).

-N-

NACHTIGAL, (DR.) GUSTAV, 1834-1884. German explorer and diplomat. Born at Eichstedt, Germany, Nachtigal trained to become a military physician. Arriving in North Africa in 1862, he acquired a passion for exploration. In 1869, at the head of his own expedition, he crossed the Sahara and reached Lake Chad in June, 1870. On July 6, 1870, he entered the Bornuan capital, Kukwa, bringing with him presents and a letter from the Prussian king to the Sultan of Bornu. Continuing westward, Nachtigal traversed the Waddai, came up through Egypt, and finally reached Europe in

1875. In 1882 he was named Imperial Consul-General in Tunis. He left Tunis in 1884 by ship, and headed south along the west African coast, charged with establishing German rule over the several coastal territories where Imperial interests had become important. On his way he established the Togo Protectorate (July 1), and arrived at Douala on July 12, 1884, in time to give formal recognition to the treaty establishing the German Kamerun Protectorate and to witness the raising of the German flag at Douala. Nachtigal died on his way back to Germany.

NATIONAL ARMY OF KAMERUNIAN LIBERATION (ALNK). The name given by the UPC to its guerrilla forces in Cameroun during the 1955-62 rebellion. Organized by the Central Executive Committee (Comité Directeur) of the UPC in exile, the ALNK directed the various maquis operations of violence and sabotage in southern and western Cameroun in 1958-1959. The Comité Directeur, consisting of Moumié, Ouandié and Kingué, attempted to coordinate ALNK operations from such foreign capitals as Cairo, Conakry and Accra. Under the local leadership of Osende Afana, Singap Martin and Paul Momo, the ALNK launched guerrilla attacks in the Bamiléké regions and in the larger southern towns of Douala and Yaoundé where sympathetic Bamiléké could be recruited. See "BAMILEKE" REBELLION.

NATIONAL ASSEMBLY OF CAMEROUN (ANCAM). The legislative body of the Cameroun Republic from April 1960 to October 1961. Before independence this parliamentary body was known as the Legislative Assembly of Cameroun (q.v.) and after the creation of the federation, as the Legislative Assembly of East Cameroon. Following independence and the ratification by popular referendum of the Constitution of the Cameroun Republic, the first and only election to the new ANCAM was held on April 10, 1960. Like its predecessors in East Cameroon, the National Assembly was composed of political groups elected on a regional and/or ethnic base. The Union Camerounaise (q.v.), representing the north and east, won 45% of the total vote and a majority of 51 seats in the 100-seat ANCAM. Other groups represented were the PDC, the legal or rallié UPC, the FPUP, the Progressistes and two independents from Douala (Dr. Marcel Bey-

bey-Eyidi and Alexandre Douala Manga Bell, both
q.v.).
   On May 5, the Assembly elected Ahidjo (the only
candidate) the first President of the Cameroun Republic by a vote of 89 for, 10 abstentions and one absent.
The dissolution of opposition parties and their fusion
with Ahidjo's UC, which was to culminate in a one-
party state in 1966, began during the short life of the
National Assembly. See FRONT POPULAIRE POUR
L'UNITE ET LA PAIX; MOUVEMENT D'ACTION NA-
TIONALE CAMEROUNAISE; PARTI UNIFIE.
   The National Assembly was unicameral and elected
by direct universal suffrage. It was given the power
to legislate in six general areas: (1) the guarantees
to, and fundamental obligations of citizens; (2) the status of persons and property; (3) political, administrative, and judicial organization involving the functioning
of the national and local assemblies, national defense,
the creation or elimination of administrative jurisdictions, penal and civil procedure, the magistracy, and
the civil service; (4) financial and budgetary matters;
(5) social and economic programs; and (6) policies and
programs of education. See CONSTITUTION OF THE
CAMEROUN REPUBLIC (1960). Compare: CONSTITUTION OF THE FEDERAL REPUBLIC OF CAMEROON
(1961); CONSTITUTION OF THE UNITED REPUBLIC
OF CAMEROON (1972).

NATIONAL COUNCIL OF NIGERIA AND THE CAMEROONS
   (NCNC). A Nigerian political party founded in August
   1944 by Dr. Nnamdi Azikiwe to which such early Cameroonian nationalists as Endeley, Namme, Kale and
   Mbile (all q.v.) belonged. Out of this participation
   grew the first Southern Cameroonian interest in developing political organizations with a particularly Southern Cameroonian nationalist orientation. See CAMEROONS FEDERAL UNION; KAMERUN UNITED NATIONAL CONGRESS. The NCNC brought under one organizational apparatus the Cameroons Youth League,
   the Bamenda Improvement Association and the Bakweri
   Union (all q.v.). After the prolonged governmental
   crisis in the Nigerian Eastern Regional House of Assembly in early 1953 over Azikiwe's leadership of
   the NCNC, Cameroonian members of the NCNC split,
   a majority calling for separate regional autonomy for
   Southern Cameroons (see KAMERUN NATIONAL CONGRESS), and the rest calling for continued association

with the Eastern Region (see KAMERUN PEOPLES' PARTY).

NATIVE AUTHORITIES. As part of their system of "indirect rule" in the Southern Cameroons during the interwar period, the British created, recognized or appointed local chiefs to leadership positions in the Native Authority system. On the basis of a series of systematic reports and studies, the British were able to accurately identify the locus of political power in many of the tribal groups, clans and chiefdoms and thus created a colonial authority system that mirrored the traditional ones with considerable fidelity. The creation of Native Authorities was part of the scheme of administrative devolution envisaged by Britain's Governor-General for Nigeria, Sir Frederick Lugard. Some of the Native Authorities were Fons (q.v.), and some were village chiefs while others consisted of a council of elders. Lacking sufficient funds and personnel to administer the mandate "directly," the British relied on the Native Authorities (with their councils and courts) to deal with various aspects of local government: taxation, criminal offenses, health and roads. The Native Authorities were allowed to keep half the revenues obtained through taxation and court fines.

NDONGMO AFFAIR. In August 1970 the Bishop of Nkongsamba, Msgr. Albert Ndongmo, was arrested by the government and put on trial for aiding Ernest Ouandié and his UPC maquis during the 1960s. Since 1961 Ndongmo had been in contact with the UPC maquisards, providing aid and shelter to UPC leaders and repeatedly denouncing the government. A military court found him guilty of subversion and conspiracy to overthrow the government and assassinate President Ahidjo. In December, 1970 he was condemned to death, along with Ouandié, but had his sentence commuted to life imprisonment, partly through the intervention of Pope Paul VI, who asked for clemency on his behalf. The local Church hierarchy, through Archbishop Zoa, declared its support for the government and formally disavowed Msgr. Ndongmo's actions, but the government is said to be suspicious of the Church's repeated assertions of "non-partisanship" in politics. See CATHOLICISM.

NDOP. An ethnic group among the Tikar peoples.

NEW KAMERUN see SEITZ, THEODOR

NGOM, JACQUES, 1920- . Trade union leader. Born on July 5, 1920, at Makak, Ngom was educated locally. In 1944 he helped found the Cameroon branch of the French Confédération Générale de Travail, and during the 1950s was a member of the French Economic and Social Council. Between 1960 and 1965 he was a member of the East Cameroon Economic and Social Council, and after 1965 became Budget, Personnel, and Material Director in the Federal Ministry of Planning and Development.

NGONDO. The Douala people's traditional "council of notables," converted in the late 1940s into an organizational adjunct of the UPC which supported Cameroonian reunification and independence. Like its Bamiléké counterpart Kumsze, the ethnically-based Ngondo became disenchanted with UPC goals and activities and later opposed the party.

NIGERIAN YOUTH MOVEMENT (NYM). A political group of young Nigerian nationalists organized about 1938 in Lagos. The NYM's political success in the 1938 elections for the Legislative Council may have been a factor in prompting young Cameroonian nationalists to form the Cameroons Youth League (q.v.) in 1939. Indeed, membership in the two youth groups did overlap to some extent, and the CYL was modeled after the NYM. An important Nigerian political party, the National Council of Nigeria and the Cameroons (q.v.), was an offshoot of the NYM.

NJOYA, AROUNA, 1908- . Former Minister, co-founder of the Union Camerounaise. Arouna Njoya was born in Foumban in 1908, and is an uncle of the incumbent Sultan of Bamoun, El Hajj Seidou Njimoluh (q.v.). Between 1922 and 1927 Arouna attended the École d'Etat in Dchang; from 1927 to 1929 he was employed by the French administration in Dchang as a clerk and interpreter. From 1927 to 1947 he served as a Bamoun chief under the Sultan, turning to territorial politics in 1946 as a delegate to the first Cameroun Territorial Assembly. He was re-elected to each of the Cameroon's legislatures (in 1952, 1956, 1960, and 1962), and also served in the Senate of the French Republic from 1947 to 1957. When Ahmadou Ahidjo became Prime Minister in 1958, Arouna served in his cabinet first as Finance Minister, then as Minister for Health and Population. Arouna was a vice-President of the country's principal party, and played a major role in the negotiations that led to the formation of the Cameroom Federal Republic in 1961. After independence, he served in Ahidjo's cabinet as Minister of Interior (1960-61), and as Minister of Justice (1961-64) in the first Federal Cabinet. In 1964 he resigned from the Cabinet and retired from active politics for reasons of health.

NJOYA, (SULTAN), 1876(?)-1933. Sultan of Bamoun and one of the most notable traditional rulers in Cameroun history. Njoya's father, the Sultan Nsangou, died in 1888; Njoya was too young to assume the Bamoun throne, so for two years (during which his brothers tried to seize power) Njoya's mother acted as regent. Njoya succeeded to the throne in 1890, when he was only fifteen years old. He accommodated himself to German rule and was considered an imperial official. In 1923, after a series of disputes with the French administration (who had taken over after the German Kamerun protectorate ended in 1916), Njoya was deposed and his territory devided into 17 chieftaincies. In 1931 he was exiled to Yaoundé, where he died on May 30, 1933. Njoya was a highly creative individual endowed with unusual intellect. He developed an original alphabet of 83 letters and 10 numbers and had a <u>History of the Customs and Laws of Bamoun</u> written in it. Njoya was the 16th Sultan in the Bamoun dynasty, but the first to become Muslim. For some time, after 1906, he fell under the religious influence of a German missionary, Goehring. Subsequently, disappointed with both Islam and Christianity, Njoya decided to create his own religion, which was a mixture of Islam, Christianity, and animism. The new religion died with Njoya's conversion to Islam in 1916. Among Njoya's other accomplishments was the construction of a large palace in Foumban, a pharmaceutical compilation by which he fixed standard medical dosages in his kingdom, the construction of a mechanical mill to grind corn, the drawing of the first maps of Bamoun, a compilation of Bamoun legends and tales, and the founding of a private museum to preserve Bamoun art and artifacts. The museum and palace still stand today.

NORTHERN CAMEROONS CASE. (Cameroon v. United Kingdom.) One result of the United Nations plebiscite of 1961 was that the inhabitants of the Northern Cameroons chose to integrate with Northern Nigeria, rather than join the proposed Cameroon federation. The Northern Cameroons subsequently became the Sardauna Province of Northern Nigeria. The Cameroon government charged Britain with responsibility for alleged voting irregularities in the Northern Cameroons during the plebiscite. Moreover, it argued that the votes in the north should have been tallied with those in the Southern Cameroons, which would have resulted in a clear majority for reunification. Cameroon took the matter to the International Court of Justice, which rendered its verdict in 1963. The Court dismissed Cameroon's action, contending that since the United Nations General Assembly had ratified the results of the plebiscite in 1961, the matter was no longer justiciable.

NORTHERN KAMERUN DEMOCRATIC PARTY (NKDP). A small party which campaigned throughout Northern Cameroon before the 1959 UN plebiscite, urging citizens to vote for continued trusteeship and a postponement of the decision whether to join Nigeria or the French Cameroun. It was the only party in the campaign which envisioned the "final reunification of the former German Cameroons." See KAMERUN IDEA, THE. The NKDP was highly successful in using local and ethnic issues to mobilize the non-Fulani and pagan inhabitants of the trust territory, especially in the Chamba district. In the 1961 plebiscite in Northern Cameroon, the NKDP campaigned for separation from Nigeria and Union with Cameroun. See PLEBISCITES, UNITED NATIONS.

NORTHERN PEOPLES CONGRESS (NPC). The dominant political party in the Northern Region of Nigeria led by the traditional elite of the Hausa-Fulani peoples. It was founded in December, 1949, but was banned, along with all other parties in Nigeria, in May, 1966. The NPC was able to exert its influence and superior organization on behalf of the pro-Nigerian alternative in the February 1961 plebiscite in Northern Cameroons. See PLEBISCITES, UNITED NATIONS.

NSANGU (or NSANGGUF). A Bamoun king who attempted to extend his influence over the Nsaw and other Tikar groups. He was beheaded in a battle with the Nsaw in 1888. Nsangu was succeeded by the remarkable sultan Njoya. See BAMOUN; NJOYA, (SULTAN).

NSAW. A tribal unit among the Tikar peoples.

NSHARE, 17th Century. Founder of the Bamoun people. Sometime during the Seventeenth Century, one Nshare, the son of a Tikar chief, left his tribe with a part of its people. He headed south, crossed the Mbam River, and after several engagements with hostile villages, settled his followers at Nji-Mom, in the country of the Pa-Mbam, some twenty miles north of present-day Foumban. Nshare's subsequent wars brought some seventeen neighboring chiefs under his domination, and he had himself proclaimed chief of the Pa-Mbam, from which the name Bamoun is derived. Nshare eventually extended his kingdom even further, and fixed his capital at a place called Mfom-Ben, from which the name Foumban is derived. The dynasty founded by Nshare has continued unbroken through seventeen kings to the present incumbent, Sultan El Haj Seidou Njimoluh, who is himself a son of the celebrated Sultan Njoya. See NJOYA, SULTAN; SEIDOU NJIMOLUH).

NTUMAZAH, NDEH, 1926- . West Cameroon politician. Ntumazah was born in 1926 at Mankon/Bamenda, and was educated locally until 1944, when he left to join his brother in Douala. In 1948, he probably joined the newly-formed Union des Populations du Cameroun (UPC) party and returned to the Southern Cameroons, where he became involved in several local political disputes in Bamenda. In 1957, when the UPC leadership was in temporary residence in Bamenda following the party's abortive revolt in 1955, Ntumazah founded the One Kamerun party, designed as the Southern Cameroons' wing of the UPC. In 1957, 1958, and 1959, he appeared several times at the United Nations as a petitioner to plead the reunification cause. In 1960 and 1961 he led the One Kamerun delegations to the several conferences that discussed the nature of the Federation between East and West Cameroon.

-O-

OKALA, RENE-GUY CHARLES, 1910- . Former Foreign Minister. Born on October 19, 1910 at Bilomé (Mbam), he attended the Roman Catholic Seminary in Yaoundé until 1929, when he left to become a teacher. In 1931 he was employed by a British firm, and in 1938 joined the civil service as an interpreter. He was a co-founder of one of the earliest Cameroun political organizations, the Jeunesse Camerounaise Française in 1939. In 1946 he was elected to the Representative Assembly, and was re-elected to a seat in the several Cameroun legislatures that followed (1949, 1952, 1956), and became a deputy of the National Assembly in 1960. From 1945 to 1955 he also served as a Senator to the French Council of the Republic. He held various ministerial posts in the Cameroun government: Minister of Public Works, Transport and Mines (1958-59), Minister of Justice (1959-60), and Minister of Foreign Affairs (1960-61). In June, 1962, along with several other opposition leaders, he was arrested, tried and convicted of conspiracy and libel, and sentenced to four years imprisonment. Okala was released in 1965, and immediately helped to dissolve the Cameroon Socialist Party, which he had helped to found in 1959 as a branch of the African Socialist Movement. Reconciled with President Ahidjo, he joined the dominant Cameroon Union party, and in 1968 was rewarded by being appointed Itinerant Ambassador to the President. Okala failed to survive the transformation of Cameroon to a unitary state in 1972, losing his position and retiring.

ONANA AWANA, CHARLES, 1923- . Minister of Finance. Onana Awana was born ca. 1923 at Ngoulemekong, and attended primary and secondary schools in Cameroon. He occupied a number of important administrative positions before being named (1957) Principal Secretary to the then Deputy Prime Minister Ahidjo. Between 1958 and 1960 he was Permanent Secretary of the Cameroon Government in Paris, during which period he completed his studies at the École Nationale de la France d'Outre-Mer (ENFOM). Upon his return to Cameroon (1960), he was named Federal Minister of Finance, then (1961) Federal Minister Delegate to the Presidency for Territorial Administration, then (1963)

Federal Minister of Finance and the Plan. In 1964 he
became Secretary-General of the Central African Customs
and Economic Union (UDEAC), and in 1970 was
named Federal Minister of Planning and Territorial Development,
a position he held until 1972, when he returned
as Minister of Finance in the new unitary government.

ONE KAMERUN PARTY (OK). A rump party of the UPC
which the latter left behind in Southern Cameroons after
its abortive collaboration with the KNDP and after
the British banned the UPC from the territory. The
OK was founded in 1957 and headed by Ndeh Ntumazah
(q.v.), a former member of the UPC directorate. The
OK maintained a liaison with the external Moumié faction
of the UPC. It was partially successful in capturing
the support of the West Cameroon radical left:
university students studying abroad, some urban migrants
and workers in the Victoria and Kuma areas,
and a scattering of local intellectuals with educational,
labor union and cooperative ties.
 The extremist OK won no seats in the March 1957
elections to the Southern Cameroons House of Assembly.
In the January 1959 elections, it advocated secession
from Nigeria and immediate unification with
Cameroun, but won no seats and obtained very few
votes. The OK's principal stronghold was in Kumba
(q.v.) where it helped mobilize the population with its
anti-Ibo propaganda in the February 1961 plebiscite.
At this time Ntumazah claimed 3,000 dues-paying members
for the OK in the Southern Cameroons. One OK
candidate (from Mamfe North) was elected to the 37-
seat West Cameroon Legislative Assembly in the December
1961 elections but immediately declared his
support for the Foncha government. The OK dwindled
in significance after 1961 when federation removed its
raison d'être.

ORGANISATION COMMUNE AFRICAINE, MALGACHE ET
MAURITIENNE (OCAMM). The Joint African, Malagasy,
and Mauritian Organization is a grouping of former French
colonies of Africa and the island of Mauritius. It is a linear
descendant of the former "Brazzaville Group" and the
Union of African and Malagasy States. President Ahidjo
often presides over the meetings of OCAMM at its headquarters
in Yaoundé. OCAMM was founded in 1965 by
eleven states including Cameroon. Its goal is to acceler-

ate the economic, social, technical and cultural development of member states within the framework of the Organization of African Unity (q.v.). To this end, a series of gradual cooperative steps have been taken, such as a common international airline (Air Afrique), regional industrial development, sugar and meat marketing agreements, shared schools of veterinary medicine and engineering, and joint telecommunications systems. OCAMM became the most influential regional bloc within the Organization of African Unity, and its member states often voted together at the United Nations. In spite of these achievements, member cleavages have caused concern for OCAMM's viability. Cameroon withdrew in 1973.

ORGANIZATION OF AFRICAN UNITY (OAU). The OAU is a loose association of independent African states, including Cameroon, which aims at promoting unity and international cooperation among African states and to eradicate all forms of colonialism in Africa. President Ahidjo helped draft the OAU charter and found the OAU at Addis Ababa in 1963. In accordance with the OAU's policy of non-interference in the affairs of other member states, Ahidjo's government maintained a strict neutrality in the Nigerian civil war (1967-70) and in the disturbances preceding the coup in neighboring Equatorial Guinea in 1969. Ahidjo was chosen OAU Chairman for 1969-1970.

OUANDIE, ERNEST, 1924-1971. Revolutionary politician. Ouandié was born in 1924 in the Bamiléké division of east Cameroon. Educated locally, he entered the teaching profession in 1940. In 1944 he joined the Cameroon branch of the French Confédération Général du Travail, and in 1948, helped to found the radical Union des Populations du Cameroun party, becoming its Vice-President in 1952. He left Cameroun with the leadership of the party in 1955, following its abortive revolt, taking refuge first in Bamenda, then later in Egypt and Ghana. In 1961 or 1962 he returned clandestinely to Cameroon to take charge of several UPC guerrilla groups still active in the country. Ouandié appeared several times at the United Nations to plead the UPC case, was co-editor of the party newspaper, Voix du Cameroun (q.v.), and authored a number of political pamphlets. In August 1970, he was captured at Mbanga by government security forces; four months later a military court sentenced him to death, and he was executed on January 15, 1971.

OUDNEY, WALTER see CLAPPERTON, HUGH

OUSSOURA TAXES. A form of traditional tribute to Fulani
chiefs (or lamibê, q.v.). The Oussoura tax was suppressed by the Union Camerounaise party (q.v.) as a
source of support for the "less progressive" (some
said "reactionary") elements in society.

-P-

PALM OIL. West Cameroon's fifth most valuable export
crop, extracted from the crushed kernels of oil palm
fruit clusters. It is cultivated on industrial plantations such as the CDC and Pamol. The palm oil produced in East Cameroon, on the other hand, is mainly consumed locally.

PAN-AFRICAN INSTITUTE FOR DEVELOPMENT (PAID). A
non-profit international body organized in 1964, based
in Geneva, and concerned with rural and agricultural
development in Africa. PAID has two colleges in
Cameroon for the training of civil servants in African
development. The first is the Ecolé des Cadres,
founded in 1965 and located in Douala (q.v.). It has
a two-year course for civil servants fom francophone
nations. The other school, Sautoy College, is located
in Buea (q.v.), where one-year courses in community
development and agricultural economics are offered to
civil servants from anglophone Africa. Trainees at
the two colleges get practical experience by doing field
work in Cameroon. In addition to the two colleges,
PAID maintains an Applied Research Center in Douala
which produces monographs and overseas various rural development projects.

PARTI DE L'UNION CAMEROUNAISE see UNION CAMEROUNAISE

PARTI DES DEMOCRATES CAMEROUNAIS (PDC). Known also as the Démocrates Camerounais, the PDC (1958-66)
under A. M. Mbida (q.v.) was the successor to L. P.
Aujoulat's Catholic-oriented party, the BDC, in East
Cameroon. The PDC's Beti leaders were generally
opposed to reunification because of the idea's currency
among the Douala and Bamiléké peoples with whom
they were in conflict. The party's strength lay in the

Nyong-et-Sanaga Region (Yaoundé and its environs) and among the central tribes (mainly Eton and Ewondo). In its heyday the PDC also enjoyed the support of the Catholic hierarchy throughout the country (see CATHOLICISM) and claimed some 30,000 active members in December 1960. The PDC won about 21% of the popular vote and 20 (of 70) seats in the December 1956 elections to ATCAM (which became ALCAM in May 1957). Mbida was confirmed as Premier at the head of a coalition government, but was forced to resign in February 1958. Confused and leaderless, the Démocrates could only provide ineffective opposition, as twelve PCD deputies had, by January 1959, crossed to the government side. The PDC was able to muster only six votes against Ahidjo's proposal for a pleins pouvoirs law in October 1959 (see LEGISLATIVE ASSEMBLY OF CAMEROUN) and did not participate in the preparations for the table ronde (q.v.). Following his thirteen-month self-imposed exile in Guinea, Mbida returned in February 1960 (after independence) to try to revive the PDC. The party campaigned unsuccessfully against the constitutional referendum in February 1960. The April 1960 elections to ANCAM saw a drop in both the percentage of PDC votes and number of Assembly seats: from 21% to 10% and from 20 (of 70 seats) to 11 (of 100 seats). In May the PDC deputies joined Ahidjo's coalition government but were expelled when they opposed his policies for federation. PDC representation in the Eastern Legislative Assembly dropped to eight when three of its deputies joined the Union Camerounaise (q.v.) majority in early 1962. The arrest of Mbida and other members of the Front National Unifié (q.v.) in July 1962 further demoralized the PDC. The party was unable to gain any seats in the 1964 federal elections to AFCAM (due the harassment and fraud, it claimed) and did not even contest the 1965 elections for the East Cameroon Legislative Assembly.

PARTI SOCIALISTE CAMEROUNAISE (PSC). Organized in November 1959 by Charles Okala from the Union Sociale Camerounaise (q.v.), the PSC never enjoyed much popular support in Cameroon. Basically it provided Okala with a platform for his pronouncements, a staff of campaign workers, and the appearance of a mass following to echo his positions. Okala and his

PSC resisted the trend toward a one-party state in Cameroon, joining a loose coalition of opposition parties in June 1962 (the Front National Unifié, q.v.) to reject President Ahidjo's concept of a parti unifié (q.v.). With the arrest of Okala and other opposition leaders the following month, on charges of "inciting hatred and conflict," two PSC deputies decided to join the Union Camerounaise (q.v.). By the beginning of 1963 there were no PSC deputies in the Eastern Assembly, and by September 1966, the PSC had been dissolved and then officially merged with the new single national party, the Union Nationale Camerounaise (q.v.).

PARTI TRAVAILLISTE CAMEROUNAIS (PTC). A short-lived political party in East Cameroon organized in March 1962 by Dr. Marcel Beybey-Eyidi (q.v.), who became its national secretary, and by Mbandja Malanga, a former UPC activist. The PTC became moribund in July 1962 after the arrest and imprisonment of Dr. Beybey. See FRONT NATIONAL UNIFIE. The PTC was one of many opposition groups which succumbed to the pressures which ultimately led to a one-party state in Cameroon.

PARTI UNIFIE. After independence in 1960 President Ahidjo continually elaborated on his concept of a parti unifié, or "unified party," and the need for an entente among existing parties, for a "common minimum program," so that unity and national development could be achieved in the Federal Republic. As parties in opposition to Ahidjo's governing Union Camerounaise (q.v.) disintegrated and/or merged with the UC, often under the threat of legal sanctions or the promise of reward, the concept was made reality. Some parties gave in easily or voluntarily (e.g., MANC), while other groups (e.g., FNU) had to be physically disbanded. Some opposition leaders (e.g., Okala) saw hidden in the concept of a parti unifié the possible dictatorship of a monolithic parti unique, or single party, with an unwarranted concentration of power. By late 1962 East Cameroon, for all intents and purposes, had evolved into a one-party system, with the only seven opposition deputies in the Assembly (six PDC and one UPC) having been rendered ineffective. Several parties still existed in the western part of the federation (i.e., KNDP, CPNC, CUC), but they dissolved themselves four years later and merged with the UC to form a new national single party, the Union Nationale Camerounaise (q.v.).

PASS-ALL, "KING." Traditional chief of the Malimba people. In 1883, the French consular officer Mattei, on board the ship Voltigeur, signed a treaty of protection with "King" Pass-all. This was immediately challenged by "King" Bell (q.v.), who claimed to be Pass-all's superior, and who warned the French that his country was already on offer to Britain.

PAYSANS INDEPENDANTS. A loose parliamentary grouping of ex-UPC Bamiléké deputies from the western areas of East Cameroon. The Paysans Independants organized around the nine seats they won in the 1956 elections to the new Legislative Assembly (q.v.). The group was headed by Mathias Djoumessi and Michel Njiné. Njiné became vice-premier in Ahidjo's coalition government in February 1958. The Paysans Independants won no seats in the 1960 elections to ANCAM, however.

PEACE CORPS. Invited by the Cameroon Federal Republic to aid in the development of the country, the first contingent of 29 Peace Corps Volunteer teachers arrived in West Cameroon in September 1962. They taught such subjects as history, mathematics and science in the local schools and also worked in teacher training colleges. More teachers and agricultural workers came over the years. In East Cameroon the use of PCVs since their arrival in September 1963 reflected that state's language needs; they were primarily English teachers. See BILINGUALISM. By 1972 there were almost a hundred Peace Corps Volunteers in Cameroon.

PEANUTS (GROUNDNUTS). The tenth most valuable agricultural crop in Cameroon, most of which is exported or processed for oils.

PERMANENT MANDATES COMMISSION (PMC). A League of Nations body set up to secure compliance to the principles of the League mandate system by checking on the activities of the mandatory powers. The eleven-member Commission was not empowered to enforce policies in the mandates but did receive annual reports from France and the United Kingdom regarding the status of their respective Cameroonian territories, frequently criticized the mandatories for their administrative shortcomings, and brought international pressure to bear on various colonial malpractices. See MANDATE SYSTEM. One notable instance was its investigation of France's use of corvée labor in Cameroun. This violation of the mandate agreement was widely criticized and, as a result of the adverse publicity, the French administration ameliorated working conditions after 1927. See FORCED LABOR. The counterpart of the League's Permanent Mandates Commission is the United Nations Trusteeship Council. See TRUSTEESHIP SYSTEM.

PHILLIPSON REPORT. A financial study made by Sir Sydney Phillipson in 1959 to determine the capacity of the Southern Cameroons to finance its own way without Nigerian assistance. Commissioned by Prime Minister Foncha to study the economic consequences of separation from Nigeria, the Report concluded: (1) that the Southern Cameroons could not be financially viable as an independent state; and (2) that the Southern Cameroons had been since 1954 a net creditor to the Federation of Nigeria in that it had contributed more to Nigerian revenues than it had received in aid. See "CHICK FORMULA." The first conclusion seemed to verify the contention of those Southern Cameroonian politicians who wanted continued economic and political association with Nigeria, while the second conclusion pleased those who wanted Southern Cameroonian independence or unification with the Cameroon Republic to the east.

PHILLIPSON, SIR SYDNEY. British financial and administrative expert. Chairman of an all-party conference at Mamfe, Southern Cameroons, on August 10 and 11, 1959, which met to decide on the alternatives to be put to the voters in the South in the forthcoming plebiscite and the qualifications for voting. The conference deliberated for two days but failed to reconcile the different views of Foncha and Endeley. Phillipson also headed a study team which analyzed the extent of Southern Cameroonian economic dependence on Nigeria. See PHILLIPSON REPORT.

PIDGIN ENGLISH. Acquired by contacts with early British and American traders and missionaries, pidgin English is still spoken in many parts of the former West Cameroon, in spite of attempts by the schools in that area to teach formal, non-jargon English. Pidgin English began as a mixture of native dialects with a simplified form of English, and developed because neither British nor American traders were concerned about linguistic purity in their commercial dealings with the local populations. The prevalence of pidgin English has caused some concern about the possibility of achieving true bilingualism (q.v.) in the federation, since in many cases it has interfered with the widespread learning and acceptance of standard English. See WES-KOS.

PLEBISCITES, UNITED NATIONS. Three UN-administered plebiscites or referenda were held in the British Cameroons in 1959 and 1961 to determine the future political status of these territories. The November 1959 plebiscite, held in the Northern Cameroons, posed the following alternatives: unification with Northern Nigeria or deferral of any decision until a later date. The voters opted for the latter, 70,401 to 42,797.

In preparation for the two plebiscites to be administered simultaneously in the Northern and Southern Cameroons on February 11-12, 1961, the United Nations produced and distributed numerous posters, handbills and copies of an official brochure, outlining "The Two Alternatives" to the electorate. The question posed in both Cameroons was whether to join Nigeria (which had become independent on October 1, 1960) or to unite with the Cameroun Republic (which had become independent on January 1, 1960). Polling in the Southern Cameroons resulted in an overwhelming vote (233,571 to 97,741) for unification with the Cameroun Republic. By contrast, the voting in the Northern Cameroons this time produced a sizable margin (146,296 to 97,659) for joining Nigeria. The Ahidjo regime protested this result, but to no avail. See INTERNATIONAL COURT OF JUSTICE; NORTHERN CAMEROONS CASE. On June 1, 1961, the Northern Cameroons formally became the Sardauna Province of the Northern Region of Nigeria, while on October 1, 1961, the British Southern Cameroons became the state of West Cameroon within the Cameroon Federal Republic.

PRE, ROLAND. Former French governor of Gabon, Guinea, Upper Volta and Somaliland. Pré was appointed High Commissioner of Cameroun in November, 1954 (replacing Jean Soucadaux). He took a hard line toward UPC activities and propaganda and, in addition, alienated the moderates in ATCAM with his "strict construction" of the Assembly's powers. In February 1955 Pré announced his intention to "crush Communist activity." In March the CGCT launched a series of short strikes on the Douala waterfront. In April the UPC and its affiliates (the JDC, UDEFC, and USCC) demanded the termination of the territory's trusteeship, while demonstrations occurred throughout south and southwest Cameroun. In May even more widespread violence took 26 lives. The UPC was banned in July, but many African legislators blamed Roland Pré for the May riots. Pré was replaced in April 1956 by Pierre Messmer, the former governor of the Ivory Coast, who initially took a more tolerant attitude toward the UPC. See "BAMILEKE" REBELLION.

PRESBYTERIAN SECT see PROTESTANTISM

PRESTATION. A form of compulsory labor obligation which the French introduced in the Cameroun in the 1920s. Imposed on Camerounians of sujet status, the prestation system required all males to furnish the government with ten days of free labor a year. Commutation of the prestation was possible at the rate of two francs per day of labor, but was rarely allowed in practice. The recruitment of workers was done initially by local chiefs, but when they began to recruit free labor for themselves, the task was taken over (in 1930) by government administrators. See FORCED LABOR; MISE EN VALEUR.

PROGRESSISTES, GROUPE DES. A ten-member parliamentary grouping of MANC and PSC deputies in the National Assembly of Cameroun (q.v.) during 1960-61. Its two most prominent members were Charles Assalé and Charles Okala (both q.v.). The Progressistes participated in President Ahidjo's coalition government in May 1960, Assalé being appointed the first Prime Minister of the Cameroun Republic and Okala the first Foreign Minister. The Groupe des Progréssistes dissolved itself the following year and united with Ahidjo's Union Camerounaise (q.v.).

PROTECTORATE POLICY (POLITIQUE DE PROTECTORAT).
The generic name for French policy toward its overseas colonies. The two main strands of the policy were: a policy of "assimilation" which developed out of the libertarian ideals of the French Revolution; and a policy of "association," which arose in the latter part of the nineteenth century in response to European imperial expansion. In practice, however, the two policies often overlapped, and sometimes complemented one another. See ASSIMILATION, POLICY OF; ASSOCIATION, POLICY OF.

PROTESTANTISM. The Protestants were among the first of the early Christian missionaries who settled along the Cameroon coast in the mid-eighteenth century. The Baptists under Alfred Saker (q.v.) gained the first foothold in 1845, but suffered schisms and an unsettled existence due to the change in colonial rulers and the First World War. The Presbyterians were largely successful among the Bassa and Bulu peoples and continue to operate outstanding secondary and higher schools such as the American Presbyterian mission school at Foulassi, the Presbyterian school at Elat and, with the French, the higher school at Libamba.
   An American Lutheran mission, dating from 1919, worked in north Cameroun and today maintains two Bible schools in Garoua and Yagoua and a printing house and leper hospital in Kaélé. Other Protestant groups which have evangelized, proselytized and eventually consecrated Cameroonian pastors are the Norwegian Lutherans, the Adventists and Jehovah's Witnesses. West Cameroon today is largely Protestant owing in part to the efforts of these missions. Contrast: CATHOLICISM; ISLAM. See BASEL MISSION SOCIETY; MISSIONS, PROTESTANT.

PUTTKAMER, JESCO VON. The Kamerun's third Governor (1895-1907). Puttkamer encouraged penetration into the northern area and was instrumental in getting plantations established on a large scale. He also helped create a private trading corporation, the Gesellschaft Süd-Kamerun (1898), which succeeded in establishing a German monopoly in the rubber and ivory that abounded in the rich southeast forest region. A similar concessionaire, the Gesellschaft Nordwest-Kamerun, was created in 1899 to exploit the Bamoun and Bamiléké regions. Puttkamer also had built the Governor's mansion in Buea known as the Schloss. See BUEA. Puttkamer was dismissed as Governor after his conviction at Potsdam for unjust behavior toward and physical abuse of Africans. See SEITZ, THEODOR.

PYGMIES. An ethnic group in the equatorial forest in the Cameroon southeast, near the Congo basin. Pygmies were probably the original inhabitants of the southern forest area, but now number only about 6,500 and are widely dispersed in small villages or families. Shy of contact with their taller neighbors, the pygmies have a monogamous family structure and are highly religious. They practice totemism and consider certain animals sacred. Some pygmies live in the southeastern towns where they are often respected and protected for their supposed magical qualities.

-R-

RABEH (or, RABAH). Bornuan ruler who conquered the Kanembu and overthrew the Kanembu dynasty in the northern parts of Cameroun circa 1895. Rabeh established his capital at Dikwa. He was killed in a battle against the French in 1900.

RALLIEMENT. (figuratively: return to legal life.) An amnesty campaign by the Ahidjo government in 1958-1959 to entice UPC rebels and guerrilla maquisards out of their armed underground opposition and back into open, legal channels for the pursuit of nationalist objectives. Over 2,000 rebels reportedly defected and surrendered. Moreover, some of the leaders of the outlawed UPC (e.g., Mayi Matip, Pierre Kamden Ninyim) were allowed to organize a political group, known colloquially as the ralliè UPC, which won six seats in the Cameroon Legislative Assembly in the April 1959 by-elections. This development encouraged further defections from the rebel forces. See "BAMILEKE" REBELLION.

RASSEMBLEMENT CAMEROUNAISE (RACAM). A short-lived political party in Cameroun organized in April by left-wing trade unionists after their failure to take over Unicafra. Racam was allied to the RDA and the French Communist Party and was the seminal group for the UPC, the Cameroun's first well-organized and truly nationalistic party. Reuben Um Nyobé (q.v.), Secretary-General of the USCC and later UPC militant, was one of the nine founders of Racam. It demanded independence for Cameroun, attacked the assimilationist policies of France, and was then immediately banned by the French administration. See UNION DES POPULATIONS DU CAMEROUN.

RASSEMBLEMENT DEMOCRATIQUE AFRICAIN (RDA). The first African political party to operate on an interterritorial basis in France's sub-Saharan territories, the RDA was an alliance dedicated to seeking greater political rights for French-speaking Africans. It was founded in September 1946 by Félix Houphouet-Boigny and his colleagues at Bamako, Sudan, in order to provide a broad entente of African parties and groups in the struggle against colonialism. The RDA won seats to the French National Assembly in 1946 and until 1955 was allied with the French Communist Party. In 1955 the RDA broke with the Communists; its Cameroun branch retained the connection, and subsequently became the Union des Populations du Cameroun (q.v.).

RASSEMBLEMENT DU PEUPLE CAMEROUNAIS (RAPECA). One of the many short-lived political groupings organized in 1946 in French Cameroun. In the heady atmosphere of postwar nationalism, numerous new trade unions and political parties began to exercise their recently-gained opportunities to organize, rally, strike and run candidates for office. Rapeca lasted only a few months, but its name was revived by André Fouda (q.v.) in Yaoundé in January 1959 when he formed a party allied to Soppo Priso's Démocrates Camerounais (q.v.). Rapeca was one of the participating groups in the Committee for the Table Ronde (q.v.).

RENAISSANCE CAMEROUNAIS (RENAICAM). An anti-UPC political group which, like Esocam and Indecam, Renaicam, was created with administration help ca. December 1948 at Abong-Mbang in the eastern part of French Cameroun. It was primarily an ethnic political grouping composed of Ewondo-Maka and had virtually disappeared by 1957.

REPRESENTATIVE ASSEMBLY OF CAMEROUN (ARCAM). Created as a result of the new French Constitution and reforms of 1946, ARCAM was Cameroun's first legislature. Thirty-four of its members (sixteen Europeans and twenty-four Africans) were elected from dual electoral rolls whereby at least two-fifths of the members had to be elected from the "first college" of French citizens and the remainder from the "second college" of Africans. In addition, six seats were appointive. ARCAM had few independent legislative powers but could "deliberate" on fiscal and economic matters (subject to the metropolitan Conseil d'Etat's veto), was entitled to pass resolutions for submission to the appropriate metropolitan ministry, and was to be consulted by the French administration on all regulations concerning the disposition of public lands, labor conditions, education and the execution of development programs.

During its first session in 1946 ARCAM began demanding more than simply these "advisory" powers, affirming its desire to have greater initiative and responsibility in preparing its own agenda. The first elections to the Assembly were fought and won on the personal appeal of the candidates involved, not over issues or between rival parties with differing programs. Aujoulat, Ahidjo, Soppo Priso, Okala and Betoté Akwa (all q.v.) were members of the first ARCAM, while UPC spokesmen such as Kingué, Moumié, Nyobé, and Ouandié (all q.v.) tried unsuccessfully over the years to win seats in the ARCAM and its successor legislatures. ARCAM's name was changed in 1952 to the Territorial Assembly of Cameroun (q.v.) or ATCAM.

"REUNIFICATION ROAD." A highway project begun in 1966 with US AID help to link Douala and Victoria, the principal commercial and port districts of East and West Cameroon, respectively. It was completed and opened with fanfare in 1969, thus reducing what was a 200-kilometer detour to a 56-kilometer, hard-surface highway.

ROGOZINSKI, STEPHEN. A Polish adventurer and former lieutenant in the Russian Imperial Army who, in British pay, concluded thirty-five "temporary" treaties with native chiefs (e.g., the Bakweri) in the Cameroons in 1885, much to the displeasure of the Germans who had hoisted their imperial flag over the Cameroonian coastal area several months earlier. See NACHTIGAL,

GUSTAV. The land ceded by the native chiefs under these treaties was annexed to the British colony of Victoria (q.v.). British-German relations became strained over Rogozinski's activities and over their overlapping land claims in the region. By February 1885, Great Britain had relented in this treaty-making contest and agreed to surrender many of the claims based on Rogozinski's treaties.

RUBBER. The seventh most valuable agricultural crop of Cameroon, produced principally in the southeast and southwest. Almost all of it is exported.

-S-

SAKER, (DR.) ALFRED, 1814-1880. English missionary. Saker was born in England and, at the age of 29, having studied for the Baptist Missionary Ministry, he accepted a mission post in Jamaica. In 1844, after a short stay in Jamaica, he left to assist the mission settlement at Clarence, on the island of Fernando Po. Under pressure from the Spanish Jesuits on the Island, Saker left Clarence in 1845 for Douala where, on June 22, 1845, he established the first Christian mission on the Cameroon coast. He performed his first baptisms in 1849, after having firmly settled his mission at Bimbia. Saker learned the Douala language and published Douala versions of the Old and New Testaments on a press built by Joseph Merrick at the Bimbia Mission. Saker founded two more missions at Deido and Bonaberi, and in 1858, after having purchased some land at the foot of Mount Cameroon from King William of Deido, founded the mission of Victoria on Ambas Bay. Victoria became the first permanent English settlement on the Cameroon coast. Saker remained in Cameroon thirty years, finally retiring to England in 1876, where he died four years later. See MERRICK, JOSEPH.

SAMBA, MARTIN-PAUL, 1870(?)-1914. Samba was born ca. 1870 near the village of Biba, in the Ebolowa district. His family soon moved to Kribi, on the coast, where he met and was taken into the service of the German explorer Kurt von Morgen. Morgen took Samba with him to Germany, where he spent six years in German schools, finally completing military training and emerging as a Lieutenant in the Imperial Army. He served with the Imperial General Staff, rising to the rank of Captain. In 1895 Samba returned to Cameroon, and between 1895 and 1910, in his capacity as a German officer, participated in several campaigns to pacify the center and northern parts of the protectorate. In 1910 Samba resigned his commission, became a traditional chief at Ebolowa, and began preparing a revolt of the hinterland tribes in concert with Rudolph Douala Manga Bell (q.v.) and several other traditional chiefs. When war broke out in 1914, Samba drafted a letter to the French governor at Brazzaville declaring his intention to attack the German forces in Cameroon, and asking for support. The letter was intercepted and shown to the German commandant at Ebolowa, Von Hagen, who had Samba arrested immediately. Charged with high treason, Samba was shot by a firing squad on August 8, 1914. Following his death, he became a popular hero, and legends about him began to circulate.

SANGEMELIMA. A southern town inhabited primarily by the Bulu and Fang peoples. It was the site of a 1956 ethnic riot against immigrant Bamiléké. See BULU; ETHNIC CONFLICT; LE PROBLEME BAMILEKE.

SEIDOU NJIMOLUH (NJOYA), EL HADJ, 1904- . Sultan of Bamoun. Sultan Seidou succeeded to the Foumban throne in 1933. He was elected to the Territorial Assembly in 1952, and served in every succeeding legislature up to and including the 1970 Federal Assembly. He is also Mayor of Foumban and President of the Bamoun Customary Court. One of several northern Cameroon traditional magnates in the Cameroon legislature, he remains one of the most powerful traditional chiefs in the country.

SEITZ, THEODOR. The Kamerun's fourth governor (1907-1910). Seitz was a humanitarian administrator who was determined to remedy the abuses and scandals of previous governors. See PUTTKAMER, JESCO VON. He favored increased native representation on local councils, the elimination of certain kinds of domestic slavery and an end to forced labor and flogging. Seitz's term also saw negotiations begin with France for the acquisition of a large part of the French Congo. In return for ceding German rights in Morocco to

France, Germany received from France about 107,000 square miles of the French Congo, virtually doubling the size of the Kamerun. The final agreement (1911) gave the Germans an outlet to the Congo River and drew the southern boundary so that it enclosed Spanish Rio Muni. This additional area acquired by the Germans was known as "New Kamerun." See GLEIM, OTTO.

SLAVE TRADE. The early Portuguese visitors to the Cameroon coast opened up the area to the slave trade. This commerce in human booty began to flourish after 1530, when the burgeoning plantations in the New World found imported African labor increasingly necessary. For the next three centuries Portuguese, Spanish, French, British, American and German traders competed for a share in the slave market. The island of Fernando Po was one of the main collection points for slaves taken along the Bight of Benin. French, British and German traders established semi-permanent posts along the coast, principally at the mouth of the Wouri, where the indigenous Douala acted as middlemen in the slave trade. See CALABAR. In 1807 the British declared their own slave trade illegal and began policing the Gulf of Guinea in an attempt to suppress it altogether. The slave trade gradually faded as commerce in ivory and palm oil became more lucrative for the Douala and as missionary activity began.

SOCIETE D'EXPANSION ET DE MODERNISATION DE LA RIZICULTURE DE YAGOUA (SEMRY). A company created in 1954 to develop a rice cultivation and processing enterprise in the Yagoua (q.v.) area of the far northern Cameroon. SEMRY has raised rice production in the Logone River (q.v.) valley from nil in 1953 to 6,000 tons annually by 1972. The rice produced is cheap, of good quality, and helps offset the cost of importing rice. In April 1972 the World Bank agreed to finance an expansion of SEMRY's activities with a loan of $3.7 million. The French Fonds d'Aide et de Coopération (q.v.) also offered money (in excess of 2,000 m. CFA francs) for the extension work, which will expand acreage under cultivation and provide a new dike and drainage system. The SEMRY system encouraged and aided local farmers in rice production; it did not establish a large industrial farm. The rice is grown on small plots of between 40 and 60 acres. See also MASSA.

SODEN, JULIUS VON. The Kamerun's first governor (1885-1891) and an advocate of a gradual rather than the rapid and forceful opening of the hinterland that the traders favored. Under his governorship the German flag was raised at Buea in 1885; German firms started plantations on the lower slopes of Mount Cameroon, trebling the land under cultivation by 1913; the Germans consolidated their hold on the coastal region and expanded their trade and commercial establishments; and the Basler Mission, which had taken over the English Baptists' mission at Victoria, set up a mission at Douala. See ZIMMERER, EUGEN VON.

SOPPO PRISO, PAUL, 1913- . Politician, businessman. Soppo Priso was born in Douala on July 19, 1913, of humble origins, his mother having been a non-Douala household slave. Educated in Douala in French Protestant primary and secondary schools, in 1938 he rallied the educated young Doualas in urging continuation of the French mandate in the face of German agitation for the return of the territory. He was president of Jeucafra (Jeunesse Camerounaise Française), the first prewar political organization to have official sanction. During the war he was employed by the Public Works Department, and by 1946 had struck out on his own as an independent building contractor. His commercial activities have made him one of Cameroon's wealthiest men. He served in the Cameroun Legislative Assembly (1947-52), the Territorial Assembly (1952-55) and the Legislative Assembly, 1956-60. He was President of the Territorial Assembly 1953-55, and was co-founder of a political party, the Groupe d'Action Nationale. He also served in the French National Assembly of the French Union, 1953-55.

STATUTE OF THE CAMEROUN. A law passed by the French National Assembly in late 1956 and ratified by the new Cameroun Legislative Assembly (q.v.), on February 22, 1957. The statute was designed to implement the reforms of the French loi-cadre (q.v.) of 1956, giving the Cameroun a wider measure of autonomy within the trusteeship framework.

SUJETS INDIGENES. So-called "native subjects" in the
French colonies, subject to special laws (such as the
indigénat, q.v.) from which the indigenous elite (assimilés, evolués) was exempt. Assimilés had rights
equal to those of French citizens; sujets indigènes
could not vote, were tried by summary courts, were
subject to forced labor and the préstation (q.v.).

-T-

TABLE RONDE. A policy of reconciliation and rapproche-
ment initiated by the ralliés and supported by Soppo
Priso and the Démocrates Camerounais (q.v.) in 1959,
which was offered to members of the "external" UPC
(q.v.). See RALLIEMENT. The idea was to have a
series of round-table discussions with all Camerounian
political elements participating so that mutually satis-
fying decisions could be made regarding Camerounian
unity and the end of internal strife before independence
on January 1, 1960. A Committee for the Table Ronde,
consisting of leaders from five parties, was created in
Yaoundé, but with the ralliés and the Démocrates con-
spicuously absent. The Committee established such
conditions for the participation of the "external" UPC
that the latter could not accept without branding itself
responsible for terrorism and without relinquishing its
ideals of "national liberation." As a result, the idea
of a table ronde faded quietly in that same year.

TCHOUNGUI, (DR.) SIMON-PIERRE, 1916- . Former
Prime Minister of East Cameroon, physician. Born
on October 28, 1916 at Nkolmending/Mefou, he was
educated locally and in 1938 became a medical aide,
serving in Yaoundé and Mbalmayo. In 1942 he enlisted
in the Free French forces, taking part in the military
campaigns in France. Demobilized in 1946, he studied medicine in Dakar, returning to Cameroon (1947)
and medical duties in Bafoussam and Yaoundé. From
1950 to 1956 he continued his medical studies in Paris,
earning his medical doctorate. On returning to Cameroon, he served two years in the Ministries of Public
Health and Public Administration. He was appointed
medical superintendent of the Yaoundé Hospital in 1960,
and in 1961 was named Director of Public Health, then
Federal Minister of Public Health that same year. In
1964 he was named Minister of National Economy, then

(1965) Minister without Portfolio. In October, 1965, he was designated Prime Minister of East Cameroon, a position he held until 1972, when the Federal Republic was transformed into a unitary state.

TERRITORIAL ASSEMBLY OF CAMEROUN (ATCAM). The name "Representative Assembly" of Cameroun (q.v.) or ARCAM was changed in 1952 to "Territorial Assembly" or ATCAM, to stress a greater role for the legislature in the actual governing of the territory. Indeed, by 1952, the number of elected seats had increased from 34 to 50, the six appointive positions had been dropped, the proportion of members to be elected from the (European) "first college" had dropped from two-fifths to one-third, registered voters in the (African) "second college" had increased from 39,000 to 521,000, and the number of candidates for the fifty seats had increased from about 40 (for the 34 elective seats in ARCAM in 1946) to over 300. The actual legislative powers exercised by ATCAM, prior to the loi-cadre of 1956 (q.v.), were restricted to certain "advisory" votes on fiscal and economic matters (as was ARCAM), but over the years fewer of its decisions were annulled by the Conseil d'État and more of ATCAM's recommendations were followed.

Within the Assembly the various chairmanships passed increasingly into African hands. Moderates such as Aujoulat, Ahidjo, Soppo Priso, and Okala (all q.v.) were re-elected to the Assembly in 1952, while again the radical nationalist UPC won no seats. In contrast to the elections to ARCAM, those to ATCAM in 1952 were contested by a full panoply of parties, including BDC, UPC, Esocam and the Camerounian branches of various French parties, both socialist and Gaullist. Article 10 of the loi-cadre of 1956 abolished the dual college electoral system and provided for elections to ATCAM on the basis of universal suffrage from a single electoral college. Voter registration continued apace until over 1.7 million Camerounians were on the electoral rolls.

ATCAM was dissolved in November 1956 to prepare for elections the following month so that a new assembly could pass judgment on the French government's newly-drafted Statute of the Cameroun, giving Cameroun a wide measure of autonomy. Nearly one million people (about 55% of those registered) cast ballots on December 23 for the enlarged (to 70) Assem-

bly. More than five parties split the vote with the
Union Camerounaise (q.v.) gaining a plurality of the
votes (34%) and of the seats (30). The Statute of the
Cameroun was passed by ATCAM on February 22,
1957, and it went into effect on April 4. On May 9
ATCAM took the title of Legislative Assembly of Cameroun (q.v.) or ALCAM, and on the following day André Mbida (q.v.) was invested as the first Prime Minister, heading a coalition government.

TIKAR. A term designating the various related tribes of
the Bamenda Plateau who comprise the second largest
grouping (about 400,000) among the Cameroon Highlanders. The various Tikar tribes (e.g., Bafut, Kom,
Ndop, and Nsaw) are also known as "grassfielders,"
after the characteristic cover of the Bamenda highlands, a name that is also often used by the Bamiléké.
The Tikar reside in both the former eastern and western states of Cameroon, with the overwhelming majority in the western portion.

TIKO. The second largest town in West Cameroon. Originally a trading station on the coast, the Germans converted it into a port. In an attempt to integrate the
economies of the two states after federation, the Federal Republic modernized Tiko and made it a subport
of Douala. Tiko was connected to Douala by a new
French-financed road (56 kilometers) in April 1969.

TIMBER. The production of wood for both export and local
consumption is in the hands of some twenty timber
companies in Cameroon. As of 1971 there were thirty
sawmills, two plywood mills at Dimako and Douala, a
plywood factory, a match works, and ten furniture or
industrial carpentry works. The timber reserves of
the tropical forest are an area of considerable potential growth. Estimates as to the amount of timber reserves vary from 29 to 39 million acres, of which
less than one-fifth was being exploited in 1971 due to
problems of access. Nevertheless, timber constituted
Cameroon's fourth leading export commodity.

TOBACCO. An increasingly important commercial crop in
Cameroon; until recently, most production was used
locally (or by the Bastos cigarette factory in Yaoundé),
but quantities are now exported.

TOMBEL MASSACRE. The slaughter of 236 Bamiléké by a mob of Bakossi in the town of Tombel on December 31, 1967. The immediate catalyst for the violence was the robbery and murder of four Bakossi, including a school-teacher, by a group of bandits (widely assumed to be Bamiléké) shortly before Christmas. The deeper cause was the underlying and continuing ethnic tension between the two groups, as the Bakossi resented increasing Bamiléké economic control of commerce in the area. See LE PROBLEME BAMILEKE. One hundred and forty-three Bakossi were eventually tried by a military court and various sentences meted out.

TRANSCAM RAILWAY. A rail line which will link Yaoundé and Ngaoundéré, a distance of 630 kilometers, in order to exploit the large deposits of bauxite found in the Martrap-Tibati areas in the north and to improve connections between north Cameroon and the southern coastal areas. See ALUMINUM. Over $80 million from a consortium of French, American and Common Market sources has helped finance the project, which may be completed by 1975. The Transcameroon railway, at present the single most important development project in the country, will eventually extend northward to the Chad basin, and possibly eastward to the Central African Republic. The rail system will not only provide a new and profitable means of access to the sea but also should promote closer integration of the equatorial African states. See BAUXITE; UNION DOUANIERE ET ECONOMIQUE DE L'AFRIQUE CENTRALE.

TRUSTEESHIP SYSTEM. Established under Chapter XII of the Charter of the United Nations, the trusteeship system replaced and went considerably beyond the aims of the mandate system of the defunct League of Nations. Article 76 of the UN Charter provided that the purpose of trusteeship was to "promote the political, economic, social and educational advancement of the inhabitants of the trust territories, and their progressive development toward self-government or independence...." The mandate system had called only for "the well-being and development of [dependent] peoples."
    The manner in which the trust territories were to be governed by the Administering Authorities (e.g., France and the United Kingdom, in the two Cameroons) was to be supervised by the Trusteeship Council of the

of the United Nations. Annual reports on each territory and periodic on-the-spot investigations by UN Visiting Missions (q.v.) were designed to monitor adherence to the Charter and the Trusteeship Agreements. The opportunity given to Cameroons politicians to reach world opinion through the organs of the trusteeship system probably speeded progress to self-government, independence, and eventually, reunification. Trusteeship status terminated for French Cameroun when it achieved independence on January 1, 1960. On October 1, 1961, the two Cameroons were united, and the trusteeship over the British Southern Cameroons came officially to an end.

-U-

UM NYOBE, REUBEN, 1913-1958. Nationalist leader. Um was born in Boumnyébel. After attending Protestant schools in the Bassa area, he was admitted to the Teacher Training School at Sangmélima, but had to leave after only one year, in 1932. He then found a minor post in the government finance office in Douala, and in 1939, was employed as clerk to the civil court in Yaoundé. In 1944, when two French civil servants formed discussion groups designed to initiate Cameroun public employees to French trade unionism (particularly the Confédération Générale du Travail), Um Nyobé became an active participant. In 1947 he joined the CGT, and entered Cameroon political life. In April, 1948, he and several trade union colleagues founded the Union des Populations du Cameroon (UPC) party (q.v.) whose aim was the immediate grant of independence to the territory and reunification with the British Cameroons. The UPC remained a legal entity until 1955, contesting elections, but without much success. In May 1955, it instigated a territory-wide insurrection, which failed, and Um Nyobé and several UPC leaders took refuge in the British Cameroons. That same year, Um and his lieutenant, Mayi-Matip, returned to Cameroon to organize guerrilla resistance. On September 13, 1958, he was killed in a skirmish with government troops near Boumnyébel.

UNION BAMILEKE. Organized in February 1948 at Bafoussam in French Cameroun, the Union Bamiléké was an ethnic-based organization with solidarity, security and political objectives. It was the first anti-UPC political group and was created by pro-Administration Bamiléké chiefs in order to counter the pro-UPC Kumsze (q.v.). When the latter renounced its UPC ties in 1950, the Union Bamiléké lost much of its raison d'être but continued to function as a loose grouping of peasants and planters. It was dissolved in 1961, when its members formally committed themselves to support the Union Camerounaise (q.v.).

L'UNION CAMEROUNAISE (1937-1938). A quasi-political organization comprised of Camerounian évolués in Douala which petitioned the League of Nations in 1937 to convert the Cameroons into an "A" mandate. The president of this organization and signer of the petition was one Mandessi Bell, apparently of the politically-experienced Douala Bell family. In 1938 on the eve of World War II, the organization sent identical letters to Franklin D. Roosevelt, Neville Chamberlain and Premier Daladier of France, protesting against any possible return of the territory to Germany. The instigation for these letters was twofold: German propaganda which demanded the return of its former colonies (see DEUTSCHE KOLONIALGESELLSCHAFT); and talk by some British and French leaders that colonial concessions to Germany might be a way to avert war.

UNION CAMEROUNAISE (UC). Organized in May 1958 by Ahmadou Ahidjo (q.v.) from a northern-based parliamentary group in ALCAM, the UC was the governing party in East Cameroon from 1958 to 1961 and the governing party in the federation from 1961 to 1966. The UC was founded at Garoua (q.v.) at a meeting of five small local northern political groups. The parliamentary base of the new party consisted of twenty-nine northern deputies (primarily Muslim Fulani) plus five other apparentés (electorally allied deputies) to the UC parliamentary group. As the first political party in the north of East Cameroon, the UC was the principal channel to the national political arena for northern politicians. The UC had the support of many traditional northern lamibé (q.v.) and relied on ethnic solidarity among the Fulani for its electoral strength. It sought to Islamize and politicize the Kirdi (q.v.) to gain additional adherents.

The UC became a mass party as it incorporated over the years the leadership and following of a num-

ber of other smaller parties and groups. At the UC's
fourth party congress at Ebolowa in July 1962, the
treasurer-general claimed 300,000 dues-paying, card-
carrying members, representing the largest number of
adherents ever claimed for a political organization in
Cameroon. The party was hierarchically organized,
with the base composed of a large number of cells at
the village or neighborhood level and a decision-making
Comité-Directeur (Executive Committee) at the top.
After independence, reunification and reconciliation
(with the UPC), the UC developed a new party ideology
more suitable to a less revolutionary atmosphere. See
FOUMBAN CONFERENCE; PARTI UNIFIE. Besides
Ahidjo, Arouna Njoya and Moussa Yaya (both q.v.)
were the most influential voices in UC party affairs.
 In the 1956 elections to ATCAM, the UC parliamentary group garnered 34% of the popular vote (a
plurality) and 30 of the 70 Assembly seats. Ahidjo
was appointed Vice-Premier and Minister of the Interior in the Mbida government. When the latter fell in
February 1958, Ahidjo became the new Prime Minister.
In the 1960 elections to ANCAM, Ahidjo led his party
to a greater plurality of votes (45%) and a majority
(51) of the 100-seat Assembly. See LEGISLATIVE
ASSEMBLY OF CAMEROUN. After federation in 1961,
opposition parties in Cameroon either joined the UC
voluntarily or were disbanded by threat of legal, political or physical sanctions. By 1965 the UC had
emerged as the only party in East Cameroon. See
FRONT NATIONAL UNIFIE; FRONT POPULAIRE POUR
L'UNITE ET LA PAIX; MOUVEMENT D'ACTION NA-
TIONALE CAMEROUNAISE; PARTI DES DEMOCRATES
CAMEROUNAIS; PAYSANS INDEPENDANTS. In 1966
the remaining parties in the West dissolved themselves
and then joined with the UC to form a single national
party, the Union Nationale Camerounaise (q.v.). See
CAMEROON PEOPLES NATIONAL CONVENTION;
CAMEROON UNITED CONGRESS; KAMERUN NATION-
AL DEMOCRATIC PARTY.

UNION CAMEROUNAISE FRANÇAISE (UNICAFRA). The successor organization to Jeucafra. Unicafra was founded
in late 1945 by André Fouda (q.v.) and dissolved in
1947 to become Rassemblement Camerounais (q.v.).
During its brief life, Unicafra pleaded both Camerounian causes and devotion to France, as its name im-
plied. Trade unionists, especially the militant USCC,

sought unsuccessfully to overwhelm Unicafra and capture its leadership positions in order to gain political leverage in the postwar struggle in Cameroun among various unions and nascent parties.

UNION DEMOCRATIQUE DES FEMMES CAMEROUNAISES (UDFC). The women's wing of the Union des Populations du Cameroun (q.v.) and successor to the earlier Comité féminin de l'UPC. UDFC was led by Mmes. Moumié and Kingué and like its youth-oriented counterpart, the JDC, was a propaganda organ, recruitment center and petition-writing agency in the UPC's hierarchical organization. It was outlawed in Cameroun along with its parent UPC in July 1955, but continued its activities across the border in Kumba, West Cameroon. See JEUNESSE DEMOCRATIQUE CAMEROUNAISE.

UNION DES POPULATIONS DU CAMEROUN (UPC). An East Cameroon political party founded in 1948, the UPC was the first true nationalist party in the Cameroons. It urged the achievement, by violence if necessary, of unification of the two Cameroons and independence from France. On April 10, 1948 Ruben Um Nyobé, Felix Moumié, Ernest Ouandié, Abel Kingué (all q.v.) and several other trade union leaders formed the UPC from the remnants of the Rassemblement Camerounais (q.v.). Within two months the UPC became the Cameroun branch of the Rassemblement Démocratique Africain (q.v.) and had begun to attract support from influential "traditional" organizations such as Ngondo and Kumsze (both q.v.).

The UPC was organized pyramidically, with local party cells at the base, Central and Regional Committees in the middle and a Central Executive Committee at the peak. The UPC created subsidiary and complementary affiliates, such as UDFC and JDC, and published a monthly newspaper, Voix du peuple du Cameroun. The UPC was strongest in urban and plantation centers (e.g., Douala, Nkongsamba) as well as in the Sanaga Maritime Region, home of the Bassa people. See BASSA-BAKOKO; UNION DES SYNDICATS CONFEDERES DU CAMEROUN. By the time the first UN Visiting Mission (q.v.) arrived in November 1949, the UPC was the best organized political party in French Cameroun.

Between 1949 and 1955 anti-UPC groups emerged

Union des Populations 118

(e.g., Union Bamiléké, Esocam, Renaicam, all q.v.), as well as other political parties in East Cameroon, such as the precursors to the PDC and the PSC. Many of the latter parties preempted the UPC's nationalist program for their own use. Unable to win seats in the Cameroun assemblies (ARCAM and ATCAM) and with the French administration hostile to its goals, the UPC decided to turn from verbal extremism to more violent action. See PRE, ROLAND. During May 1955, the UPC launched a series of riots and demonstrations in Douala and Yaoundé but failed to ignite their hoped-for nationwide insurrection. The UPC was banned in July, its leaders either fleeing into exile or going underground. See "BAMILEKE" REBELLION; MAQUIS; NATIONAL ARMY OF KAMERUNIAN LIBERATION.

The underground UPC at home carried on a campaign of sabotage, intimidation, and assassination to discourage voting in the December 1956 elections to ATCAM. The Mbida government during 1957, and the Ahidjo government until 1962, used French troops to help quell UPC violence and terrorism. See also ZONE DE PACIFICATION. The continuing rebellion in many parts of southern and western East Cameroon plus the UPC's propaganda campaign waged at the United Nations brought to the fore another theme in Cameroonian politics: "reconciliation" with the banned UPC and amnesty for its leaders. The ban was eventually lifted in February, 1960. See: COURANT D'UNION NATIONALE; MOUVEMENT D'ACTION NATIONALE CAMEROUNAISE. The Ahidjo government also passed an amnesty law to encourage UPC defections. See RALLIEMENT. Even though Um Nyobé was killed in September 1958, ending the Bassa phase of the revolt, the external wing of the UPC, from foreign capitals in Africa, continued to stoke the fires of unrest in the principal towns and in the countryside. At the UN the UPC agitated for general elections in Cameroun before independence on January 1, 1960, arguing that since the UPC had not been permitted to participate in the 1956 elections to ATCAM, the Assembly was not "representative." See UNITED NATIONS, "CAMEROONS SESSION" OF GENERAL ASSEMBLY. Rebuffed at the UN, its leadership split, dead, "rallied," or captured, its membership down from defections, and its goals pre-empted by other parties, by October 1961 the UPC had lost much of its raison d'être and revolutionary élan. Maquis groups were sporadically active in the southeast and southwest during the 1960s but were increasingly contained by the Ahidjo government and disavowed by the populace. Politically, the UPC's final act of submission came in September 1968, when Theodore Mayi-Matip (q.v.), out of jail since 1965 and presumably reconciled with Ahidjo, joined the ruling single party, the Union Nationale Camerounaise (q.v.). See also BAMENDA CONFERENCE (1955); CATHOLICISM, INFLUENCE OF; CHINA, PEOPLES REPUBLIC OF; KAMDEN NINYIM, PIERRE; KAMERUN IDEA, THE; KAMERUN UNITED NATIONAL CONGRESS; KANGA, VICTOR; NDONGMO AFFAIR.

UNION DES SYNDICATS AUTONÔMES CAMEROUNAIS (USAC). Considered one of the most radical of the Cameroon's trade unions, the USAC merged with other large unions in 1963 to form the giant Fédération des Syndicats du Cameroun (q.v.)

UNION DES SYNDICATS CONFEDERES DU CAMEROUN (USCC). In September 1944, the Confédération Générale du Travail, the Communist-dominated and largest trade union in France, helped found the USCC under Charles Assalé (q.v.) as the CGT's local Camerounian branch. The USCC advocated the "general strike" as the best strategy for bringing about the establishment of a sovereign Camerounian state. USCC aims (and to some extent leadership) coincided with those of the UPC. Reuben Um Nyobé (q.v.) was at one time Secretary-General of the USCC. See also RASSEMBLEMENT CAMEROUNAIS. The USCC challenged France's overseas labor laws and took part in a series of wildcat strikes, which degenerated into riots, in Douala between September 21 and 30, 1945. Following the riots, strikes, and demonstrations which occurred in Douala and Yaoundé in April and May 1955, the leaders of the USCC were arrested.

UNION DES SYNDICATS CROYANTS DU CAMEROUN (USCC). An East Cameroon trade union federation formed in 1962 by the merger of two Christian trade unions, the Confédération Camerounaise des Syndicats Croyants and the Union Camerounaise des Travailleurs Croyants. It was affiliated with the ATUC and the Pan-African Union of Believing Workers, the regional branch of the

IFCTU. By 1963 mergers had reduced the number of
union groups in East Cameroon to two: the USCC and
the Fédération des Syndicats du Cameroun (q.v.). In
1969 these two united with the West Cameroon Trade
Union Congress (q.v.) to form a single national body,
the Union des Travailleurs Camerounais (q.v.).

UNION DES SYNDICATS LIBRES DU CAMEROUN (USLC). An
East Cameroon trade-union grouping affiliated with the
ICFTU. It was one of the major unions to merge in
1963 to form the Fédération des Syndicats du Cameroun (q.v.).

UNION DES TRAVAILLEURS CAMEROUNAIS (UTC). This
trade union grouping is the "umbrella" organization of
the principal West and East Cameroon trade union federations. Paralleling the centralization of party control in the Cameroons, the UTC was formed in October
1969 by a merger of the two remaining union groups
in the East (USCC and FSC) with the one remaining
large union in the West (WCTUC). The three component federations of the UTC were united at Ahidjo's instigation for their alleged "powerlessness" (in Ahidjo's
words).

UNION DOUANIERE ET ECONOMIQUE DE L'AFRIQUE CENTRALE (UDEAC). The Central African Customs and
Economic Union was established by the Treaty of
Brazzaville and went into force on January 1, 1966.
Its founding members are five neighboring former
French territories in Equatorial Africa: Cameroon,
Chad, Gabon, Central African Republic, and Congo
(Brazzaville). The Union, with its twelve million potential consumers, comprises a free trade area and
enforces common tariff and taxation policies. The
member countries, like the European Economic Community (q.v.), are attempting economic integration
through regional association. See also TRANSCAM
RAILWAY. The supreme organ of the Union is the
Council of Heads of State, of which Ahidjo was President during 1970.

Cameroon is perhaps the strongest member of
UDEAC and may in fact become the industrial center
for the equatorial region. In 1966, for example, the
gross domestic product of the five-country UDEAC area
was estimated at about $1.4 billion, of which almost
one-half was generated in Cameroon. UDEAC has ben-

efited Cameroon in many ways: it forced the harmonization of internal customs differences between East and West Cameroon, completed in July 1966; it increased the trade for the port of Douala as well as spurred the development of inland transportation facilities to the land-locked member states of Chad and Central African Republic; and it doubled the potential market available for Cameroonian products.

UNION GENERALE DES TRAVAILLEURS D'AFRIQUE NOIRE (UGTAN). A "militant" pan-African trade union organization formed in January 1957 at Cotonou, Dahomey, by various Black African trade unions in an attempt to gain greater autonomy from their metropolitan centrales. UGTAN denounced the loi-cadre (q.v.) as a balkanizing attempt to break up workers' unity. Two East Camerounian unions, the UGTC and the CGCT, maintained close liaison with UGTAN until 1963 when the former merged with other unions at home to form the Fédération des Syndicats du Cameroun (q.v.).

UNION GENERALE DES TRAVAILLEURS DU CAMEROUN (UGTC). A radical East Camerounian trade union which maintained close ties with both the "militant" UGTAN and the Communist WFTU. In 1963 the UGTC merged with other East Camerounian unions to form the Fédération des Syndicats du Cameroun (q.v.).

UNION NATIONALE CAMEROUNAISE (UNC). The Cameroon National Union (CNU/UNC) was the single ruling party in the Cameroon Federal Republic from 1966 to 1972 and thereafter in the United Republic of Cameroon. It came into formal existence on September 1, 1966, after months of interstate and inter-party consultation, with the merger of the governing party of each state (the UC in the East and the KNDP in the West), along with the two opposition parties in the West Cameroon, the CUC and the CPNC. This merger took place just five years after the federation itself had come into existence, and it converted Cameroon into a national single-party system. (Technically, new parties could still be formed, and any party if it wished could stay out of the UNC, but these possibilities did not occur.) The UNC may be described as a party of Cameroonian elites rather than as a mass party, for the merger united the leadership of the nation rather than the diverse groups which comprise the population. Moreover, political initiative primarily comes from the party and government leaders at the top rather than from local or regional representatives. During 1967 the UNC successfully displaced the members of the once-powerful KNDP in the West with its own new regional branch. Augustin N. Jua (q.v.), West Cameroon Premier and last symbol of West Cameroonian political autonomy, was replaced by Solomon T. Muna (q.v.), a "federation man" and Ahidjo's appointee. In the December 1967 elections to the West Cameroon Legislative Assembly, the UNC, the only party to present candidates, won all 37 seats. In simultaneous elections on June 7, 1970 to the East Cameroon Legislative Assembly (100 seats) and to the National Federal Assembly (50 seats), the UNC presented a single set of candidates to the electorate and won all seats.

The 1969 UNC party congress was held in Garoua (q.v.), where the Union Camerounaise (q.v.) had been founded eleven years earlier. The party congress elected a Political Bureau containing thirty-five of the most important governmental figures and including the federal President and Vice-President, the two prime ministers, and a dozen federal and state ministers. The UNC Charter, outlining the party's internal and external policies, was published in April 1969. It supports efforts towards the liberation and unification of Africa; it respects a democratic system of government within Cameroon; and it states that economic and social development should be achieved in Cameroon through encouraging private initiative while reserving for the state a determining and organizing role. The UNC also publishes a weekly party newspaper, l'Unité.

UNION NATIONALE DES ETUDIANTS KAMERUNAIS (UNEK). The principal Cameroon students' organization in France. UNEK was left-oriented and made no pretense at concealing its hostility to the Ahidjo government, being sympathetic instead to the aims of the UPC. UNEK was affiliated with the Union Internationale des Etudiants (International Students' Union), which was a prime organizer of the various International Youth Festivals. UNEK published a monthly magazine, l'Étudiant Kamerunais. In 1960, UNEK's anti-government activities became so irritating to the Cameroun authorities that UNEK was asked to disband, and five of the organization's leaders were deprived of their government scholarships. Pierre Kamden Ninyim (q.v.) began his militant nationalist career in Paris as a member of the pro-UPC UNEK.

UNION SOCIALE CAMEROUNAISE (USC). A Cameroun Socialist party founded in January 1953 by Charles Okala (q.v.) after his defeat in the 1952 elections to ATCAM. Launching itself on a program of anti-capitalism and anti-imperialism, the USC attempted to set up a number of sections in Bulu Territory and in Douala but failed to gain much mass support among either workers or peasants. The USC joined Soppo Priso's short-lived Courant Mouvement d'Union Nationale (q.v.) in 1956 and in 1959 became the Parti Socialiste Camerounaise (q.v.).

L'UNITE. Official newspaper of the Cameroon National Union, published weekly in Yaoundé.

UNITED NATIONAL FRONT see FRONT NATIONAL UNIFIE

UNITED NATIONS. Cameroon became a member of the UN in 1960 and maintains a permanent mission in New York. Within the General Assembly the Federal Republic's representatives orient themselves according to the postures developed by the "African caucus," and more particularly to the positions of the OCAM (q.v.) group at the UN. Cameroon, on the whole, gives only qualified support to the United Nations, but it participates fully in the various UN agencies such as the Economic Commission for Africa, the World Health Organization, the International Labor Organization, the Food and Agriculture Organization, and the UN Educational, Scientific and Cultural Organization (UNESCO). See PLEBISCITES, UNITED NATIONS; TRUSTEESHIP SYSTEM.

UNITED NATIONS, "CAMEROONS SESSION" OF GENERAL ASSEMBLY. An extraordinary session of the UN Thirteenth General Assembly, which convened on February 20, 1959 to deal definitively with the future of British and French Cameroons. For three weeks the General Assembly's Fourth (Trusteeship) Committee debated the key issues raised by the report of the 1958 Visiting Mission (q.v.): the question of independence, the character of the Camerounian Assembly elected in December, 1956, the demand for pre-independence elections, the status and activities of the UPC, the legitimacy of the Ahidjo regime, and the nature of French intentions toward the Cameroun. Ahidjo and representatives of his government were present at the UN, as were some fifteen UPC petitioners. On March 13, 1959, the General Assembly approved independence for Cameroun as of January 1, 1960, endorsed its prospective admission to the United Nations, and expressed confidence that elections would take place in the Cameroun "at the earliest possible date" after independence.

The Fourth Committee also discussed the future of the Cameroons under British administration and decided that there would be a plebiscite in November, 1959, at which the voters in Northern Cameroons would decide between joining Northern Nigeria or deferring any decision until later. See PLEBISCITES, UNITED NATIONS. The decision about Southern Cameroons' future was delayed until October, 1959, owing to unresolved differences between Foncha and Endeley. The formula finally decided upon by the General Assembly called for a plebiscite not later than March 1961, with clear alternatives between joining Nigeria or the Cameroun Republic.

UNITED NATIONS VISITING MISSIONS. The United Nations Trusteeship Council periodically sent visiting missions to investigate conditions in the trust territories and to hold hearings. Four such missions within ten years visited one or both of the Cameroons: in 1949, 1952, 1955, and 1958. The missions received petitions and complaints from various local political groupings regarding independence for the territories, reunification with the East, customs and boundary restrictions along the frontier separating the two Cameroons, and various alleged colonial malpractices. The prospect of a UN mission visit had the effect of stimulating nationalist activity among Cameroonian groups. Numerous meetings were held, petitions circulated and proposals prepared for presentation to the Visiting Mission. The report of the 1958 Visiting Mission was instrumental in prompting termination of the Trusteeship Agreement for French Cameroun. See TRUSTEESHIP SYSTEM; UNITED NATIONS, "CAMEROONS SESSION" OF GENERAL ASSEMBLY.

"UNITY GROUP." A parliamentary alliance in the Federal Assembly (q.v.) between the Union Camerounaise and the Kamerun National Democratic Party (both q.v.), the governing parties of East and West Cameroon, respectively. In April 1962 the UC and KNDP set up a Coordinating Committee to "harmonize their actions" and committed themselves to a single party at the national level. See PARTI UNIFIE. The "Unity Group" was the precursor to the single national party which was to emerge in 1966, the Union Nationale Camerounaise (q.v.).

UPECISTES. Generally, members of the UPC party. Also, adherents of the UPC who "returned to legal life" and stood for election to the National Assembly (q.v.) in 1960. Eight Upécistes were elected under the UPC banner from among the Bassa and Douala. See RALLIEMENT.

-V-

VICTORIA. Victoria was an early British missionary colony on Ambas Bay facing Fernando Po (q.v.) and the first permanent European settlement in the Cameroons. It was founded in 1858 and governed by the British missionary Alfred Saker (q.v.). Victoria was officially proclaimed a British possession and annexed to the British empire by Consul E. H. Hewett (q.v.) on July 19, 1884. In 1887, after the German occupation, the Victoria settlement was eliminated when the British Baptist Missionary Society sold its holdings to the German Basel Mission Society (q.v.). Under German administration, the Victoria area was built up and cultivated. An agricultural school was opened there by the Germans to prepare the local peoples for work on the plantations. The Victoria Division was one of four administrative divisions mapped out by the British when they regained control of Southern Cameroons after World War I. After federation in 1961, the Bota-Victoria-Tiko area was expanded into the major port of West Cameroon. In 1969 the "Reunification Road" linking Douala with Victoria was officially opened.

VOGT, FRANCIS-XAVIER, 1870-1943. Catholic missionary. Born on December 3, 1870 at Marlenheim, France, he was educated in France and ordained in 1899. At the age of 35 he was named apostolic vicar to central Zanguebar, German East Africa, and in 1906, was

consecrated bishop. After 16 years in Bagamoyo
(Zanguebar), he was posted to Cameroon (1922), with
the task of reviving the Church's efforts in the territory; of some 16 missions set up by the Germans, only 5 survived. During the next twenty years Vogt devoted himself to building missions, schools, seminaries,
hospitals, and other Church-related establishments. In
1925 he published an Ewondo-French syllabus, and later,
an Ewondo catechism that was later translated into
Bassa and Douala. See MISSIONS, CATHOLIC.

VOLLARBE (or BORORO). One of the two large Foulbé families which have traditionally dominated the Cameroon
north. The Vollarbe are found chiefly in Ngaoundéré
(q.v.) and Banyo. See YILLAGA.

-W-

WES-KOS. Designation of the variety of Pidgin English
(q.v.) spoken along the West African coast from St.
Louis (Senegal) to Kinshasa. Wes-Kos has both grammatical structure and conventional usages; many Wes-Kos words have found their way into American English
via the slave trade. For example, "pickaninny," used
in the U.S. South as a semi-derogative term for a
Black child, derives from Wes-Kos "picken," which
simply means "child."

WEST CAMEROON TRADE UNION CONGRESS (WCTUC).
Formed in 1962, the WCTUC embraced most of West
Cameroon's trade union organizations, such as those
among teachers, postal and telegraph workers, bank
employees, commercial and clerical workers, various
public employees and the important CDCWU. It
claimed 20,000 members in 1965. The WCTUC was
affiliated with the International Confederation for Free
Trade Unions (ICFTU). In 1969 the WCTUC merged
with the two principal unions in the East to form a
single national body, the Union des Travailleurs Camerounais (q.v.). See FEDERATION DES SYNDICATS
DU CAMEROUN; UNION DES SYNDICATS CROYANTS
DU CAMEROUN.

WOERMANN, ADOLF, 1843-1919. An influential Hamburg
trader and head of the C. Woermann Company. The
Woermann firm was established in 1837 and began trad-

ing operations in West Africa in 1849. Its first trading station in the Cameroons was opened in 1868. Its agents cooperated with the British on the Court of Equity (q.v.). Johann Thormählen, later of the rival firm of Jantzen and Thormählen (q.v.), was the Woermann agent in the Cameroons in the 1870s. Woermann placed his ships and agents at the disposal of Nachtigal (q.v.), who formally established the German protectorate over the Cameroons on July 14, 1884. However, all the preliminary arrangements had been made by Woermann agents in the colony, including Woermann's brother Eduard (q.v.), as the British Consul Hewett (q.v.) was to discover to his everlasting chagrin a week later. Besides virtually arranging the annexation of the Cameroons through his agents and close contact with Chancellor Bismarck, Woermann developed the colony's first plantation, practically created the Kamerun government himself and worked out the colony's educational program. By 1905 he had over 30 trading stations in the Kamerun and had his hand in such diverse operations as river dredging, wharf building, railway construction, cotton production, exploring, plantation directing, and missionary activities. See GERMANY, COLONIAL POLICY AND LEGACY OF; KRIBI.

WOERMANN, EDUARD. Younger brother of Adolph Woermann (q.v.); German trader and official. Eduard arrived in Douala in 1884, and helped to convince the Douala chiefs to sign the treaty of annexation (July 12, 1884) that established the German Kamerun Protectorate.

WORLD FEDERATION OF TRADE UNIONS (WFTU). A Communist-dominated international trade-union organization with which both the Union Générale des Travailleurs du Cameroun and the Confédération Générale Camerounaise du Travail (both q.v.) had maintained close liaison prior to the merger of trade unions in East Cameroon in 1963. See FEDERATION DES SYNDICATS DU CAMEROUN.

WORLD WAR I, KAMERUN CAMPAIGNS. The Kamerun campaigns lasted from 1914 to 1916, and resulted in the defeat of German forces. Three Allied groups conducted the campaigns: (1) the northern columns led by Brisset and Ferrandi, which struck from Chad, and the British column from Nigeria, led by Gen. Cunliffe; (2) the southeast columns commanded by Gen. Aymerich (q.v.), including French and Belgian troops, striking from Gabon; and (3) the coastal forces including French and English colonial troops from Sierra Leone, Gold Coast, and Nigeria, which struck at Douala and were to move inland along the railway. The British troops eventually occupied much of what became West Cameroon, the French and their Belgian allies, the East Cameroon. The German forces, led by Col. Zimmerman, numbering less than half the Allied troops, were gradually forced south and into internment in Spanish Guinea and Fernando Po. The Allied forces met in Yaoundé in January, 1916, marking the end of the campaigns. The last German stronghold, Mora in the north, finally surrendered on February 20, 1916.

WORLD WAR II, CAMEROON PARTICIPATION IN. With the defeat of France in 1940 and the creation of the puppet French regime in Vichy led by Marshal Petain, it was expected that the French colonies would fall under Vichy control. The then Governor of the French Cameroon, Brunot, was thought favorable to Vichy, and on August 26-27, a military mission led by Col. Philippe Leclerc took possession of the French Cameroun on behalf of the Free French regime-in-exile of General de Gaulle. Brunot promptly surrendered his civil and military powers to Leclerc. On October 8, 1940, en route to Brazzaville, de Gaulle landed at Douala, symbolizing the first step of his return to France. Leclerc subsequently launched a surprise attack on Gabon, which had remained loyal to Vichy, and took Libreville on November 8, 1940. Chad, led by Governor Eboué, "rallied" to de Gaulle in August of that same year. Leclerc then established his headquarters in Fort-Lamy, and from that base organized a number of trans-Saharan actions against the German and Italian rear in Libya and other north African areas. Cameroon troops later participated in the liberation of France, and were among the French soldiers that entered Paris with de Gaulle and Leclerc.

-Y-

YAGOUA. A town in the Cameroon north on the Logone River (q.v.) near the border with Chad. It has become a principal rice-growing area. See MASSA; SOCIETE D'EXPANSION ET DE MODERNISATION DE LA RIZICULTURE DE YAGOUA.

YAOUNDE. The capital of the Cameroun Republic (1960-61), the capital of both East Cameroon and the Cameroon Federal Republic (1961-72), and the capital of the United Republic since May 1972. After Douala, Yaoundé is the second most populous town (120,000 people in 1971) in the country. Yaoundé was not occupied by Europeans until after 1890 when the Germans, having put down the resistance of the indigenous Ewondo, opened a station there. The French administered Cameroun through a Commissioner and a Conseil d'Administration situated in Yaoundé. Rapid urbanization after 1946 brought pressure on housing and consumer goods in Yaoundé as well as large numbers of unemployed. Many of the urban migrants were Bamiléké who, as in Douala, came to dominate petty commerce, industry and transport in the face of opposition from the traditionally dominant local ethnic groups. See LE PROBLEME BAMILEKE. A large proportion of the population of Yaoundé is Catholic owing to the efforts of missionaries, who opened a seminary there in 1927. See CATHOLICISM.

YILLAGA. One of the two large Foulbé families which have traditionally dominated the Cameroon north. The Yillaga have been the rivals of another large Foulbé family--the Vollarbe (q.v.)--for control over lands or for the political upper hand in the north. This historic schism belies the common assumption among many southern politicians that the Cameroon north is monolithic and cohesive and controlled en bloc by powerful lamibé (q.v.). The lamido of Rei-Bouba is the chief representative of the Yillaga family.

-Z-

ZIMMERER, EUGEN VON. The second Governor of the Kamerun (1891-1895). Under his rule beginnings were made by German explorers to open up the interior of the Kamerun to trade and administrative control. Native rebellions among the Bakweri, Bassa, and Bulu broke out against German penetration of the hinterland, but were put down during this period. See PUTTKAMER, JESCO VON; ZINTGRAFF, EUGEN.

ZINTGRAFF, EUGEN. An imaginative German explorer who helped open up the interior of the Kamerun during the governorship of Soden and Zimmerer (both q.v.). Zintgraff explored the area between the Cameroon River and the Rio del Rey in 1886-87. He established stations at Barombi and Bali and traveled as far north as the Benué River in an attempt to open a northern overland route. This venture resulted in a series of hardfought battles against the Tikar, Bamiléké, Bali and Fulani peoples. The idea of a northern overland route was subsequently abandoned. Zintgraff sent samples of cotton to Germany in 1888, arousing hopes of ending the German dependence on British and American cotton. However, efforts to produce cotton in Kamerun met with little success.

ZOA, MSGR. JEAN, 1924- . Archbishop of Yaoundé. Msgr. Zoa was born in Saa, and was educated at the Parish School in Efok, the Petit Séminaire at Akono, the Grand Séminaire at Mvolye, and the Collegium de Propaganda Fide in Rome. He was ordained a priest in 1950, and became, successively, Vicar in Ombessa (Bafia), 1953-57; Parish priest at the Sacred Heart of Paris, in Yaoundé (1957-58); and Director of Operations for the Archdiocese of Yaoundé (1958-61). In 1961 he was named Archbishop of Yaoundé. Msgr. Zoa holds a number of other ecclesiastical offices, and is the founder of the order of Nova et Vetera. During his career Msgr. Zoa has several times brushed with the Cameroon government, particularly during the 1970-71 period, when one of his bishops, Ndongmo, was implicated, tried, and condemned of conspiring against the state. See CATHOLICISM, INFLUENCE OF.

ZONE DE PACIFICATION (ZOPAC). An area along the main roads between Douala and Yaoundé in which the Mbida government in the fall of 1957 regrouped some ten to fifteen thousand civilians. The populations were resettled within stockades and supplied with alarm signals and weapons. Zopac's purpose was to deprive roving maquisards of hostages and shelter and to allow the authorities to systematically hunt out the bands of terrorists. By the end of the year over one hundred rebels had been arrested and others forced to take refuge in the forests. See "BAMILEKE" REBELLION.

## A CHRONOLOGY OF CAMEROON HISTORY

(Note: Names in capitals are discussed in the Dictionary)

| Date | Event(s) |
|---|---|
| 500 BC | The first possible written mention of the Cameroon coast: HANNON, a Carthaginian seafarer, records in his Periplus, a visit to volcanoes south along the "Lybic coast." |
| 8th-10th Centuries | The Sao settle around Lake Chad. |
| 1472 | The discovery of FERNANDO PO and the estuary of Wouri River by the Portuguese; they name it Rio dos Cameroes (River of Prawns). |
| 16th Century | Bantu migrations, settlement of the southeast Cameroon by the Bantu; the Portuguese and Dutch trade along Cameroon coast; disappearance of the Sao. |
| 17th Century | The Bamiléké settle on the plateaux in the western part of Cameroon. The Kanem-Bornu empire is extended to Lake Chad and the northern Cameroon area. |
| 1715 | Islamization of the Mandara. |
| 1806 | MODIBO ADAMA becomes Emir of Yola and founds Adamawa; Islamization of the Fulani peoples of North Cameroon. |
| 4 February 1823 | The English explorers DENHAM, CLAPPERTON, and HOUDNEY reach Lake Chad by crossing the Sahara from Tripoli. |

| Date | Event(s) |
|---|---|
| 10 June 1840<br>7 May 1841<br>28 April 1852 | Treaties ending slavery along Cameroon coast are signed by British traders and Douala "kings" AKWA and BELL. |
| 1843 | JOSEPH MERRICK, a Black Jamaican pastor, founds a Protestant Mission at Douala. |
| 10 June 1845 | ALFRED SAKER arrives at Douala and founds Bethel Mission; in 1858 he founds Victoria. |
| 1856 | Creation of a merchant's Court of Equity at Douala. |
| 6 November 1881 | Douala KINGS BELL and AKWA write to British government asking for protection; they are rebuffed. |
| 12 July 1884 | EDUARD WOERMANN, the chief German trader at Douala, signs a treaty with Douala chiefs establishing the German protectorate. |
| 14 July 1884 | GUSTAV NACHTIGAL arrives in Douala on July 12 to take possession of the new protectorate for Germany; raises the German flag. |
| 1884-1916 | Period of the German Kamerun Protectorate. |
| 1872 | NACHTIGAL explores the Cameroon hinterland. |
| 1878 | RABAH begins conquest of the Lake Chad area. |
| 21 April 1885 | Britain cedes the territory around Mt. Cameroon (including Victoria) to Germany. |
| 24 December 1885 | An agreement between Germany and France fixes the Rio Campo as the southernmost limit of the Kamerun protectorate. |

| Date | Event(s) |
|---|---|
| 1886 | VON SODEN, the first German governor, opens the first official school, directed by THEODOR CHRISTALLER. |
| 1888 | The British open a trading station at Garoua; Tappen Beck opens the trading station that eventually becomes Yaoundé. |
| 1891 | A German expedition to Buea clashes with local Bakweri people; the Bakweri are subdued, but a German officer (Gravenreuth) is killed. |
| 1895 | The German governor VON PUTTKAMER arrives at Douala; he makes his first headquarters in Douala, later installs the protectorate's administration at Buea. |
| 1899-1901 | The Bulu, resisting European penetration to the interior, fight a running war with Germans between Kribi and Ebolowa but are eventually overcome. |
| 22 April 1900 | Battle between French forces and those of RABAH near Kousseri (now Fort Foureau); RABAH is killed, as is French Commandant LAMY; Rabah's empire comes to an end. |
| 1902 | The Germans reach Foumban. |
| 26 April 1909 | Mt. Cameroon erupts; the German government leaves Buea for Douala. (Mt. Cameroon also erupts in February, 1922 and February-March, 1959). |
| 4 November 1911 | French cedes to Germany some 275,000 sq. km. of its equatorial African possessions; the new Kamerun encircles Spanish Rio Muni, touches the Congo River at Bonga and the Congo's tributary, the Ubangui, at Zinga. |
| 11 April 1911 | Opening of the Douala-Nkongsmaba railway on which construction was begun in 1907. |

| Date | Event(s) |
|---|---|
| 2 August 1914-<br>20 February 1916 | Period of hostilities in Kamerun during the First World War. |
| 8 August 1914 | PAUL-MARTIN SAMBA executed by the Germans in Ebolowa; RUDOLF DOUALA MANGA BELL executed by the Germans in Douala. |
| 27 September 1914 | The British capture Douala. |
| 13-14 October 1914 | The British capture Victoria and Buea. |
| 10 June 1915 | Garoua falls to the Allies. |
| 1 January 1916 | Yaoundé falls to the Allies. |
| 20 February 1916 | The fortress of Mora finally surrenders to the allies; the war in Cameroon ends; the Germans leave Cameroon and are interned in Spanish Rio Muni. |
| 4 March 1916 | Britain and France sign accords dividing the former Kamerun into occupation zones; the accords are confirmed by the Peace Treaty signed 19 June 1919. |
| 20 July 1922 | France receives a Mandate from the League of Nations to administer its part of the former Kamerun; Britain becomes a Mandatory for its parts of the Kamerun. |
| 1922-1946 | Period of British and French Cameroons Mandates. |
| 1922-27 | Completion of the Eseka-Yaoundé section of the central railway (the Douala-Eseka section was built by the Germans). |
| 1922 | EUGENE JAMOT, a French military doctor, arrives in Cameroon to conduct a campaign against sleeping sickness; Jamot dies in 1937 in Paris, his campaign nearly won. |

| Date | Event(s) |
|---|---|
| 30 May 1933 | Death of SULTAN NJOYA of Foumban, exiled in Yaoundé since 1931. |
| 27 August 1940 | COLONEL LECLERC lands at Douala, rallies Cameroon to General de Gaulle's Free French cause. |
| 1 September 1943 | Death of CHIEF CHARLES ATANGANA at Mvolye-Yaoundé. |
| 30 January 1944 | Brazzaville Conference opens. |
| 24-25 September 1945 | A strike in Douala degenerates into a riot; several people are killed. |
| 1945 | The decrees of 9/10/1945 and 25/10/1945 give Cameroun a Representative Assembly (ARCAM), elected from dual electoral rolls. |
| 13 December 1946 | Cameroun becomes a United Nations Trusteeship under French Administration; British Cameroons becomes a Trusteeship under British administration. |
| 1946-1960 and 1961 | Period of UN Trusteeship over the two Cameroons. |
| 10 April 1948 | RUBEN UM NYOBE founds the Union des Populations du Cameroun (UPC), as the local branch of the interterritorial Rassemblement Démocratique Africaine party. |
| 1952 | ARCAM is replaced by the Cameroun Territorial Assembly (ATCAM), also elected from dual rolls; ATCAM lasts until 1956. |
| 25 May 1955 | UPC launches strikes, demonstrations, and violence in the southern part of Cameroun; hundreds of people are killed or injured; on 13 July 1955 the UPC is outlawed and goes underground to continue a guerrilla struggle that lasts until 1970, when the last of the UPC maquis leaders (ERNEST OUANDIE) is captured and exe- |

| Date | Event(s) |
|---|---|
| 25 May 1955 (continued) | cuted. Um Nyobé is himself killed in a skirmish with police on 13 September 1958. During 1955-70 period, perhaps 10-15,000 die as a result of the violence. |
| 23 December 1956 | Elections for a new 70-man Assembly that will operate under a new statute granting internal autonomy to Cameroun. |
| 16 April 1957 | New Camerounian institutions come into being: a Cameroun government with a Prime Minister named by the (French) High Commissioner and invested by the Assembly. Cameroun citizenship is recognized, and Cameroun chooses its own flag, national anthem, and seal. |
| 1957 | ANDRE-MARIE MBIDA is invested as Prime Minister of the first Cameroun government on May 10; on May 9, the Territorial Assembly becomes the Legislative Assembly (ALCAM). |
| 18 February 1958 | AHMADOU AHIDJO becomes Prime Minister following fall of the Mbida government on May 13. |
| 24 October 1958 | ALCAM adopts a resolution inviting the Cameroun government to demand ending of the trusteeship and accession to independence on January 1, 1960. |
| 1 January 1959 | Cameroun attains virtual autonomy under a new statute. |
| 1 January 1960 | The UN Trusteeship comes to an end and the Cameroun Republic comes into being in the presence of the UN Secretary-General and numerous foreign dignitaries; the occasion is marred by UPC-inspired violence in Douala and Yaoundé. |
| 21 February 1960 | The new constitution of the Cameroun Republic is adopted by national referendum. |

| Date | Event(s) |
|---|---|
| 10 April 1960 | General elections to the first National Assembly of independent Cameroun. |
| 5 May 1960 | Ahmadou Ahidjo is elected first President of the Cameroun Republic. |
| 20 September 1960 | Cameroun is admitted to the United Nations. |
| 11 February 1961 | UN plebiscite in the British Cameroons; the Southern Cameroons votes to join the Cameroun Republic in a federal union; the Northern Cameroons elects to join Nigeria and subsequently becomes Sardauna Province of Northern Nigeria; the British trusteeship ends. |
| 1 June 1961 | The Northern Cameroon becomes part of Northern Nigeria; President Ahidjo proclaims June 1 a Day of National Mourning. |
| 9 July 1961 | Foumban conference outlines terms for reunification. |
| 14 August 1961 | The National Assembly adopts the Constitution of the Cameroon Federal Republic. |
| 1 October 1961 | The Cameroon Federal Republic comes into existence. Ahidjo becomes Federal President, J. N. FONCHA, Vice-President. |
| 1 September 1966 | Fusion of the principal political parties of East and West Cameroon into a single national party, the Cameroon National Union (CNU). |
| October 1969 | The three principal trade union organizations merge to become the trade union arm of the CNU. |
| March 1970 | Federal presidential elections: President Ahidjo is re-elected by 97% of the vote; S. T. MUNA becomes Vice-President, replacing J. N. Foncha |

| Date | Event(s) |
|---|---|
| August 1970 | Conspiracy trials of ERNEST OUANDIE (last of the UPC maquis leaders), BISHOP NDONGMO of Nkongsamba, and several others. Ouandié, Ndongmo, and three others are found guilty and sentenced to be executed. Ndongmo's sentence is commuted to life imprisonment by President Ahidjo, but Ouandié and two others are executed on January 15, 1971. |
| 20 May 1972 | National referendum on the creation of a unitary state: the proposed Constitution receives 3,217,056 votes to 158. East and West Cameroon, their governments and separate institutions, cease to exist; the federal Vice-Presidency is abolished; President Ahidjo remains chief executive and a single national legislature replaces the three previously in existence. The Cameroon Federal Republic formally becomes the United Republic of Cameroon. |

SOURCES: Engelbert Mveng and Beling-Nkoumba, Manuel d'Histoire du Cameroun: Engelbert Mveng, Histoire du Cameroun; V. T. Le Vine, The Cameroon Federal Republic; Neville Rubin, Cameroun; V. T. Le Vine, "Political Integration in Cameroon," in K. Bentsi-Entchill and D. Smock, National Integration in Africa. (Full citations may be found in the bibliography.)

# INTRODUCTION TO THE STUDY OF CAMEROON: A BIBLIOGRAPHIC ESSAY*

## by V. T. Le Vine

This essay cannot, of course, mention all the important published work on Cameroon; our selection was, therefore, highly idiosyncratic, stressing those items most likely to be available in the better university libraries (though a few will, undoubtedly, be difficult to obtain), or which can be obtained through inter-library loan. Works in the social sciences predominate in our selection, though the bibliography that follows includes works in other disciplines. English and French publications are most frequently cited, since these are principal languages in which Camerooniana appears. One or two major contributions by German scholars are also noted. Above all, selection has been of works deemed most useful to those embarking on the study of Cameroon; the specialist will probably find little here with which he is not already familiar.

Before turning to a discussion of the Cameroon materials themselves, a word about bibliographies of Cameroon is in order. To begin with, there is at this time no complete bibliography of Cameroon in print. The bibliography in this book is quite extensive, and partial bibliographies may be found in the several volumes (to be discussed below) by Fr. Mveng, Profs. Rubin, Welch, Johnson and Le Vine. The historian will find the Library of Congress' Official Publications of French Equatorial Africa, French Cameroons, and Togo, 1946-1958 of considerable value, and the recent Bibliography of Cameroon Folklore, by Virginia and Mark Delancey (African Studies Association, USA, 1972), represents a basic research tool for the anthropologist, ethnologist, and of course, the folklorist.

---

*(Revised from the Journal of Cameroon Affairs, Vol. 1, No. 2, March-June, 1972, pp. 4-10.)

## 1. KAMERUN, CAMEROONS, CAMEROUN--to 1960

There was a time, as few as a dozen years ago, when even the most casual interest in Cameroon could find little satisfaction. The largest amount of printed material on Cameroon available before 1960 turned out, surprisingly, to be German, published during the German protectorate (1885-1916) or, more likely, during the inter-war period when Germany campaigned for the return of her former colonies. Besides being in the German language, and hence inaccessible to most francophones and anglophones, it tended to be largely composed of materials (travelogues, memoirs, romances, pseudo-histories) of a polemic or propagandistic nature. There was also a body of French materials--official reports, memoirs, and the like--which dwelt on aspects of France's "civilizing mission" in Cameroon, tended to be self-congratulatory, but which offered little of concrete value (save some doubtful statistics) on the life, society, and internal development of the country. The only solid intellectual fare in French was to be found in the publications of the local IFAN center (now IRCAM), to which Cameroon owes an immense debt of gratitude for having placed Cameroon scholarship and research on a sound basis. Of particular note were two studies on Sultan Njoya and the Bamum (Histoire et Coutûmes des Bamum, 1952, and Dugast and Jeffreys' L'Ecriture des Bamum, 1950); Bouchard's excellent study of the Cameroon coast in history (La côte du Cameroun dans l'histoire et la cartographie, 1952); Lambezat's Kirdi, les populations paiennes du nord-Cameroun (1950); Delaroziere's study of the Bamileke, Les institutions politiques et sociales des populations dites Bamiléké (1950); and Guilbot's labor survey of Douala (Petite étude sur la main-d'oeuvre à Douala, 1949). In addition, IFAN published a quarterly journal reporting its research, Etudes Camerounaises. Scholars working in the British Cameroons also produced a limited, but solid body of work, mainly anthropological and ethnographic. In the small group thus involved were Phyllis Kaberry (Women of the Grassfields, IMSO, 1952), M. D. W. Jeffreys, E. M. Chilvers, and Edwin Ardener (Coastal Bantu of the Cameroons, IAI, 1956) and his wife, Shirley. Ardener also helped to produce, in 1958, the first historical study of the Southern Cameroons (Victoria, 1858-1958).

There were other scholars in both Cameroons who produced notable work (for example, Jean Hurault's and

Raymond Lecoq's monographs on the Bamiléké; Dizain and Cambon on the New Bell populations; Kuszinski's demographic study of Cameroons and Togoland; C. K. Meek on land tenure in Nigeria and the Cameroons, etc.) but the point must be made that most of their work dealt with anthropological and ethnographic matters; what political and economic information there was had to be gleaned from peripheral material in the above literature, or from official reports and monographs. The only scholarly study of the German period was Harry Rudin's superb Germans in the Cameroons (Yale, 1938), and practically the only outside reporting on the Cameroons mandates (apart from the League of Nations materials) was incorporated into Prof. Raymond Leslie Buell's monumental two-volume work, The Native Problem in Africa (Macmillan, 1928). Finally, for the record, mention must be made of two non-scholarly books, only the second of which achieved wide circulation: Andre Mikhelson's Kings and Knaves in the Cameroons (Van Rees Press, 1938), a badly-written, semi-fictional, "it happened to me" tale, and Gerald Durrell's delightful Bafut Beagles (1957), the naturalist's true account of animal collecting in the Bafut area of West Cameroon. The late Fon Achimbiri II is the book's real hero.

In a very real sense, 1960 marked a turning point for scholars interested in Cameroon, and for Cameroonian scholars themselves. For various reasons, some undoubtedly connected with the long-festering UPC revolt, the French administration had long been reluctant to grant political scientists and economists access to the French Cameroon. Some journalists penetrated the veil from time to time, and much that we have on politics in Cameroon before 1960 came from such astute observers as George Chaffard and Philippe Decraene. Independence provided scholars interested in Cameroon with an opportunity to come and see for themselves, and attempt some unbiased reconstruction of Cameroon's political, social, and economic development. Even more important, independence meant that Cameroonian scholars could now strike out on their own and develop the study of Cameroon along authentic national lines. Thus, since 1960, the serious student of Cameroon affairs has had available to him an increasing number of useful and sometimes illuminating works by Cameroonian and non-Cameroonian scholars alike. Above all, the serious lack of analytical studies of Cameroon politics and economics has finally been rectified. One further observation is in order before we turn to the post-1960 materials: what is now available represents one of the best arguments for bilingualism, since almost all of this body of published work is either in English and French, and the well-informed student of Cameroon must be able to read in both languages to get a balanced view of his subject.

## 2. HISTORY AND POLITICS

The bilingual mix is apparent in the works under this rubric. To begin with, there is no general history of Cameroon available in English, but for those who read French, East Cameroon historians have provided both excellent surveys and special histories. Perhaps the starting point should be Fr. Englebert Mveng's Histoire du Cameroun (Presence Africaine, 1963), which treats the pre-1945 period exhaustively but only covers the 1945-1960 years in a most sketchy fashion. Fr. Mveng and M. Beling-Nkoumba have also produced a school text, Manuel d'histoire du Cameroun (Yaoundé, 1969), which contains much interesting matter, but is of little use to the scholar. Two other Cameroon historians have contributed important studies: Eldredge Mohammadou, who has attempted a reconstruction of northern Cameroon history in the pages of the bi-annual Cameroon review, Abbia (he also wrote a short Histoire de Tibati, Editions CLE, 1970), and René Douala Manga Bell, who did a Douala-centered study of the 1884-1914 period in the pages of the Catholic newspaper, L'Effort Camerounais (Oct., 1969-Jan. 1970). Unfortunately Manga Bell's study is not generally available, and the Abbé Thomas Ketchoua's useful Contribution à l'histoire du Cameroun (1962) is now out of print. Until 1960, Rudin's study of the German period was the principal source on the Protectorate, but two collections of studies edited by the East German scholar Helmuth Stoecker (Kamerun unter deutscher Kolonialherrschaft, vol. 1, 1960; vol. 2, 1965, Rutten & Loening, Berlin) provide additional data and insights, though from a Marxist perspective.

The rather limited West Cameroonian historical and political literature is almost all in English. Pride of place in this category must go, of course, to the indefatigable Ardeners. Dr. Ardener's contributions to Victoria 1858-1958 (Victoria Centenary Committee, 1958), his "Political History of Cameroon" (World Today, XVIII; 8, 341-350), "The Nature of the Reunification of Cameroon" (in A. Hazelwood, ed., African Integration and Disintegration, OUP, 1967) and Shirley Ardener's Eyewitness to the Annexation of

Cameroon (Government Printer, Buea, 1968) constitute a solid body of highly valuable work. Needless to say, all scholars of the politics of Cameroon have relied heavily on their efforts. Other, more extended discussions of the political history and politics of West Cameroon are included in the several books by Profs. Le Vine, Gardinier, Welch, Johnson, and Rubin, all to be discussed in detail below.

One further note is in place here. Apart from political pamphleteering and electoral literature, West Cameroonians have written little on the history and politics of their area. Virtually the sole exception is the late Peter M. Kale, who was involved in West Cameroon politics from the beginning (i.e., from the start of West Cameroon nationalist activity, in 1946), and eventually became speaker of the West Cameroon legislature. In 1968, the West Cameroon government posthumously published his Political Evolution in the Cameroon (Buea: Government Printer), which is interesting not only because of its subject matter, but because it presents the West Cameroon political story from the perspective of a key participant.

It would, perhaps, be amusing to speculate why Americans have published so much about Cameroon, but hardly worthwhile to do so. The fact remains that Americans have long found Cameroon fascinating, and the bulk of the contemporary analyses of Cameroon politics and political history has been by American scholars. We have mentioned the seminal studies by Profs. Buell and Rudin; these appeared in 1928 and 1938, respectively. In 1963, David Gardinier, a student of Rudin's, published his Cameroon: United Nations Challenge to French Policy (OUP), a short but careful study of the internal and international politics of the UN trusteeship in both Cameroons. Also in 1963, Victor Le Vine published "The Cameroon Federal Republic," a general political study, in G. Carter (ed.), Five African States (Cornell U. Press), which was followed in 1964 by The Cameroons from Mandate to Independence (U. of Calif. Press), both the result of field research in the two Cameroons during 1959, 1960 and 1961. The latter study represented the first full-scale attempt to examine the political history of both French and English-speaking Cameroons during the mandate and trusteeship periods. It included a survey of the German period, an interpretation of the socio-political consequences of modernization in the Cameroons, and a relatively close look at the politics of Cameroon reunification. (The latter book appeared in French in 1969 as Le Cameroun, Editions Nouveaux Horizons.) Le Vine also undertook an extended examination of Cameroon political parties in his section in J. S. Coleman and C. Rosberg (eds.), Political Parties and National Integration in Tropical Africa (U. of Calif. Press, 1964.)

The next American essay into Cameroon politics was by Prof. Claude Welch, whose Cameroon chapters in his Dream of Unity (Cornell, 1966) specifically treat the politics of reunification, and include the best published analyses of the UN plebiscites of 1959 and 1961. Then, in 1970, Prof. Willard Johnson published his excellent The Cameroon Federation (Princeton U. Press), which covers much the same ground as Welch, but does so in a fresh perspective, and, more important, deals with the political, social, and economic realities of the first five years of reunification. Finally, in 1971, two shorter books appeared that attempted an assessment of Cameroon's first ten years of independence: Neville Rubin's Cameroun, An African Federation (Praeger), and Le Vine's The Cameroon Federal Republic (Cornell U. Press). Both treat briefly Cameroon's political evolution, and both deal extensively with the political, economic, and social realities of federation. Rubin's work does more with the constitutional and legal aspects of the federation; that by Le Vine is more concerned with Cameroon's internal politics. Rubin, incidentally, is an English don, and his work represents one of the first efforts by British scholars to examine the politics of francophone Cameroon. To cite Rubin, Johnson, Welch, Ardener, and the present writer is not to suggest that anglophone scholars have monopolized the study of Cameroon politics; the Cameroon sections in Franz Ansprenger's seminal Politik in Schwarzen Afrika (Westdeutschen Verlag, 1961) have been widely cited and used by both the American and British scholars.

Unhappily, studies of Cameroon politics by Cameroonians have not been numerous, and regrettably, little of that work has found its way into print. Several important studies, in form theses done at French universities, must nonetheless be mentioned here. Noteworthy are: J. M. Zang-Atangana, Les forces politiques du Cameroun rûnifié (Faculté de droit et des sciences économiques de Paris, 1963); A. Eyinga, Le pouvoir de décision au Cameroun (Faculté de droit, Paris, 1971); Paul Biya, Les institutions et la vie politique du Cameroun dépuis l'indépendance (Faculté de droit, Paris, 1971); Philémon Beb a Don, L'évolution du régime politique du Cameroun de l'indépendance à nos jours (Faculté de droit, Paris, 1968). An abstract from Zang-Atangana's thesis, "Les Partis politiques camerounais," appeared in Recueil Penant, No. 684, 1960. Eyinga, long identified with the political opposition in Cameroon, created quite a stir with his thesis, during the defense of which he is reported to have denounced President Ahidjo in most uncomplimentary terms.

Finally, under this rubric, we must note several studies of the Union des Populations du Cameroun (UPC) and the rebellion it inspired. The latest publication on the subject is a UPC apologia, L'U.P.C. parle (François Maspero, 1970), which appeared just about the time that rebel leader Ernest Ouandié was being tried in Cameroon. Other materials of an analytical and descriptive nature include discussions in the books by Profs. Johnson and Le Vine; Prof. Johnson's "The UPC in Rebellion: The Integrative Backlash of Insurgency," in R. Rotberg and A. A. Mazrui (eds.), Protest and Power in Black Africa (Oxford U. Press, 1971); and a French account of the early stages of the rebellion, Col. J. Lamberton's La pacification de la Sanaga-Maritime (Paris, 1961).

## 3. CONSTITUTIONS, INSTITUTIONS, AND LAWS

Cameroon scholars have done exceptionally well in this area; a number of their doctoral theses on the legal-constitutional development of Cameroon have appeared in print. In English, H. N. A. Enonchong's excellent Cameroon Constitutional Law (Yaoundé, 1967) is the first extended discussion of the subject in print. French-language materials by Cameroonians are more numerous, but of varied quality. The theses by Messrs. Beb a Don and Biya, which overlap into this area, have already been mentioned. Two earlier works are Victor Kanga's Le Droit coutumier Bamiléké au contact avec des droits européens (Yaoundé, 1959), and Enoch Katte Kwayeb's Les Institutions de droit public du pays Bamiléké (Cameroun): Evolution et régime actuel (Paris, LGDJ, 1960). Both works deal with what can be called "legal acculturation," that is, the consequences of contact between two legal systems, in this case the traditional Bamiléké and the superimposed French code systems. Kanga's study is the weaker of the two; Kwayeb does a much more thorough and scholarly job. Of the materials by non-Cameroonians, the most recent are the discussions on the Cameroon constitution in the books by Profs. Le Vine, Rub-

in and Johnson, and in P. F. Gonidec's short but useful La
République Fédérale du Cameroun (Berger-Levrault, 1971),
in the series of booklets, edited by M. Gonidec, of the Encyclopedie Politique et Constitutionelle sponsored by the International Institute for Public Administration.

Students interested in the legal and institutional aspects of the mandate, the trusteeships, and the first Republic (1960) may find useful information in Le Vine's first Cameroon book (The Cameroons from Mandate to Independence).
Prof. Gardinier's study of the trusteeship has already been noted. In French, of interest are a thesis on the mandates and the trusteeships by Paul Blanc (Le régimes du mandat et de tutelle, Montpelier, 1953); P. Vergnaud's "La levée de la tutelle et la réunification du Cameroun" (Revue Juridique et Politique, no. 4, Oct.-Dec. 1964), which deals with the termination of the trusteeship and the transition to the Federal system; and the ubiquitous M. Gonidec's two articles, "Les institutions politiques de la république fédérale du Cameroun," (Civilisations, XI, 1961, no. 4, and XII, 1962, no. 1).

Finally, in English, Le Vine's article in Abbia (no. 15, 1971), on "The Termination of Trusteeship in the British Cameroons," combines discussion of both legal and political aspects of that problem.

4. ECONOMICS

A basic, complete and recent study of Cameroon's economy is Philippe Hugon's Analyse du sous-développement en Afrique noire: l'exemple de l'économie du Cameroun (Presses Universitaires de France, 1968). A different point of view, that of a revolutionary Marxist, is expressed by the late Osende Afana in his L'économie de l'ouest africain (Maspero, 1966). (Afana, who had joined the UPC guerrillas in Cameroon, was killed during a skirmish with police in 1967). In English, there is Reginald H. Green's structural study of the Cameroon economy, "The Economy of Cameroon Federal Republic," in P. Robson and D. A. Lury (eds.), The Economies of Africa (Allen & Unwin, 1969); a chapter on Cameroon in the International Monetary Fund's Surveys of African Economies, Vol. 1 (Washington, D.C., 1968); and discussions of various aspects of Cameroon's economy in the recent volume by Profs. Rubin and Le Vine. Also, in 1971, EDIAFRIC published a massive study of Cameroon's economy: L'Economie du Cameroun. A somewhat specialized study focussing on economic integration in Africa, including a section on the UDEAC (Customs and Economic Union of Central Africa, of which Cameroon is a member), is Economic Co-operation and Integration in Africa (UN Doc. ST/ECA/109, 1969). Along similar lines is another UN study, Report of the ECA Mission on Economic Co-operation in Central Africa (UN Doc. ECN. 14/L. 320/Rev. 1, 1966), which stresses the possibilities of economic harmonization among the equatorial African states and Cameroon.

Not surprisingly, French sources often provide useful material on Cameroon's economy. A set of such sources is the annual reports of the Monetary Committee of the Franc Zone, usually titled La Zone Franc en (and the year). The reports are issued two years late; the 1969 report was published in 1971. These reports, however, are extremely valuable for the comparative data they provide.

5. THE SOCIAL, ETHNIC, AND PHYSICAL MILIEUX

As was noted earlier, it was precisely within anthropological, demographic, geographic, linguistic, and natural scientific areas that most pre-1960 scholarship was pursued. And it was here that the Cameroon section of IFAN (Institut Francais d'Afrique Noire, now the Institut d'Etudes Camerounaises, IRCAM) made its greatest contributions. Obviously, space does not permit a complete listing of the IFAN-IRCAM publications, but suffice it to point out that the Institute's output has been prodigious, including not only the representative works mentioned earlier, but immensely valuable contributions in the fields of cartography (the IRCAM Atlas du Cameroun, for example), pedology, geology, agronomy, meteorology, and natural history. The serious student of these matters can do no better than work in IRCAM's excellent library, in which are gathered not only the IFAN-IRCAM materials, but the research and publications on Cameroon by scholars from a dozen countries. For those not so fortunate, a few suggestions may serve by way of introduction.

First, geography: Pierre Billard's Le Cameroun Fédéral, Vol. 1, Essai de géographie physique (Lyon, 1963) is basic and highly detailed. (Billard's second volume, which deals with social and institutional contexts, is badly done, inaccurate, and should be avoided.)

Second, social and ethnographic works: here, the list of important work is longer and more varied, including studies both in English and French. Once, again, the indefatigable Ardeners head the list. In 1960, with Alan Warmington, they published what amounted to a socio-economic ecology of the Southern Cameroons: Plantation with Village in the Cameroons (Oxford U. Press). That same year, Warmington contributed a study of the Cameroon Development Corporation Workers' Union, A West African Trade Union (Oxford U. Press), a pioneering effort in the rather neglected field of African labor sociology. The West Cameroon grassfields have also had their devotees; we have already noted the contributions by Kaberry, Chilvers, and Jeffreys. Also of note is the monograph by Robert and Pat Ritzenthaler, Cameroons Village (Milwaukee Public Museum, 1962), an anthropological description of Bafut; and the Rev. Paul Gebauer's Spider Divination in the Cameroons (Milwaukee Public Museum, 1964), a delightful study of this unusual practice among the Kaka people of the Mbem area of Bamenda province. Finally, mention must be made of two French studies of the Bamiléké, important because of the light they cast on the socio-demographic roots of "le problème Bamiléké,": Claud Tardits' Les Bamiléké de l'ouest Cameroun (Berger-Levrault, 1960), and Jean Hurault's rather more detailed La Structure sociale des Bamiléké (Mouton, 1962).

Education in Cameroon has not been the object of much scholarly inquiry, but the student may find relevant materials in the recent books by Profs. Rubin, Johnson, and Le Vine. Also, H. O. Vernon-Jackson has explored the language question in Cameroon education in a short monograph: Language, Schools, and Government in Cameroon (Columbia U., Teachers College Press, 1967), and an interesting Cameroonian point of view on educational philosophy is given by former education minister William Eteki Mbumua in his Un certain humanisme (Ed. CLE, 1970).

As we indicated at the beginning of this short essay, our selections have been idiosyncratic, including mainly titles in the social sciences, history, and politics. If we have slighted other areas, such as literature and poetry, we have done so because our interest lay in sketching a scholarly introduction to Cameroon and not because we thought the work of such authors as Mongo Beti and Ferdinand Oyono were unimportant. Certainly, the serious scholar of Cameroon must read their work, since they often reveal the inner

Bibliographic Essay 149

dimensions of matters that social scientific analysis can only describe or dissect. Thus Oyono's Une Vie de Boy and Le vieux negre et la medaille, and Mongo Beti's Le pauvre Christ de Bomba and Ville cruelle speak more directly to the heart of the colonial situation than could any sociological or political study. Regrettably, not much Cameroonian fiction has been published in recent years, save in the pages of Abbia magazine and other occasional journals.

Abbia, Cameroon's only truly bilingual journal, deserves particular mention. Since it began publication in 1962, its pages have included poetry, fiction, articles on Cameroon history, politics, educational policy, art, and, in fact, on all aspects of Cameroon culture. Published in Yaoundé under the auspices of the Federal Ministry of Education and edited by Dr. Bernard Fonlon, the journal has now 15 issues to its credit; it is hoped that financial stringencies (reported in 1971) will not prevent its further publication.

In 1971, Cameroon celebrated its tenth anniversary as a federation, and its eleventh year of independence. It need hardly be added that President Ahidjo's leadership during these years has been crucial to Cameroon's present enviable political and economic state. Three books describe the President's policies and philosophy: Contribution à la construction nationale (Présence Africaine, 1964), The Political Philosophy of Ahmadou Ahidjo (CNU Political Bureau, 1968), and Ahmadou Ahidjo par lui-même (CNU, 1968). The President's official biography is by Beat Baeschlin-Raspail, Ahmadou Ahidjo, pionier de l'Afrique moderne (Ed. Bory, Monaco, 1968).

Last, but not least, is a recent and fascinating biography by Jacques Kuoh Moukouri, former Cameroon Ambassador to the USA, Doigts noirs (Montréal, Editions à la page, 1963). M. Moukouri "rose from the ranks" of the colonial civil service, and recalls his experiences both before and after independence. The book is recommended for its view of East Cameroon politics by an insider.

7. KEEPING UP WITH CAMEROON

Probably the most regularly frustrating problem faced by students of Africa is how to keep up with contemporary events on the continent. The problem is no less acute for students of Cameroon, who must cope with irregular mails, long delays in obtaining Cameroon newspapers, and the fact that Cameroon news seldom if ever appears in American or European news media. The fact is that most of us are reduced to covering a fairly wide spectrum of sources in order to glean a minimum of information on even the most important Cameroonian events. That said, a few sources do provide that minimum, and sometimes, extended discussions or articles. Most important in this respect are several periodicals: West Africa (weekly, from London), Afrique Nouvelle (weekly, from Dakar), Jeune Afrique (monthly, Paris), Africa (monthly, London), Europe-France-Outremer (monthly, Paris), and Marchés tropicaux et mediterranéens (monthly, Paris). The prestigious French daily newspaper, Le Monde, and its monthly offspring, Le Monde Diplomatique regularly carry Cameroon news in small quantity, and summaries of the most important monthly events in Cameroon can usually be found in the Africa Research Bulletin (monthly, London) and Africa Diary (monthly, New Delhi).

# BIBLIOGRAPHY

## BOOKS

Abs, P[aul] J[oseph] M[aria]. Der Kampf um Unsere Schutzgebiete. Essen/Rhur: F. Floeder, 1926.

Ahidjo, Ahmadou. Contributions à la construction nationale. Paris: Présence Africaine, 1964.

Alexandre, Pierre and J. Binet. Le Groupe dit Pahouin. Paris: Presses Universitaires de France, 1958.

Ansprenger, Franz, Politik im Schwarzen Afrika; Die Modernen politischen Bewegungen im Afrika Französischer Prägung. Koln and Opladen: West-deutchen Verlag, 1961.

Ardener, Edwin. Coastal Bantu of the Cameroons. London: International African Institute, 1956. (Ethnographic Survey of Africa, no. 9.)

Ardener, Edwin and Shirley, and A. Warmington. Plantation and Village in the Cameroons. London: Oxford University Press, 1960.

Ardener, S., Eyewitness to the Annexation of Cameroon, 1883-1887. Buea: Government Printer, 1968.

Aujoulat, L[ouis] P[aul]. Aujourd'hui l'Afrique. Paris: Casterman, 1960.

Aymerich, Joseph G. (General). La Conquête du Cameroun. Paris: Payot, 1931.

Baeschlin-Raspail, Beat C. Ahmadou Ahidjo: Pionnier de l'Afrique Moderne. Monaco: Edition, Paul Bory, 1968.

Balandier, Georges. Sociologie des Brazzavilles Noires. Paris: Presses Universitaires de France, 1957.

Baumann, H., and D. Westerman. Peuples et civilisations de l'Afrique. Paris: Presses Universitaires de France, 1948.

Becker, T. H. Das Schulwesen in Afrika. (Band XII 1/2, Afrika Handbuch der praktischen kolonialwissenschaften). Berlin: Walter de Gruyter, 1943.

Bederman, Sanford, The Cameroons Development Corporation: Partner in National growth. Bota: CDC, 1968.

Beer, George Louis. African Questions at the Paris Peace Conference. New York: Macmillan, 1923.

de Belleau, de Lyée. Du Cameroun au Hoggar. Paris: Alsatia, 1945.

Benjamin, Jacques. Les Camerounais occidentaux: La Minorité dans un État bicommunautaire. Montréal: Les Presses de l'Université de Montréal, 1972.

Bentwich, N. C. Le système des mandats. Hague: Hague Academy, 1929.

Bergfeld, Ewald. Die Französischen Mandatsgebiete Kamerun und Togo. Greifswald: H. Adler, 1935.

Beti, Mongo (pseud., Alexandre Biyidi). Mission to Kala. London: Heinemann, 1964. (Trans., Mission Terminée).

_____. King Lazarus. London: Heinemann, 1969. (Trans., Le Roi Miraculé).

_____. Le Pauvre Christ de Bomba. Paris: R. Laffont, 1956.

_____. Ville Cruelle. Paris: Ed. Africaines, 1954.

Betts, Raymond F. Assimilation and Association in French Colonial Theory, 1890-1914. New York: Columbia University Press, 1961.

Billard, Pierre. Le Cameroun Federal. 2 vols. Lyon:

Bibliography 153

Imprimerie des Beaux-arts, 1968.

Binet, Jacques. Budgets Familiaux des planteurs de cacao au Cameroun. Paris: Office de la recherche scientifique et technique de la France d'Outre-Mer, 1956.

Biyidi, Alexandre. see Beti, Mongo.

Bockel, Alain. L'administration Camerounaise. Paris: Berger-Levrault, 1971.

Bola, H., and R. Lagrave. J'Aime Mon Pays: Le Cameroun. 2nd ed. Yaoundé: Federal Republic of Cameroon, Ministry of National Education, 1963.

Bouchaud, Joseph, C.S.E. La Côte du Cameroun dans l'histoire, et la cartographic dès origines à l'annexion Allemande. Yaoundé: IFAN, Centre au Cameroun, 1952. (Memoirs de l'IFAN.)

─────. L'Eglise en Afrique Noire. Paris: La Palatine, 1958.

─────. Histoire et geographie du Cameroun. Douala, 1944.

Bridgeman, Jon, and David E. Clarke. German Africa. Stanford: The Hoover Institution, 1965.

Bruel, G. La France équatoriale Africaine. Paris: Larose, 1935.

Bruel, Max. Kampf im Urwald, von Urwald Göttern und Schicksalen Deutscher Pflanzer und Soldaten in Kamerun. Leipzig: Julius Klinkhardt, 1940.

Brunschwig, Henri. L'Expansion allemande outre-mer du XV siècle à nos jours. Paris: Presses Universitaires de France, 1957.

Brzezinski, Zbigniew. Africa and the Communist World. Stanford: Stanford University Press, 1963.

Buell, Raymond Leslie. The Native Problem in Africa. Vol. II. New York: Macmillan Co., 1928.

Cameroon National Union, Political Bureau. Ahmadou

Ahidjo, par lui-même. Printed in Monaco, 1968, distributed in Yaoundé by the CNU.

──────. The Political Philosophy of Ahmadou Ahidjo. Yaoundé: CNU. 1968.

Celarie, André. Les Moyens d' Information au Cameroun. Vols. I and II. Paris: Office de Cooperation radiophonique, 1965.

Chambre du Commerce du Cameroun. Bilan economique de 1957-1960. Douala: Chambre du Commerce, April 1964.

──────. Le Cameroun Occidental--Pays Essentiellement Agricole. Douala: Chambre du Commerce, December, 1961.

Chauleur, Pierre. L'Oeuvre de la France au Cameroun. Yaoundé: Imprimerie du Gouvernment, 1936.

Chazelas, Victor. Territoires sous mandat de la France, Cameroun et Togo. Paris: Société d'éditions géographiques, maritimes et coloniales, 1931.

Chot, Robert, ed. Le Cameroun, aspect géographique, historique, touristique, adminisitratif du territoire. Paris: Editions Alepie, 1954.

Coleman, James S. Nigeria: Background to Nationalism. Berkeley and Los Angeles: University of California Press, 1958.

Cooley, John K. East Wind Over Africa. New York: Walker & Company, 1965.

Cornevin, Robert. Histoire de l'Afrique dès origines à nos journs. Paris: Payot, 1956.

Corret, A., J. Gorse, Y. Gillet, and F. Pattier. Les Regroupements en Pays Bamiléké. I. Yaoundé: Imprimerie Nationale, 1963.

Costeodat, Rene. Le Mandat français et la réorganization des territoires du Cameroun. Besançon: Jacques et Demontrond, 1930.

# Bibliography

Delarozière, R. Les Institutions politiques et sociales des populations dites Bamiléké. Yaoundé: IFAN, Centre au Cameroun, 1950.

Delavignette, Robert. Freedom and Authority in French West Africa. New York: Oxford University Press, 1957.

de Lusignan, Guy. French-Speaking Africa Since Independence. London: Pall Mall, 1969.

Denis, Jacques, S.J. Le Phénomène urbain en Afrique centrale. Brussels: Academie Royale des Sciences Coloniales, 1958. (Classe des Sciences Morales et Politiques, Memoires en 8vo, Nouvelle Serie, Tome XIX, fasc. 1, 1958.)

Deschamps, Hubert. Les Methodes et doctrines de colonisation de la France. Paris: Armand Colin, 1953.

Deutsch, Karl W. Nationalism and Social Communication. New York: John Wiley and Sons, 1953.

Diel, Louise. Die Kolonien Warten! Afrika im umbruch. Leipzig: P. List, 1939.

Diziain, R., and A. Cambon. Étude sur la population du quartier New-Bell à Douala. Yaoundé: Institut des Recherches Camerounaises, 1956.

Drews, Max. Frankreich versagt in Kamerun. Berlin: Junker und Dünhaupt, 1940. (Schriften des Deutsches Instituts fur Aussenpolitische Forschung, Heft 79.)

Dubois, Marcel. Systèmes coloniaux et peuples colonisateurs. Paris: G. Masson, 1895.

Duchène, Albert. La Politique coloniale de la France. Paris: Payot, 1928.

du Gard, Martin. L'Appel du Cameroun. Paris: Flammarion, 1939.

Dugast, I[delette]. Inventaire ethnique du Sud-Cameroun. Yaoundé: IFAN Cameroun, 1949. (Memoires de l'IFAN Cameroun: Populations, No. 1.)

Enonchong, H. N. A. Cameroon Constitutional Law: Fed-

eralism in a Mixed Common-law, Civil-law System.
Yaoundé: Centre d'Edition et de Production de Manuels et d'Auxiliaires de l'enseignment. 1967.

Epanya Yondo Elolongue. Kamerun, Kamerun. Paris: Présence Africaine, 1960.

Escherich, Georg. Kamerun. Berlin: H. Riegler, 1938.

Eteki 'a Mbumua, William. Un Certain Humanisme. Yaoundé: Eds. CLE, 1970.

Ferrandi, Jean. La conquête du Cameroun-nord, 1914-15. Paris: Charles Lavanzelle, 1928.

Fitzgerald, Walter. Africa. 8th ed. London: Methuen. 1955.

Franceschi, Roger. Le Mandat Francais au Cameroun. Paris: Sirey, 1929.

Froelich, J. C. Cameroun-Togo. Paris: Editions Berger-Levrault, 1956.

Gardinier, Davis. Cameroon, United Nations Challenge to French Policy. London: Oxford University Press, 1963.

Gaston, Joseph. Ce qu'il faut savoir du Cameroun. Brazzaville: Agence économique de l A.E.F., 1920.

Gebauer, Paul. Spider Divination in the Cameroons. Publications in Anthropology, No. 10. Milwaukee, Wisc.: Milwaukee Public Museum, 1964.

German Colonial Society, D. K. V. Das Buch der Deutschen Kolonien. Leipzig: Wilhelm Goldmann, 1937.

Gonidec, P[ierre] F. La République fédérale du Cameroun. Paris: Berger-Levrault, 1969. 88 pp.

Gorges, E. H. The Great War in West Africa. London: Hutchinson, 1927.

Grosclaude, Pierre. Menaces allemandes sur l'Afrique. Paris: F. Sorlot, 1938.

Groves, Charles P. The Planting of Christianity in Africa.

Bibliography 157
Vol. IV. London: Lutterworth Press, 1958.

Guernier, Eugene, and René Briat, eds. Cameroun, Togo. Paris: Editions de l'Union Française, 1951. (Encyclopedie de l'Afrique Française.)

Guilbot, J. Petite Etude sur la main d'oeuvre à Douala. Yaoundé: IFAN, Centre au Cameroun, 1948.

Hailey, [William Malcolm] Lord. An African Survey. Revised, 1956. New York: Oxford University Press, 1957.

Hall, Hessel Duncan. Mandates, Dependencies and Trusteeship. Washington: Carnegie Endowment, 1948.

Hardy, George. Histoire de la colonisation française. Paris: Larose, 1928.

_____. Histoire sociale de la colonisation française. Paris: Larose, 1953.

_____. La Politique coloniale et le partage de la terre aux XIXe et XXe siècles. Paris: Editions Albion Michel, 1937.

Harmand, Jule. Domination et colonisation. Paris: Payot 1940.

Harris, Norman D. Intervention and Colonization in Africa. New York: Houghton Mifflin, 1914.

Herskovits, Melville J. The Human Factor in Changing Africa. New York: Alfred A. Knopf, 1962.

Hertslet, Sir Edward. The Map of Africa by Treaty. Vol. I. London: HMSO, 1894.

Hugon, Philippe. Analyse du sous-developpement en Afrique noire: L'exemple de l'économie du Cameroun. Paris: Presses Universitaires de France, 1968.

Hurault, Jean. Mission d'études au Cameroun, 1955. Paris: Institut Géographique National, 1956.

_____. Notes sur la structure sociale des Bamiléké. Paris: Institut Géographique National, 1951.

_____. La Structure sociale des Bamiléké. Paris: Mouton, 1962.

Ingold, J. (General). L'Epopée LeClerc au Sahara, 1940-1943. Paris: Berger-Levrault, 1945.

Joelson, F. S. Germany's Claim to Colonies. London: Hurst and Blackett, 1939.

Johannssen, G. Kurt, and H. H. Kraft. Germany's Colonial Problem. London: T. Butterworth, 1937.

Johnson, Willard R. The Cameroon Federation: Political Integration in a Fragmentary Society. Princeton, N.J.: Princeton University Press, 1970.

Kaberry, Phyllis M. Women of the Grassfields. London: HMSO, 1952.

Kale, P[eter] M. Political Evolution in the Cameroons. Buea: West Cameroon Government Printer, 1968.

Kanga, Victor Jean-Claude. Le droit coutumier Bamiléké en contact avec des droits Européens. Yaoundé: Imprimerie du Gouv't., 1959.

Kemner, Wilhelm. Kamerun dargestellt in kolonialpolitischer, historischer, verkehrstechnischer, rassenkundlicher, und rohstoffwirtschaftlicher Hinsicht. Berlin: Freiheitsverlag, 1937.

Kern, Gottfried. Deutsche Kämpfe in Kamerun. Berlin: Verlagshaus fur Volksliteratur und Kunst, 1913.

Ketchoua, Thomas (Abbé). Contributions à l'Histoire du Cameroun de 450 avant Jésus-Christ à nos jours. Yaoundé: Imp. St. Paul, 1962.

Kirk-Greene, Anthony H. M. Adamawa Past & Present. Oxford: Oxford University Press, 1958.

Kittler, Glen D. The White Fathers. New York: William Allen, 1958.

Kom, David. Le Cameroun. Essai d'analyse économique et politique. Paris: Editions Sociales, 1971.

Bibliography 159

Kuczynski, R. R. Cameroons and Togoland: A Demographic Study. London: Oxford University Press, 1939.

Kuoh Moukouri, Jacques. Doigts Noirs. Montréal: Ed. à la page, 1963.

Kwayeb, Enoch. Le Droit coutumier Bamiléké au contact des droits européens. Yaoundé: Imprimerie du gouvernement, 1959.

Labouret, Henri. Le Cameroun. Paris: P. Hartmann, 1937.

_____. Colonisation, colonialisme, décolonisation. Paris: Payot, 1952.

Lange, Fried. Massa, wann kommst du wieder; zwischen Tschadsee und götterberg, Erlebnisse in Kampf in Kamerun. Düsseldorf: Völkischer Verlag, 1942.

Lecoq, R. Les Bamiléké. Paris: Présence Africaine, 1953.

Lembezat, Bertrand. Le Cameroun. 3rd ed. Paris: Editions Maritimes et Coloniales, 1954.

_____. Kirdi, les populations paiennes du nord-Cameroun. Yaoundé: IFAN, Centre au Cameroun, 1950. (Memoires de l'IFAN, Centre au Cameroun, Serie, Populations, no. 3.)

Le Vine, Victor T. The Camerooons from Mandate to Independence. Berkeley and Los Angeles: University of California Press, 1964.

_____. The Cameroon Federal Republic. Ithaca: Cornell University Press, 1971.

Lewin, Evans. The Germans in Africa. New York: Cassell, 1915.

Lewis, Thomas. These Seventy Years. London: Carey Press, 1929.

Lieb, A. Deutsche Kolonialarbeitung: Zehn Jahre Mandatscherrschaft in Kamerun. Berlin: Freiheitsverlag, 1932.

Lloyd, Christopher. The Navy and the Slave Trade. New York: Longmans, Green, 1949.

Logan, Rayford W. The African Mandates in World Politics. Washington: Public Affairs Press, 1948.

──────. The Operation of the Mandate System in Africa, 1919-1927. Washington, D.C.: The Foundation Publisher, 1942.

Lugard, Sir F[rederick] D. The Dual Mandate in British Tropical Africa. London: William Blackwood, 1923.

McCullough, Merran; Margaret Littlewood, and I. Dugast. Peoples of the Central Cameroons. London: International African Institute, 1954. (Ethnographic Survey of Africa, no. 9.)

MacLean, Eva. Unser Kamerun von Heute. München: Fichte Verlag, 1940.

Mair, Lucy P. Native Policies in Africa. London: Routledge and Sons, 1936.

Mandeng, Patrice. Auswirkungen der deutschen Kolonialherrschaft in Kamerun, Die Arbeiterkräftebeschaffung in den Südbezirken Kameruns während der deutschen Kolonialherrschaft 1884-1914. Hamburg: Helmut Buske Verlag, 1973.

Manue, Georges R. Cameroun, Création Française. Paris: F. Sorlot, 1938.

Marabail, Henri J. J. Etude sur les territoires du Cameroun. Paris: Ed. Larose, 1919.

Marshall, D. Bruce. The French Colonial Myth and Constitution - Making in the Fourth Republic. New Haven: Yale University Press, 1973.

Masson, Georges. Le mise en valeur des territoires du Cameroun placés sous mandat Francais. Paris: Librairie Coloniale et Orientale Larose, 1928.

Mathiot, André. Les territoires non-autonomes et la Chartre des Nations-Unis. Paris: Librairie Générale de Droit et Jurisprudence, 1949.

Maywald, Fritz. Die Eroberer von Kamerun. Berlin: O. Stollberg, 1938.

# Bibliography 161

Meek, C. K. Land Tenure and Land Administration in Nigeria and the Cameroons. London: HMSO, 1957.

Merat, L. L'Existence au Cameroun. Paris: Larose, 1928.

Mercier, M. A. Rapport sur les Possibilites du Developpement industriel du Cameroun. Paris: Société d'études pour le développement économique et social, 1960.

Mohammadou, Eldridge, Histoire du Tibati. Yaoundé: Editions CLE, 1968.

_____. Contes et Poemes Foulbé de la Benoué. Yaoundé: Ed. CLE, 1965.

Mortimer, Edward. France and the Africans, 1944-1960. A Political History. New York: Walker & Co., 1969. 390 pp.

Moynet, Paul. Victory in the Fezzan. London: Fighting France Publications, 1944.

Murdock, George Peter. Africa: Its People and Their Culture History. New York: McGraw-Hill, 1959.

Murray, James N. The United Nations Trusteeship System. Urbana, Ill.: University of Illinois Press, 1958.

Mveng, Engelbert. Histoire du Cameroun. Paris: Présence Africaine, 1963.

Nguini, Marcel. La Valeur politique et sociale de la tutelle Française au Cameroun. Aix-en-Provence: Faculté de Droit, 1956.

Nicolas, Raoul. Le Cameroun depuis le Traité de Versailles. St. Armand/Cher.: Imprimerie A. Leclerc, 1922.

Njoya, Idrissou Mborou. Histoire et Coutumes des Bamun. (Henri Martin, trans.) Yaoundé: IFAN, Cameroun, 1951. (Memoires, IFAN, Centre Cameroun.)

Och, Helmut W. Albertus. Die Wirtschaftsgeographische Entwicklung der früheren Deutschen Schutzgebieten Togo und Kamerun. Königsberg: 1931.

Oehler, Anna. L'Oeuvre de la France au Cameroun. Yaoundé: Impr. du gouvernement, 1936.

Oxford University British Commonwealth Group, Bullock, A., ed. Germany's Colonial Demands. London: Oxford University Press, 1939.

Oyono, Ferdinand. Le Vieux Negre et la Medaille. Paris: Julliard, 1956.

──────. Chemin d'Europe. Paris: Julliard, 1960.

Passarge, Siegfried. Kamerun (Vol. II of Meyer, Hans. Das Deutsche Kolonialreich). Leipzig: 1909.

Paulin, Honoré. Cameroun-Togo. Paris: L. Eyroller, 1923.

Pouquet, Jean. L'Afrique Equatoriale Française et le Cameroun. Paris: Presses Universitaires de France, 1954.

Powell, E. Alexander. The Last Frontier: The White Man's War for Civilization in Africa. New York: Scribners, 1919.

Puttkamer, Jesco von. Gouverneurs Jahre in Kamerun. Berlin: Verlag Georg Stilke, 1912.

Rathery, Gilbert, ed. Cameroun, terre d'avenir. Chambre de Commerce du Cameroun, ed. Paris: Editions Diloutremer, 1960.

Reyher, Rebecca H. The Fon and His Hundred Wives. Garden City, N.Y.: Doubleday, 1952.

Ritter, Karl. Neu-Kamerun. Jena: Reichskolonialamt, 1912. (Veroffentlichen, no. 4.)

Ritter, Paul. Afrika Spricht zu Dir. Mülhausen/Thür.: Bergwald Verlag, 1938.

Ritzenthaler, Robert and Pat. Cameroons Village, an Ethnography of the Bafut. Milwaukee: Milwaukee Public Museum, 1962. (Publications in Anthropology, no. 8.)

Roberts, Stephen H. History of French Colonial Policy.

London: Shoestring Press, 1929.

Robinson, Ronald, and John Gallagher. Africa and the Victorians. New York: Macmillan, 1961.

Rohrbach, Paul. Deutsche Pflanzungen in Kamerun. Hamburg: P. Hartung, 1937.

Rouard le Card, Edgar. Les Mandats francais sur Togoland et le Cameroun, étude juridique. Paris: A. Pedone, 1924.

Routil, Robert. Kamerun, Land und Leute. Vienna: Gottlieb Diestel, 1914.

Rowling, Cecil W. A. Study of Land Tenure in Cameroons Province. London: Colonial Office Land Tenure Panel, HMSO, 1948.

Royal Empire Society, Information Bureau. Notes on Conditions in the British Cameroons. London: Royal Empire Society, 1956.

Royal Institute of International Affairs, Information Department. Germany's Claim to Colonies. 2d ed. London: Oxford University Press, 1939.

Rudin, Harry. Germans in the Cameroons, 1884-1914. New Haven: Yale University Press, 1938.

Sady, Emil J. The United Nations and Dependent Peoples. Washington, D.C.: Brookings Institution, 1956.

Saurrat, Albert. La Mise en valeur des colonies françaises. Paris: Payot, 1923.

Schnee, Heinrich, ed. Das Deutsche Kolonialreich. Leipzig: Deutsche Kolonialverein, 1930.

―――. German Colonization, Past, Present and Future. New York: Knopf, 1926.

Schober, Reinhold. Kamerun: Neuzeitliche Verwaltungsprobleme. Berlin: E. S. Mittler und Sohn, 1937.

Schreiber, Joachim Hans. Deutschen Kolonien unter besonderer Berucksichtigung; Hierstellung als Mandate der

Völkerbundes. Bonn: Dummler, 1939. (Volkerrechtsfragen, no. 43.)

Seitz, Theodor. Die Gouverneurs jahre in Kamerun (Vol. 2 of Vom Aufsteig und Niederbruch Deutscher Kolonialmacht). Karlsruhe: C. P. Mueller, 1927.

Sicé, A. L'Afrique Equatoriale Française et la Cameroun au service de la France. Paris: Presses Universitaires de France, 1946.

Stanford Research Institute. The Economic Potential of West Cameroon. Menlo Park, Calif.: The Institute, 1965.

Steer, George L. Judgment on German Africa. London: Hodder and Stoughton, 1939.

Stoecker, Helmuth, ed. Kamerun unter deutscher Kolonial herrschaft. Berlin (East): Rutten and Loening, 1960. Four studies, including one by Hans Peter Jaeck ("The German Annexation"), two by Adolf Rueger ("The Revolt of the Policemen," "The Rise and Condition of the Working Class under the Cameroonian Colonial Regime"), and one by Hella Winkler ("The Cameroonian Proletariat, 1906-1914").

Student, Erich. Kameruns Kampf 1914-16. Berlin: Verlag Bernard & Graefe, 1937.

Tardits, Claude. Les Bamiléké de l'ouest Cameroun. Paris: Berger-Levrault, 1960.

Thompson, Virginia, and R. Adloff. French West Africa. London: Allen and Unwin, 1958.

Townsend, Mary Evelyn. Origins of Modern German Colonialism, 1871-1885. New York: Columbia University Press, 1921.

_____. The Rise and Fall of Germany's Colonial Empire. New York: Columbia University Press, 1930.

Union des populations du Cameroun. l'u.p.c. parle. Paris: F. Maspéro, 1971.

Veicopolous, Nicolas. Traité des Territoires Dépendants,

Tome I, Le Système de Tutelle d'Après la Chartre de San Francisco. Athens: Institut Français d'Athenes, 1960.

Vernon-Jackson, H. O. H. Language, Schools, and Government in Cameroon. New York: Teachers College Press, Columbia University, 1967.

Vesse, A. Etude de l'Economie Camerounaise, en 1957. 2 vol. Yaoundé: Section de la Statistique Générale, 1957.

Victoria Centenary Committee. Victoria, Southern Cameroons, 1858-1958. Victoria: Basel Mission Book Depot, 1958.

Warmington, W. A. A West African Trade Union. For the Nigerian Institute of Social and Economic Research, London: Oxford University Press, 1960.

Welch, Claude E., Jr. Dream of Unity: Pan-Africanism and Political Unification in West Africa. Ithaca, N.Y.: Cornell University Press, 1966.

Wells, F. A. and W. A. Warmington. Studies in Industrialization, Nigeria and the Cameroons. Oxford: Oxford University Press, 1962.

Wieschhoff, Hans. Colonial Policy in Africa. Philadelphia: University of Pennsylvania Press, 1944.

Wilbois, Joseph. Le Cameroun. Paris: Payout, 1934.

Witherell, Julian T. Official Publications of the French Equatorial Africa French Cameroons and Togo, 1949-1958. Washington, D.C.: Library of Congress, 1964.

Wright, Quincy. Mandates under the League of Nations. Chicago: University of Chicago Press, 1930.

Zimmerman, E. Neu-Kamerun: Reiseerlebnisse und Wirtschaftspolitische Untersuchungen. Berlin: Mittler und Sohn, 1913.

## ARTICLES AND PAMPHLETS (By Author)

Adrianov, B. V. "Etnicheskii sostav sovremenogo Kameruna," Sovetskaya Etnografia, 1959, no. 5, p. 56.

Alima, Jos-Blaise, and Jacques de Sugny. "Cameroun: Cent peuples, deux langues, unde nation," Jeune Afrique, No. 457 (Oct. 1-7, 1969), pp. 58-68.

Amphoux, Marcel. "Le Mandat de la France au Cameroun," Revue de Science Politique. Vol. 56 (1933), pp. 276-298.

Andersen, Kjell. Report on the Economic Aspects of Reunification Presidency, Republic of Cameroon. Yaoundé: mimeographed. February, 1961.

Anjah, E. A. Kamerun Reunification, A Discussion of Reality. For Kamerun United Commoner's Party Aba/Nigeria: Ofomata's Press, 1956.

Ardener, Edwin. "The Kamerun Idea," West Africa, June 7, 1958, p. 533; no. 2148 (June 14, 1958), p. 559.

──────. "The Origins of the Modern Sociological Problems Connected with the Plantation System in the Victoria Division of the Cameroons." (Minutes of) West African Institute of Social and Economic Research, Sociological Section (March, 1953), pp. 88-105.

──────. "Cautious Optimism in West Cameroon," West Africa, September 30, 1961.

──────. "Crisis of Confidence in the Cameroon," West Africa, August 12, 1961.

──────. "The Nature of the Reunification of Cameroon," in A. Hazelwood, ed., African Integration and Disintegration. London: Oxford University Press, 1967.

──────. "The Political History of Cameroon," The World Today, XVIII, 1962, pp. 341-350.

──────. "Social and Demographic Problems of Southern

Bibliography 167

Cameroons Plantation Area," in Social Change in Modern Africa, Aiden Southall, ed., Oxford: Oxford University Press, 1963.

Bayart, J. F. "One-party Government and Political Development in Cameroun," African Affairs, Vol. 73, No. 287 (April, 1973), pp. 125-144.

――――. "L'Union Nationale Camerounaise," Revue Française de Science Politique, Vol. 20, No. 4 (Aug., 1970), pp. 706-720.

Bederman, Sanford H. "The Cameroons Development Corporation: A Unique Example of Government's Role in Commercial Tropical Agriculture," Essays in International Relations. Atlanta, Ga.: Spring, 1967, pp. 8-19.

Berrill, Dr. K. E. "The Economy of Southern Cameroons." Lagos: Government Printer (?), 1960.

Beti, Mongo (pseud. Alexandre Biyidi). "Tumultueux Cameroun," Revue Camerounaise, 2nd yr., no. 11 (Sept.-Oct., 1959), p. 155.

Bigart, Homer. "Cameroon Leader Ending His Exile," New York Times, February 28, 1960, p. 14.

――――. "Hashish-Mad Rebels Kill 74 in Cameroon," New York Times, February 25, 1960, p. 1.

――――. "A Test for Ahidjo," New York Times, February 23, 1960, p. 3.

――――. "Crushing Issues Face Cameroon," New York Times, January 25, 1960, p. 4.

――――. "Cameroon Terror Perils New State," New York Times, January 21, 1960, p. 1.

――――. "Cameroon Chief Cites Terror Rise," New York Times, January 20, 1960, p. 1.

――――. "Clashes Spread Over Cameroon," New York Times, January 3, 1960, p. 20.

Binet, Jacques. "Commandement Africain au Cameroun,"

Receuil Général de Jurisprudence, de Doctrine et de Législation d'Outre-Mer. No. 616, January 1954.

──────. "Sociologie urbaine au Cameroun," Yaoundé: Institut de Recherche scientifique de Cameroun (IR-CAM), 1956. (Pam.)

Binet, J. "Conditions des femmes dans la région cacaoyère du Cameroun," Cahiers Internationale de Sociologie, vol. 16 (Jan.-June, 1956), pp. 109-123.

Bond, Edward. "The Conquest of the Cameroons," Contemporary Review, vol. 109 (1916), pp. 620-627.

Boutillier, C. Tardits, and R. Diziain. Etude sociologique et économique des Douala, Bamiléké, Bassa. Office de la Recherche Scientifique et technique de la France Outre-Mer. Paris: 1957 (?). (Pam.)

Brutsch, Jean-Rene. "Fernando Po et le Cameroun," Etudes camerounaises, no. 43-44 (March-June 1954), pp. 67-78.

Calvert, Albert Frederick. The Cameroons. London: T. W. Laurie, 1917. (Pam.)

Cameroon National Union. "First National Congress: General Policy Report. Presentation of A. Ahidjo, National President." Garoua: CNU, March, 1969.

Cameroons Peoples National Convention. Plebiscite Message to all Workers of the Cameroons. Lagos: Times Press, February 1961.

Centre des Hauts Etudes d'Afrique Moderne (CHEAM) Studies, Paris: (Pams. and loose bound)

    Alexandre, Pierre. La Détribalisation. January 18, 1957. Study no. 2822.

    ──────. Le Mouvement Fang au Regroupement Pahouin. Study No. 2518, 1956.

    Arnould, Maurice. Musulmans et païen-Évolution Générale d'une subdivision du Nord-Cameroun, Guider. Study No. 2775, 1957.

# Bibliography

_____. Transformation des structures traditionelles du Nord Cameroun. Study No. 2877, 1957.

Binet, J. Va Vie politique traditionnelle des Bamoun. Study 2225, 1953.

Gauthier, Henri. Nord et Sud Cameroun. Study No. 3433, 1961.

Lamberton, Colonel. Les Bamiléké Camerounais d 'Aujourd' hui. Study No. 3761, March 16, 1960.

_____. La Pacification de la Sanaga Maritime. Study No. 3760, February 18, 1960.

Merlo, J. (R. P.) Le Proletariat à Douala. Study No. 3263. February 1960.

N'Kamgang, Robert. Les Chefferies traditionnelles dans l'organisation administrative du Cameroun. Study No. 3266, 1959-60.

Vincent, J. Evolution de la société dans le Sud Cameroun. Study No. 3275. January 1960.

Cercle Culturel Camerounaise, "Debat contradictoire sur la Constitution," Cahiers d'Education Civique, 3 trimestre, 1960.

Chaffard, George. "Cameroun à la veille de l'indépendance," Europe France-Outre-Mer, no. 355 (June, 1959), p. 65.

Chilver, E. M. "Native Administration in the West Central Cameroons, 1902-54." In Kenneth Robinson and Frederick Madden, eds., Essays in Imperial Government, pp. 201-215. London: Oxford University Press, 1963.

_____. "Paramountcy and Protection in the Cameroons: The Bali and the Germans, 1889-1913." In R. Prosser and W. R. Louis, eds., Britain and Germany in Africa: Imperial Rivalry and Colonial Rule, pp. 479-511. New Haven: Yale University Press, 1967.

Chilver, E. M., and P. M. Kaberry. Traditional Bamenda. Buea: Government Printer, 1966. (Pam.)

_____. "Traditional Politics in Nsaw," Africa, XXIX,

4 (Oct. 1959), pp. 366-83.

――――. "From Tribute to Tax in a Tikar Chiefdom," Africa, XXX, 1 (Jan. 1960), pp. 1-19.

――――. "Some Problems of Land Tenure in Nsaw," Journal of African Administration, Vol. 12 (Jan. 1960), pp. 21-28.

Chudeau, R. "La nouvelle situation des colonies françaises africaines Togo-Cameroun," Géographie, vol. 33, no. 2 (1920), pp. 193-218.

Coleman, James S. "Current Political Movements in Africa," The Annals of the American Academy of Political and Social Sciences (March, 1955), pp. 97-112.

――――. "La réunification avec le Cameroun meridional," Europe France Outre-mer, No. 379, June 1961, pp. 24-26.

Decraene, Philippe. "Le Cameroun en quête de paix et d'unité." Le Monde, March 12 and 13, 1965.

Delaroziére, R. "Cameroun, inventaire ethnique et linguistique du Cameroun sous mandat français," Journal de la Société des Africanistes, vol. 4, no. 2 (1934), pp. 203-208.

――――. "Etude de la stabilité de la population Bamiléké de la Subdivision de Bafoussam pendant les années 1946 et 1947," Etudes Camerounaises, no. 31-32 (Sept.-Dec., 1950, pp. 137-185.

de Schaetzen, Yves. "Cameroun 1970: Bilan et perspectives." Marchés Tropicaux et Mediterranéens, XXVI, No. 1263 (Jan. 24, 1970), 175-181.

Devernois, Guy. "Cameroons 1958-59, From Trusteeship to Independence," Civilizations, Vol. IX, no. 2 (1959), pp. 229-234.

Dietze, Karl H. "Die Englisch-Französische Mandatsgrenze in Kamerun," Gesellschaft fur Erdkunde, Zeitschrift, 1937, pp. 321-348.

Dippold, Max F. "L'image du Cameroun dans la literature

coloniale Allemande," Cahiers d'Etudes Africaines, Vol. XIII, No. 1 (1973), pp. 37-59.

Diziain, M. R. "Les Facteurs de l'expansion Bamiléké au Cameroun," Bulletin de l'Association des Géographes Français, no. 235-236 (May-June, 1953), pp. 117-126.

(La) Documentation Française, Notes et Etudes Documentaires. La République du Cameroun, Etude No. 2741. Paris, January 19, 1961.

_____. l'Organization économique et sociale de l'Etat fédéré du Cameroun occidental (République fédérale du Cameroun). Etude No. 2806. Paris, August 19, 1961.

_____. Notes et Etudes Documentaires. Le Cameroun sous tutelle britannique à l'heure du plebiscite. Etude No. 2756. Paris, March 1, 1961.

Douala Manga Bell, René. "Contribution à l'histoire du Cameroun," L'Effort Camerounais, Nos. 210, 211, 212, 214-219, 222, 233, October 25, 1959 to January 24, 1960.

Ducat, Marc. "Du Mandat à l'Indépendance," Marchés Tropicaux et Mediterranéens, No. 732, November 21, 1959, pp. 2547-2554.

_____. "Les problemes politiques et les perspectives au Cameroun," Marchés Tropicaux et Mediterranéens, No. 822, August 12, 1961.

Endeley, Dr. E. M. L. "Speech to Resumed Constitutional Conference." London, 1958. (Mimeographed)

Ekang, J. N. An Introduction to Eastern Kamerun. Ibadan: No publisher given, 1956. (Pam.)

Eyinga, Abel. Les Elections Camerounaises du 10 Avril 1960. Thèse, Faculté de Droit et Science Economique, Université de Paris, 1960.

_____. "Opposition en democratie." Cahiers d'éducation civique (Cercle Culturel Camerounais, Yaoundé), No. 4 (1963). (Pam.)

Farine, Avigdor. "Le Bilinguisme au Cameroun," Canadian

Journal of African Studies (Montreal) Spring 1968, pp. 7-12.

Fonlon, Bernard. "The Case for Early Bilingualism," Abbia, Yaoundé, December, 1963.

──────. "Will We Make or Mar," Abbia, Yaoundé, March, 1964.

──────. "Under the Sign of the Rising Sun," The Cameroon Times, Victoria, April 1965.

──────. "The Language Problem in Cameroon: An Historical Perspective," Comparative Education, Oxford, February 1969, pp. 25-49.

Frodin, Reuben. "Flies in the Trusteeship Ointment," American Universities Field Staff Reports, No. RF-1-'61, February 25, 1961. (Pam.)

Froelich, J. C. "Ngaoundéré, la vie économique d'une cité peul," Etudes Camerounaises, no. 43 (June-July, 1954), pp. 3-66.

Full, August. "Kamerun," Kolonialische Rundschau, vol. 9, no. 12 (1932), pp. 279-447.

Gardinier, David E., "The British in the Cameroons, 1919-1939." In R. Prosser and W. R. Louis, eds., Britain and Germany in Africa: Imperial Rivalry and Colonial Rule, pp. 413-555. New Haven: Yale University Press, 1967.

──────. "The Movement to Reunify the Cameroons," paper presented at 1960 meeting of the African Studies Association. (Mimeo.)

──────. "Reactions of the Douala people to loss of hegemony, 1944-45," Ohio University: Papers in International Studies, No. 3, 1966. (Pam.)

──────. "Urban Politics in Douala, 1944-1955," African Urban Notes, Vol. IV, No. 3 (Sept., 1969), pp. 20-29.

Gaudemet, Paul-Marie. "L'Autonomie Camerounaise," Revue Française de Science Politique, Vol. VIII, No.

Bibliography 173

1 (March, 1958), pp. 42-72.

George, S[ampson] A. Kamerun (Unification). London: 1956. (Pam.)

Geze, Bernard. "Notes de géographie physique et agronomique sur le Cameroun," Annales, Institut Nationale Agronomique de Paris. Alençon: 1941, tome 32, pp. 7-164.

Gironcourt, G. de. "Les conquêtes franco-anglaises en Afrique du Togo et le Cameroun," Bulletin, Société de Géographie et d'Etudes Colonials de Marseilles, tome 40, (1917), pp. 72-89.

Göhring, M. "Der König von Bamum und seine Schrift," Der Evangelische Heidenbote, Jahrg. 6, no. 80 (June, 1907).

Gonidec, P. F. "Les Institutions politiques de la République Fédérale du Cameroun," Civilisations, Vol. 11, no. 4, 1961 and Vol. 12, No. 1, 1962.

_____. "Questions internationales interessant la France: de la dépendance à l'autonomie-l'état sous tutelle du Cameroon," Annuaire Français de Droit International, III, 1957. Paris, Centre National de la Recherche Scientifique.

Gourou, P. "Problemes de géographie humaine au Cameroun septentrional," Cah. d'outre-mer, vol. 44 (Oct.-Dec., 1958), pp. 426-430.

Graham, Malbone W. "The Diplomatic Struggle for Africa," in University of California at Los Angeles, Committee on International Relations, Africa, the Near East, and the War. Berkeley: University of California Press, 1943, pp. 175-212.

Green, Reginald H. "The Economy of the Cameroon Federal Republic." in P. Robson and D. A. Lury, eds., The Economies of Africa. London: Allen and Unwin, 1969, pp. 236-286.

[Gua-Nulla, and M. Ndumu.] Kamerun Society, "The Kamerun Society and the Nigerian Constitutional Conference, and the Unification Question" (Victoria, 1957). (Mimeo, 9 pp.)

Guilbot, J. "Les conditions de vie des indigènes à Douala," Etudes Camerounaises, no. 28 (1949), pp. 179-239.

Haut Commissariat de la République Française au Cameroun, Cameroon: From Trusteeship to Independence, Paris, 1959. (Pam.)

Hodgkin, Thomas. "The French Cameroons," series in West Africa, Nov.-Dec. 1954.

Horner, George R. "Togo and Cameroons," Current History, Vol. 34, No. 198, February 1958, pp. 84-90.

_____. The Response of Selected Cameroun Ethnic Groups to French Political Institutions. Archives, Boston University Program of African Studies, November 1959.

Jeffreys, M. D. W. "An Extinct Jewish Colony (Victoria, Cameroons)," Jewish Affairs (Johannesburg) (Nov., 1954), p. 43.

Johnson, Willard R. "African-Speaking Africa?" Africa Forum, New York: AMSAC, 1, 2, 1965.

_____. "Political Instability, Political Disintegration and U.S. Policy Towards Africa," archives U.S. Department of State, Center for International Systems Research, Symposium on Great World Issues of the Next Decade, May 1966.

_____. "The Cameroon Federation: Political Union Between English-Speaking and French-Speaking Africa." In William H. Lewis, ed., French-speaking Africa: The Search for Identity. New York: Walker, 1965, pp. 205-220.

_____. "The UPC in Rebellion: The Integrative Backlash of Insurgency." in Robert Rotberg and Ali A. Mazuri, eds. Protest and Power in Black Africa. New York: Oxford University Press, 1970, pp. 671-694.

Johnston, Sir Harry. "The Africa of the Immediate Future," Journal of the African Society, Vol. XVIII, No. LXXI (April, 1919), p. 161.

Kaberry, Phyllis M. "Retainers and Royal Households in

# Bibliography

the Cameroons Grassfields," Cahiers d'Etudes Africaines, Vol. III, 1962-63, pp. 282-298.

Kaberry, P. M., and E. M. Chilver. "An Outline of the Traditional Political System of Bali-Nyonga, Southern Cameroons," Africa, XXXI, 4 (Oct. 1961), pp. 355-371.

Kamerun National Congress. Manifesto: Elections. March, 1957.

_____. Statement by Leaders of the KNC and the KPP. November 12, 1957 (forming an alliance of these parties).

_____. Opening Speech by the Hon. Dr. E. M. L. Endeley at the Nigeria Constitutional Conference, Lancaster House, London, September 1958.

_____. Memorandum presented by the KNC/KPP to Resumed Constitutional Conference, London, September 1958.

Kamerun National Democratic Party (KNDP). Newsletter, July, 1958, and sporadic.

_____. Presidential Address to the Annual Convention. June 8, 1962, Victoria; August 9, 1963, Bamenda.

_____. United Cameroons-Federal Constitution. Victoria: Cameroons Printing and Publishing Co., Ltd.

Kamerun Society, "Economic and Financial Problems of the Cameroons," Victoria, 1957. (Mimeographed)

Kanga, Victor and C. Onana Awana. "Le Cameroun Fédéral," Europe-France-Outremer, No. 398, March 1963.

Kilson, Martin. "Authoritarian and Single-Party Tendencies in Africa," World Politics, Vol. XV, No. 3, January 1963.

Kingué, Michel Don, et al. "Cameroun une entité aux visages multiples." Le Cité (Paris), No. 21 (Dec. 1964), pp. 15-41.

Kirk-Greene, Anthony H. M. (for the Government of Northern Nigeria). This is Northern Nigeria. Kaduna: Government Printer, 1956. (Pam.)

Kitchen, Helen. "Cameroun Faces Troubled Future." Africa Special Report, III, No. 1 (Jan. 1960), 14-15.

Knittle, Ingeborg. "Untersuchung uber die Kapitalinvestierung der Vereinigten Staaten von Amerika in Afrika," Beitrage zur Kolonialforschung. Berlin: Riemer and Andrew Steiner, 1943. (Band. IV.) Pp. 171-185.

Lamberton, (Colonel) J. "Les Bamiléké." Paris, Centre des Hautes Etudes de l'Afrique moderne, No. 3761.

Lancaster, C. Gordon. "Cameroons, Ethnology," Man, Vol. 33, no. 93 (1933) p. 91.

Larin, V. "The Cameroons Fight for Unity and Independence," International Affairs, No. 10, 1955, pp. 90-98.

Leeming, A. J. "A Historical Sketch of Victoria, British Cameroons," Nigerian Field, Vol. 13, no. 4 (Oct., 1950), pp. 184-189; ibid., Vol. 16, no. 1 (Jan., 1951), pp. 37-45.

LeLong, R. M. "Yaoundé, capitale du Cameroun," A.O.F. Magazine (Paris, 1955), no. 3, pp. 5-7.

Le Vine, Victor T. "P-Day in Cameroon," West Africa, March 4, 1961, p. 236.

_____. "Calm Before the Storm in Cameroon?" Africa Report, May 1961, pp. 3-4.

_____. "The Cameroun Federal Republic, in G. Carter ed., Five African States: Responses to Diversity. Ithaca: Cornell University Press, 1963.

_____. "Cameroon Political Parties," in J. S. Coleman and C. Rosberg, eds. Political Parties and National Integration in Tropical Africa. Berkeley: University of California Press, 1964.

_____. "Cameroon, 1955-1962," in D. M. Condit, Bert J. Cooper et al, Challenge and Response in Internal Conflict, Vol. III. Washington, D.C.: Center for Research in Social Systems, 1968, pp. 238-267.

Bibliography 177

———. "A Contribution to the Political History of Cameroon: The United Nations and the Politics of Decolonization--the Termination of the British Cameroons Trusteeship." Abbia (Yaoundé), No. 24 (Jan.-April 1970), 65-90.

———. "The New Cameroon Federation," Africa Report, vol. 6, no. 11 (Dec., 1961), p. 7.

———. "The Other Cameroons." Africa Report, VI, No. 2 (Feb. 1961), 5-6, 12.

———. "The Politics of Partition in Africa: The Cameroons and the Myth of Unification." Journal of International Affairs, XVIII, No. 2 (1964), pp. 198-210.

———. "Unifying the Cameroons," West Africa, (July 15, 1961), p. 774.

———, and Henri M'Ballah. "[Education in the] Federal Republic of Cameroon." In Helen Kitchen, ed., The Educated African, pp. 519-532. New York: Praeger, 1962.

Logan, Rayford W. "Operation of the Mandate System in Africa," Journal of Negro History, vol. 13 (Oct., 1928), pp. 423-477.

McKay, Vernon. "French Aid to Africa," Current History, vol. 33, no. 195 (Aug., 1957), pp. 91-98.

———. "Too Slow or Too Fast? Political Changes in African Trust Territories," Foreign Affairs, vol. 35 (Jan., 1957), pp. 295-310.

Mengot, Ako. "Pressures and Constraints on the Development of Education in the West Cameroon," Africa Today (Denver, Colo.) XIV-2, 1967, pp. 18-20.

Migeod, Frederich W. H. "The British Cameroons, its Tribes and Natural Features," Journal of the African Society, vol. 23, no. 91 (April, 1924) pp. 176-187.

Moncharville, M. "L'Execution du Mandat au Togo et au Cameroun," Revue Générale de Droit International Public, série 2, tome 7 (1925), pp. 58-78.

Moran, William. "U.S. Technical and Economic Assistance to Africa," in Haines, C. G., ed., Africa Today. Baltimore: Johns Hopkins Press, 1955.

Mouvement d'Action National du Cameroun. Rapport de Politique Générale et Resolutions Adoptées. 2nd Congress. January 27-30, 1961.

Mukoko-Mokeba, Magnus P. "Cameroon Reunification: A Case Study in the Process of Political Integration," Master's Thesis for Graduate School of Public and International Affairs. University of Pittsburgh, 1966.

Nicod, A. La femme au Cameroun. Paris: Société des Missions Evangeliques, 1927. (Pam.)

Nicolas, J. P. "Deux ports d'estuaire, St. Louis du Sénégal et Douala," Bulletin d'I. F. A. N. (Jan.-April, 1957), pp. 259-274.

Owona, Adalbert. "Comment les Allemands mirent la main sur le Cameroun," Revue Camerounaise, 2d year, no. 10 (July-Aug., 1959), p. xiii.

_____. "Le Movement d'inspiration marxiste: UPC" (unpublished paper).

_____. "La naissance du Cameroun (1884-1914)," Cahiers d'Etudes Africaines, Vol. XIII, No. 1 (1973), pp. 16-36.

_____. Le Nationalisme Camerounais. No. 5 of Serie: No. II Etude de divers types de nationalisme. Paper presented to Table Ronde, May 25-26, 1962. Association Française de Science Politique, Paris.

_____. "Le Traite protectoral Germano-Douala, 1884. Revue Camerounaise, 2nd year, No. 8 (March-April 1959).

Pavec, Albert. "l'Idee de réunification des Camerouns," Paris, Institut Nationale des Hautes Etudes d'Outre-Mer, unpublished study No. 126, 1958.

Philipe, Antoine. "L'essor des partis politiques au Cameroun," Latitude, No. 3, 1958.

Philippson, Sir Sydney. Report on the Financial, Economic and Administrative Consequences to Southern Cameroons of Separation from the Federation of Nigeria. Prime Minister's Office, Southern Cameroons, 1959.

Piquemal, Marcel. "Le Problèmes des Unions d'états en Afrique Noire," Revue Juridique et Politique d Outre-Mer, No. 1, Janvier-Mars 1962, pp. 21-58.

Potekhin, I. I. "Borba za Vossoyedinenye Kameruna," Sovetskaya Etnografia (1959), no. 5 p. 62.

Rathery, M. Les Produits d'exportation du Cameroun dans la conjoncture mondiale. Yaoundé: Chambre de Commerce et d'Industrie du Cameroun (1959). (Pam.)

Retif, André. "A propos de l'Union des Populations du Cameroun: Communisme et religion au Cameroun," L'Afrique et l'Asie, no. 33 (Nov., 1955).

Richet, Etienne. "Voyage au Cameroun et dans le Nigeria," Bulletin Société Royal Géographique, Vol. 47 (1927), pp. 1-46, 205-305; Ibid., Vol. 48 (1928), pp. 1-48, 109-176, 267-333.

Ritzenthaler, Robert E. "Anlu: A Women's Uprising in the British Cameroons," African Studies, XIX, 1960, pp. 151-156.

Rivlin, Benjamin. "Self-Determination and Dependent Areas," International Conciliation, No. 501, January 1955.

Roberts, Margaret. "Cameroons on the Eve," West Africa, December 19, 1959, p. 1105.

_____. "Political Prospects for the Cameroun," The World Today, Vol. 16, July 1960, pp. 305-312.

Robinson, Kenneth. "The Public Law of Overseas France since the War," The Journal of Comparative Legislation. 3rd series, Vol. XXXII, 1950 (or as No. 1 of Oxford University Institute of Colonial Studies, Reprint Series).

_____. "Constitutional Reform in French Tropical Africa," Political Studies, Vol. 6, February 1958, pp. 45-69.

Royal Empire Society, Information Bureau. Notes on Conditions in the British Cameroons. London: Royal Empire Society, 1956. (Pam.)

Schacht, Hjalmar. "Germany's Colonial Demands," Foreign Affairs, vol. 15 (Jan., 1937), pp. 223-234.

Schachter, Ruth. "Single Party Systems in West Africa," American Political Science Review, Vol. LV, no. 2 (June, 1961), p. 294.

Soppo-Priso, Paul. L'Armée camerounaise et le service obligatoire de solidarité nationale "So-Kono." Yaoundé: 1959 (Pensées et Actions, no. 2.) (Pam.)

Southern Cameroons (West Cameroon) Bar Association. Analytical Review of Constitutional Proposals, Buea, 1961. (Mimeographed)

_____. "Minutes of the Emergency Meeting, July 12, 1961," Buea, 1961. (Mimeographed)

Stengers, Jean. "L'Imperialisme colonial de la fin du XIX siecle: mythe ou realité," Journal of African History, vol. 11, no. 3 (1962), p. 469.

Strothmann, Dietrich. "Unter dem Diktat der Angst." Die Zeit, Mar. 8, 1969, p. 2.

Um Nyobé, Reuben. "Cameroun, Naissance du mouvement national," Cahiers Internationaux, Vol. 6, No. 52, January 1954.

_____. "Cameroun, Objectifs immediats du mouvement national." Cahiers Internationaux, Vol. 6, No. 53, February 1954, p. 75.

_____. "Cameroun, Ou en est le nationalisme camerounais?" Cahiers Internationaux, Vol. 7, No. 64, March 1955, p. 81.

_____. "Pour la dénouement de la crise-Kamerunaise," Lettre à M. Mbida, in Revue Camerounaise, No. 5, Sept.-Oct. 1958. Paris: Cercle Culturel des Etudiants Kamerunais.

l'Union Camerounaise, Parti de, Premier Stage de Forma-

# Bibliography

tion des Responsables de l'Union Camerounaise, August 1-6, 1961. Yaoundé: 1961. (Pam.)

_____. (Report) Congres, du Parti Politique de l'Union Camerounaise, I, 1958, Garoua; II$^e$ 1959, Ngaoundéré; III$^e$ 1960, Maroua; IV$^e$ 1962, Ebolowa.

_____. Bulletin Mensuel de Liaison. Monthly, 1960 on.

Union des Populations du Cameroun. Abdul Baghi Maw'ndi Mahamadu Rajn. Le bluff Ahidjo. Cairo: Service d'Information de l'UPC à l'étranger, 1958. (Pam.)

_____. Abdou Mfonzie. Les Yankees en Afrique ou l'Amitié du Loup et de la Brebis. Probably Accra: 1963.

_____. Bureau National Provisoire (legal UPC), La Ligne d'action de l'UPC. Secretariat National. Yaoundé: June 16, 1962.

_____. Circulaire a tous les organismes de l'U.P.C. No. 194/BCD/UPC/QD. Cairo: June 4, 1959. (Pam.)

_____. Comité Directeur. Le Patriote Kamerunais, Journal d'avant garde de la lutte de libération nationale et sociale du peuple Kamerunais, numero de November-Decembre 1959, saisi par la police française le 21 janvier 1960. Conakry: Jan. or Feb., 1960. (Pam.)

_____. _____. Unification Immédiate du Cameroun. 1952. No place of publication given. (Pam.)

_____. _____. The UPC Denounces Planned Systematic Tortures in the Camerun. Cairo: 1958. (Pam.)

_____. _____. Ce Que veut le peuple Kamerunaise. (Pam.)

_____. Declaration du Bureau du Comité Directeur de l'U.P.C. Cairo: April 1, 1959. (Pam.)

_____. Le Kamerun sous un régime de dictature fasciste. Probably Accra: Comité Directeur, 1960 (?)

———. Moumié, Félix-Roland. Intervention de M. Félix-Roland Moumié, chef de la délégation kamerunaise. (Second Conference, Afro-Asian Peoples, Conakry, April 11-15, 1960.) Conakry: Comité Directeur de l'U.P.C., April 1960 (mimeo.)

———. Moumié, Félix-R. Rape of the Cameroons. London: Committee of African Organizations, Nov. or Dec., 1959. (Pam.)

———. Moumié Mme. F. R., Dr. Félix-Roland Moumié, My Memories on his Life. Conakry: 1960.

———. Moumié, Felix R., and N. Njiawue. La révolution kamerunaise et la lutte des peuples africains. Conakry: Sept., 1959. (Pam.)

———. ———. Ouandié, E., and A. Kingué. Position de l'U.P.C. vis-a-vis de l'indépendance du Kamerun. Conakry: Dec., 1959. (Pam.)

———. Le fascisme n'aura aucun succes au Cameroun. Cairo: Service de l'information, 1958. (Pam.)

———. L'O.N.U. et le probleme Kamerunais. Cairo: Service de l'information, December or January, 1958-1959. (Pam.)

———. L'Oppression française au Kamerun. Probably Accra: Comité Directeur de l'UPC, 1963.

———. La révolution kamerunaise, ses objectifs, sa signification et ses repercussions dans le continent africain. Cairo: Feb., 1960. (Pam.)

———. La Tutelle Internationale à l'Epreuve, Cairo: Service de l' information, January or February, 1959. (Includes Memorandum of the Kamerun Society to the UN Visiting Mission to the British Cameroons, Dec. 1958.) (Pam.)

———. Unification Immédiate du Cameroun. Comite Directeur, 1952.

———. Unification Immédiate du Cameroon. Paris: Imprimerie speciale des Etudiants Camerounais, 1953.

Bibliography 183

_____. Unité Africaine ou Neo-Colonialisme? Le Delegation de l'UPC à la Conference des Organizations nationalistes. Accra, May 1962.

Union Nationale des Etudiants Kamerunais. Compte Rendu des travaux de la Conference Pan-Camerounais des Etudiants. Yaoundé, August 1959.

Vaast, Pierre. Petite Geographie du Cameroun. Bourges: Fernand Nathan, 1954. (Pam.)

Vandercook, John W. "The French Mandate of Cameroun," National Geographic Magazine. Vol. LIX, no. 2 (Feb., 1931), pp. 225-260.

Vaughn, James. "Culture, History, and Grassroots Politics in a Nigerian Chiefdom," American Anthropologist, LXVI (1964), pp. 1078-1095.

Warmington, Alan. "The Cameroons and the Fiscal Commission," West Africa, May 10, 1958, p. 443.

_____. "Saving and Indebtedness Among Cameroons Plantation Workers," Africa, Vol. XXVIII, no. 4 (Oct., 1958), pp. 329-343.

_____. "Some Aspects of Industrial Relations in the Cameroons Plantations," Proceedings of the Third Annual Conference of the West African Institute of Social and Economic Research, Ibadan: University College of Nigeria, 1956, pp. 16-22.

_____. "Prospects for the Cameroun Federation." West Africa, Sept. 30, 1961, p. 1073.

Welch, Claude E. "Cameroon since Reunification." West Africa, Oct. 19, 1963, p. 1175; Oct. 26, p. 1213; Nov. 2, 1241; Nov. 9, p. 1271.

Wrigley, G. M. "The Military Campaign Against Germany's African Colonies," Geographical Review, vol. 5 (Jan., 1918), pp. 44-65.

Zang-Atangana, J. M. "Les Partis Politiques Camerounaise," Recueil Penant, No. 684, December 1960, pp. 681-708.

_____. "Les forces politiques camerounais," Memoire

submitted to the Faculté de Droit de Paris, 1961.

Zoa, Abbé Jean. Pour un Nationalisme Chrétien au Cameroun. Yaoundé: Imprimerie Saint-Paul, 1957. (Pam.)


ARTICLES AND PAMPHLETS (Anonymous)

"Assembly Charts Course for Cameroons," United Nations Review (April, 1959), p. 15.

"Assembly Recommends New Date for Plebiscite in Southern Cameroons," United Nations Review (Nov., 1959), p. 10.

"Britain in the Cameroons," West Africa, July 16, 1960, p. 795.

"Building for Tomorrow in the British Cameroons," United Nations Bulletin, 16 (Feb. 1, 1954), pp. 118-24.

"Cameroon Comes to Stay." West Africa, April 30, 1966, p. 479.

"Cameroon Complexities." West Africa, April 23, 1966, p. 447.

"Cameroons' Fulani Premier," West Africa, January 2, 1960. pp. 5-6.

"Cameroon's Man in the Centre." West Africa, Feb. 24, 1968, pp. 211-212.

"Cameroons on the Eve," West Africa, September 19, 1959, p. 1105.

"Cameroons under Strain," The Economist, Vol. 196: 175-6, July 5, 1960.

"Cameroons under United Kingdom Administration and Cameroons under French Administration," International Organization, Vol. XIII, Spring 1959, pp. 302-305.

"Cameroun." Afrique, No. 6 (quarterly supplement, 1966).

"Le Cameroun a la veille de l'independance," Europe-France-Outremer, No. 355, June 1959, pp. 24-51.

"Cameroun, dix ans d'independance." Europe-France-Outremer, XLV, No. 457 (Feb. 1968).

"Le Cameroun dix-huit mois après l'indépendence." Europe-France-Outremer, XXXVIII, No. 379 (June 1961).

"Cameroun: L'Eglise contre l'Etat?" Jeune Afrique, No. 508 (Sept. 29, 1970), pp. 32-35.

"Cameroun, Situation favorable." Europe-France-Outremer, XLVI, No. 474-475 (July- Aug. 1969).

"Cameroun, six ans de gouvernement Ahidjo." Europe-France-Outremer, XLIII, No. 436 (May 1966).

"Cameroun, trois ans de réunification." Europe-France-Outremer, XLI, No. 416 (Sept. 1964).

"Changing Political Patterns in the British Cameroons," (Report of UN Visiting Mission) United Nations Bulletin 14 (June 1, 1953), pp. 392-94.

"Compromise in Cameroon." West Africa, July 7, 1962, p. 74.

"Les condamnations de Yaoundé." Jeune Afrique, No. 52 (Jan. 19, 1971), pp. 28-31.

"Conference de Mlle. Homburger; la colonie allemande du Cameroun," Géographie, vol. 40, no. 8 (June, 1923), pp. 355-386.

"Developments in the Cameroons," U.S. Dept. of State Bulletin, 38 (March 31, 1958), pp. 535-37.

"Doctor of Revolt," Drum (Oct., 1959), pp. 27-28.

"Federal Constitution for Cameroons," West Africa, July 29, 1961, p. 926.

_____. West Africa, September 23, 1961, p. 1056.

"The French Cameroons Today," West Africa, no. 2143 (May 19, 1958), p. 439.

"The Future of the Trust Territories of Cameroons," International Organization, Vol. 14, Winter, 1960, pp. 152-155.

"The German Delegation's Comments on the Condition of the Peace," International Conciliation, no. 143 (Oct., 1919), p. 1249.

"How Real Was Ahidjo's Victory," West Africa, April 23, 1960, p. 459.

"Independence Foreshadowed for French Cameroons." United Nations Review, Dec. 1958, p. 30.

"Kamerun boyetsya za svobodu," Sovremenii Vostok (April, 1958), p. 12.

"Kamerun National Congress Convention," West Africa, May 14, 1955, p. 444.

"The Last Federation." West Africa, April 2, 1966, p. 371.

"London Log," West Africa, November 19, 1960, p. 1321.

"Malgré la victoire du referendum--l'avenir du Cameroun reste chargé des nuages," Marchés Tropicaux et Mediterranéens, No. 74, March 5, 1960.

"Le Marché camerounais," special issue of Marchés Tropicaux et Mediterranéens, XX, No. 963 (April 15, 1964).

"Mission's Report on the Two Territories: End of Trusteeship Proposed for the French Cameroons." United Nations Review, March 1959, p. 31.

"Moskau's Taktik im schwarzen Erdteil." Ostprobleme, XII, No. 4 (Feb. 19, 1960), 112-115.

"Muted Triumph for Premier Ahidjo," West Africa, February 27, 1960, p. 235.

"Plebiscites Divide British Cameroons," U.N. Review, 8 (March, 1961), pp. 14-15.

"Le probleme national au Cameroun," Le Bulletin-Documents et Recherches, no. 6 (April 1, 1956), pp. 19-27.

"Progress Toward Self-Government in the Cameroons," U.S. Dept. of State Bulletin, 32 (Feb. 21, 1955), pp. 317-18.

Bibliography 187

"Prospects for the Cameroun Federation," West Africa, Sept. 30, 1961, p. 1073.

"Le referendum du 11 Fev. et les aléas de la réunification des Camerouns," Marchés Tropicaux et Mediterranéens. No. 795, February 4, 1961, p. 318.

"Renascence in the Cameroons; With News Story," U.N. Review, 4 (April, 1958), pp. 4, 12-15, (Bibliography on p. 46).

"Reunification in the Cameroons," West Africa, November 26, 1955, p. 1116.

"Swift Constitutional Gains in British Cameroons," U.N. Review, 2 (May, 1956), pp. 28-31.

"Training of Camerounian Terrorists in Communist China," Le Journal FEAPAN (Abidjan) No. 54, Nov., 1961, p. 3, translated in JPRS: 12321, pp. 1-9.

"Trusteeship Council's Recommendations on Four Territories," U.N. Review, 4 (May, 1958), pp. 51-52.

PUBLIC DOCUMENTS

a. FEDERAL REPUBLIC

Cameroon, Federal Republic of. l'Assemblée Nationale Fédérale, Journal Officiel des Debats. Annual sessions, Yaoundé: Imprimerie Nationale. 1961.--1972.

_____. Chambre de Commerce. Bulletin Mensuel, Douala.

_____. _____. Rapport Annuel, each year.

_____. Chamber of Commerce and Industry. Exposé sur la situation Economique du Cameroun au l' Janvier, 1960. Douala: February, 1960.

_____. Commissariat général à l'information, Le Chemin de fer trans-camerounais. 1960.

_____. Annuaire National, 1963, 1965, 1967, 1969, 1971--

_____. Constitution, October 1, 1961.

_____. Institute of Education, Cameroon Review of Education (Yaoundé).

_____. Journal Officiel-Official Gazette, October 1, 1961 to present. Yaoundé: Imprimerie nationale.

_____. Ministère de l'Economie Nationale, Service de la Statistique, Annuaire statistique du commerce exterieur du Cameroon Oriental. Imprimerle Nationale. Yearly.

_____. _____. Bulletin Mensuel. Yaoundé: Service de la Statistique Générale, mimeographed. (Continued from the Republic.)

_____. _____. Enquête Démographique Centre et Est, 1963. Yaoundé: Imprimerie Nationale, May, 1963.

_____. _____. Enquête Démographique Nord-Cameroun. 1962 (?) Yaoundé: Imprimerie Nationale.

_____. _____. La Population de Yaoundé, 1962. Yaoundé: Mairie de Yaoundé, Imprimerie Nationale. (1962?)

Cameroon, Federated State of West Cameroon, Official Gazette, Buea: Government Printer.

_____. Land and Survey Department. West Cameroon Tribal Boundaries (map No. M260 from data supplied by E. O. Ardener). Buea: November 1959.

_____. "Record, All Party Conference on the Constitutional Future of the Southern Cameroons, Bamenda, June 26-28, 1961." Buea: Government Printer.

_____. Record. Conference on the Constitutional Future of the Southern Cameroons, Foumban, July 17-21, 1961. Buea: Government Printer.

_____. Secretary of State for Finance, Estimates (for

each fiscal year).

_____. Quarters List and Directory. Buea: Government Printer (quarterly).

b. TRUSTEESHIP PERIOD

Cameroons under French Trusteeship. Assemblée (Territoriale) du Cameroun, Session Budgetaire de Mars-Avril 1957, Analyse des enseignements tirés du bilan d'ensemble dés premiers plans quadriennaux et solutions proposées, fait par A. Mandon (President de la commission des Grands Travaux et du Plan).

_____. Directorate of Foreign Relations. Cameroun, 1946 from Trusteeship to Independence 1960. Paris, 1959

_____. Etat du Cameroun:

a. Journal Officiel de l'Assemblée Représentative du Cameroun, (1947-1952).

b. Journal Officiel des Debats de l'Assemblée Territoriale du Cameroun (1952-1956).

c. Journal Officiel des Debats de l'Assemblée Législative du Cameroun (1957-1959).

_____. _____. Service d'Information du Gouvernement Camerounais. Discours prononcé par M. Le Gouverneur P. Messmer, Haut-Commissaire de la République, a l'Ouverture de la Session Budgetaire de 1957 l'Assemblée Territoriale du Cameroun. Yaoundé, March 25, 1957.

_____. _____. Service d'Information du Governement Camerounais. Discours d'Investiture prononcé par M. André-Marie Mbida, Premier Ministre, Chef du Gouvernement Camerounais, 15 Mai 1957, devant l'Assemblée Législative du Cameroun.

_____. _____. _____. Discours prononcé le 9 November 1957, à Boumnyebel (Subdivision d'Eseka) par M. André-Marie Mbida, Premier Ministre, Chef du Gouvernement Camerounais.

Cameroons under French Trusteeship. Etat du Cameroun, Service d'Information du Gouvernement Camerounais. Discours d'investiture prononcé par M. Ahmadou Ahidjo, Premier Ministre de l'Etat du Cameroun le 18 Fevrier 1958 devant l'Assemblée Législative du Cameroun.

_____. _____. _____. Communication de M. Ahidjo Ahmadou. Premier Ministre de l'Etat du Cameroun le 18 Octobre, 1958, à l'Assemblée Législative du Cameroun.

_____. _____. _____. Communication de M. Ahidjo Ahmadou. Premier Ministre de l'Etat du Cameroun le 6 Mai 1959 à l'Assemblée Législative du Cameroun. Yaoundé: Imprimerie du Gouvernement.

_____. Guide Economique de Cameroun 1959. Yaoundé: 1959.

_____. Information Service. Cameroons, 10 Years of Investments and Progress under the Leadership of France. Paris: Diloutremer, 1958.

_____. Ministère des affaires économiques. Service de la Statistique Generale. Annuaire Démographique du Cameroun. Edition Provisoire 1946-1956. Yaoundé: Imprimerie du Gouvernement, 1956.

_____. _____. _____. Bulletin de la Statistique Generale. Yaoundé: Imprimerie du Gouv't., 1958: nos. 1-12; 1959: nos. 1-12.

_____. _____. _____. Resultats du Recensement de la ville de Douala 1955-56. Population Autochtone. Fascicule 2 Resultats d'ensemble. Yaoundé: Imprimerie du Gouvernement, 1957.

_____. _____. _____. Resultats du Recensement de la Subdivision de Mbalmayo 1956, Population Autochtone. Yaoundé: Imprimerie du Gouvernement, 1957.

Cameroons under French Trusteeship. Ministère des affairs économiques. Service de la Statistique Generale. Resultats du recensement de la ville de Yaoundé 1957. Population autochtone. Yaoundé: Imprimerie du Gouvernement, 1958.

Bibliography 191

_____. _____. _____. Resultats du recensement de la ville d'Ebolowa, 1958. Population autochtone. Fasc. 1. Yaoundé: Imprimerie du Gouvernement, 1959.

c. CAMEROON REPUBLIC

Cameroun, Republic of. Chambre de Commerce et d'Industrie du Cameroun. Exposé sur la Situation Economique du Cameroun au 1 Janvier 1960. Douala: February, 1960.

_____. Constitution. February 21, 1960. Yaoundé: Imprimerie Nationale.

_____. Journal Officiel des Débats de l'Assemblée Nationale du Cameroun.

_____. Ministère des Affairs Etrangères. La Position de la République du Cameroun à la suite du Plébiscite des 11 et 12 Février 1961 dans la partie septentrionale du Territoire du Cameroun sous l'Administration du Royaume-Uni de Grande-Bretagne et d'Irlande du Nord. Paris: Editions Diloutremer, 1961.

_____. Ministère du Plan. Plan de développement économique et sociale, travaux preparatoires. 3 Vols. Yaoundé: 1960.

_____. _____. Rapport sur les possibilités de développement industriel du Cameroun. (Prepared by Société d'Etudes pour le Développement Economique et Social). Paris: 1960.

_____. La Présidence. Report on the Economic Aspects of Reunification. By Kjell Andersen. Yaoundé: February 18, 1961. (Mimeographed)

d. FRANCE

France. Agence Economique des colonies autonomes. Cameroun, magazine trimestriel. 1926--January 1937. (Colonial Ministry).

_____. Caisse Centrale de la France d'outre-mer (Paris). Graphiques de l'Evolution économique du Cameroun:

population, prix, budget ordinaire, investissements. Paris: 1953.

_____. Centre d'Information Documentaire (Paris). The Work of France in the Cameroons. 1939.

_____. Comité Monétaire de la zone Franc. Secrétariat Général. La zone Franc en 1957. Cinquieme Rapport Annuel du Comité Monetaire de la zone Franc. Paris: 1958.

France. Institut d'Emission de l'Afrique Equatoriale Francaise et du Cameroun. Rapport Annuel du Gouvernement Français sur l'administration du Cameroun sous Mandat. (1921-1938).

_____. _____. Rapport d'Activité, Exercice, 1958. Paris 1959.

_____. Ministry of the Colonies (Ministère des Colonies). Commissariat au Cameroun. Guide de la Colonisation au Cameroun. Paris: E. Larue. 1923.

_____. Ministry of Overseas France (Ministere de la France d'Outre-Mer.) Documentation Francaise. Notes et Etudes Documentaires. "L'evolution recente des Institutions Politiques dans les Territoires d'Outre-Mer," No. 1847, March 11, 1954.

_____. Ministry of Overseas France (Ministère de la France d'Outre-Mer and Ministère des Affaires Etrangères), Rapport Annuel du Gouvernement Français à l'Assemblée Générale des Nations Unies sur l'administration du Cameroun placé sous la tutelle de la France. (from 1947 to 1959).

e. GREAT BRITAIN

Great Britain. Colonial Office. Annual Report of H.M. Government to the Assembly of the United Nations on the Cameroons under United Kingdom Administration. 1946 to 1960.

_____. Foreign Office. Historical Section. Cameroon. Peace Handbooks, no. 111. London, HMSO, 1920.

Bibliography 193

──────. ──────. Draft Mandates, 1921. Cmd. 1350. London: HMSO, 1922.

──────. [Commissioner for the Southern Cameroons under United Kingdom Trusteeship.] Southern Cameroons Plebiscite, 1961, the Two Alternatives. [Buea: 1960.]

──────. ──────. Reports on Mandate of the Cameroons to the League of Nations. 1921-1922 issued as Cmd. 1647 with series title. 1923-1929 issued by Colonial Office as Colonial numbers. 1930-1938 issued by Colonial Office as Cmd. with series title.

──────. ──────. Nigeria, Report of the Fiscal Commissioner (A. L. Chick) on the Financial Effects of the Proposed New Constitutional Arrangement. Cmd. 9828. London: HMSO, 1953.

──────. ──────. Report by the Conference on the Nigerian Constitution, London, July-August 1953. Cmd. 8934. London: HMSO, 1953.

Great Britain. Foreign Office. Report by the Resumed Conference on the Nigerian Constitution. Lagos, January-February 1954. Cmd. 9059. London: HMSO, 1954.

──────. ──────. Partition of Africa: British Possessions. Peace Handbooks, nos. 89-95. London: HMSO, 1920.

──────. Secretary of State for Colonies. Report of the Nigeria Constitutional Conference 1957. Cmd. 207. London: HMSO, 1957.

──────. ──────. Report by the Resumed Nigeria Constitutional Conference 1958. Lagos, Federal Government Printer, 1959.

f. LEAGUE OF NATIONS

League of Nations. Twenty-first Ordinary Session of the Assembly. General Questions, Report of the First Committee to the Assembly. L. N. Doc. A. 33, 1946. Geneva April 17, 1947.

_____. Council, Mandat Brittanique sur le Cameroun. L. N. Publ. 1922 ser. 6, A., no. 13, 15.

_____. Permanent Mandates Commission. Minutes and Reports. 1921-1937.

_____. Secretariat, Mandates Section. British Mandates for the Cameroons. Cmd. 794. London: HMSO, 1923. G. Nigeria (Southern Cameroons)

g. NIGERIA AND SOUTHERN CAMEROONS

Nigeria, Federation of. Federal Information Service, Lagos, for Southern Cameroons Information Service. A Statement of Policy by Dr. E. M. L. Endeley. Lagos: 1958.

_____. Ministry of Research and Information. Information Division. Financial Assistance to the Cameroons. Lagos: 1959.

_____. Population Census of the Eastern Region of Nigeria, 1953. Bulletin no. 2 (Bamenda Province), no. 5 (Cameroons Province). Lagos: The Government Statistician, 1954.

_____. Population Census of the Northern Region of Nigeria, 1952. Lagos: The Government Statistician, 1952.

_____. Report of the Native Courts (Cameroons, Bamenda Province) Commission of Inquiry. Lagos: Fed. Gov't. Printer, 1953.

_____. _____. Information on the Northern Cameroons (Trust Territory Province). Kaduna: 1961. (Mimeo.)

_____. Southern Cameroons. Cameroons Development Corporation. Annual Report. Bota/Victoria, So. Cam.: from 1950.

_____. _____. Debates in the Southern Cameroons House of Assembly. Vol. I: First Session, October 26-November 9, 1954. Buea: So. Ca. Gov't. Press, 1955 (only to Nov. 2). Vol II: First Session, Oc-

Bibliography

tober 26-November 9, 1954. Calabar: St. Therese's Press, 1955 (only Nov. 3 to 9), Vol. III. First Session, Fourth Meeting, December 12 to 14, 1954. Calabar: St. Therese's Press, 1955.

_____. _____. Introducing the Southern Cameroons. Lagos: Federal Information Service, 1958. (Pam.)

_____. _____. Report on the Mamfe Conference on the Plebiscite Question, Aug. 10 and 11, 1959. Buea: So. Cam. Gov't Printer, undated.

Nigeria, Federation of. Federation Information Service, Lagos, for Southern Cameroons Information Service. A Statement of Policy by Dr. E. M. L. Endeley. Lagos: 1958.

_____. First Progress Report of the Economic Programme. Sessional Paper No. 2 of 1957. Lagos: Federal Government Printer, 1957.

_____. Population Census of the Northern Region of Nigeria, 1952. Lagos: The Government Statistician, 1952.

_____. Population Census of the Eastern Region of Nigeria, 1953. Bulletin No. 2 (Bamenda Province), No. 5 (Cameroons Province). Lagos: The Government Statistician, 1954.

_____. Prime Minister, Broadcast on the Southern Cameroons Plebiscite, January 22, 1961.

_____. Report of the Native Courts (Cameroons, Bamenda Province) Commission of Inquiry. Lagos: Federal Government Printer, 1952.

_____. Second Progress Report on the Economic Programme, 1955-60. Lagos: Federal Government Printer, 1958.

_____. Southern Cameroons. Cameroons Development Corporation. Annual Report. Bota/Victoria, Southern Cameroon, from 1950.

_____. _____. _____. Commissioner (Acting) Speech at opening of Budget Meeting Third Southern

Cameroons House of Assembly, 1st session, March 19, 1959.

_____. _____. _____. Southern Cameroons Plebiscite, 1961, The Two Alternatives. Buea: Printed by Authority of United Nations Plebiscite Commission, 1961.

_____. _____. Introducing the Southern Cameroons. Lagos: Federal Information Service, 1958.

_____. _____. Prime Minister's Office. Report on the Financial, Economic and Administrative Consequences to Southern Cameroons of Separation from the Federation of Nigeria, by Sir Sydney Philippson, K. B. E.

_____. _____. Report on the Mamfe Conference on the Plebiscite Question, August 10 and 11, 1959. Buea: Southern Cameroons, Government Printer, undated.

### h. UNITED NATIONS

United Nations. Industrial Development in Cameroon. New York: UNO, 1967.

United Nations. General Assembly. Official Records of the General Assembly, Thirteenth Session, Annexes. U.N. Doc. A/4094.

_____. _____. Fourth (Trusteeship) Committee. Report (The Future of the Trust Territories of the Cameroons Under French Administration and the Cameroons under United Kingdom Administration). (March 13, 1959.) U.N. Doc. A/4095.

_____. _____. _____. Official Records. 845-871 meetings. U.N. Docs. A/C.4/SR. 845-871 (New York, 1959).

_____. _____. _____. Petitions Concerning the Cameroons Under French Administration, Observations of the French Government as Administering Authority. U.N. Doc. T/OBS. 5/71 (Dec. 6, 1955).

Bibliography 197

_____. Trusteeship Council. Report of the United Nations Commissioner for the Supervision of the Plebiscite in the Cameroons under United Kingdom Administration. U.N. Docs. T/1491 (Nov. 25, 1959), T/1491 Corr. 1, T/1491 Add. 1 (Dec. 1, 1959).

United Nations. Trusteeship Council. Report of the United Nations Plebiscite Commissioner for the Cameroons under United Kingdom Administration; Plebiscites on the Southern and Northern Parts of the Territory, on 11 and 12 February 1961. U.N. Doc. T/1556 (April 3, 1961).

_____. _____. Report of the Trusteeship Council. U.N. Doc. Supp. 4 A/3822 (New York, 1958); Supp. 4 A/4100 (New York, 1959).

_____. _____. Special Report on Administrative Unions Affecting Trust Territories and on the Status of the Cameroons and Togoland under French Administration Arising out of Their Membership in the French Union. U.N. Doc. A/2151 (New York, 1952).

_____. _____. Special Report of the Trusteeship Council, The Future of the Trust Territories of the Cameroons under French Administration and the Cameroons under United Kingdom Administration. U.N. Doc. A/4094 (New York: Feb. 18, 1959).

_____. _____. Reports of United Nations Visiting Mission to Trust Territories in West Africa. U.N. Doc. Supp. 2 T/798 (New York, 1951).

_____. _____. United Nations Visiting Mission to the Trust Territories of the Cameroons under British Administration and the Cameroons under French Administration, 1955. Report on the Cameroons under French Administration. U.N. Doc. T/1240 (April, 1956). Report on the Cameroons under British Administration. U.N. Doc. T/1239 (April, 1956)

_____. _____. United Nations Visiting Missions to Trust Territories in West Africa, 1958. Report on the Trust Territory of the Cameroons under French Administration. U.N. Doc. T/1427 (Jan. 23, 1959). Report on the Trust Territory of the Cameroons under British Administration. U.N. Doc. T/1426 (Jan.

20, 1959) and Add. 1 (Feb. 6, 1959).

_____. _____. Addendum to the Report on the Trust Territory of the Cameroons under British Administration. (T/1426). U.N. Doc. T/1426 Add. 1 (Feb. 6, 1959).